D1563669

Springer Series on Behavior Therapy and Behavioral Medicine

Series Editors: Cyril M. Franks, Ph.D., and Frederick J. Evans, Ph.D.

Advisory Board: John Paul Brady, M.D., Robert P. Liberman, M. D., Neal E. Miller, Ph.D., and Stanley Rachman, Ph.D.

Thomas J. D'Zurilla, Ph.D., University of Illinois at Urbana, is Associate Professor of Psychology at the State University of New York at Stony Brook. He has been involved in research and clinical work related to social problem solving and problem-solving therapy for more than 15 years and has coauthored a number of pioneering theoretical and research articles on these topics. His 1971 article with Marvin R. Goldfried, *Problem Solving and Behavior Modification,* is one of the ten most-cited articles ever published in the *Journal of Abnormal Psychology.* Dr. D'Zurilla is one of a select list of 1,000 psychologists from the Western World and elsewhere to be included in A. J. Chapman and N. P. Sheehy's forthcoming reference work *Who's Who in Psychology,* London: The Harvester Press. He is also a practicing clinical psychologist and a consultant to industry on problem solving and behavior modification.

PROBLEM-SOLVING THERAPY

A Social Competence Approach to Clinical Intervention

Thomas J. D'Zurilla, Ph.D.

Foreword by Philip C. Kendall, Ph.D.

SPRINGER PUBLISHING COMPANY
New York

To my parents, Thomas and Mary D'Zurilla,
for letting me solve my own problems

Springer Publishing Company, Inc.
536 Broadway
New York, NY 10012

86 87 88 89 90 / 5 4 3 2 1

Library of Congress Cataloging-in-Publication Data

D'Zurilla, Thomas J.
  Problem-solving therapy.

  (Springer series on behavior therapy & behavioral medicine ; 18)
  Bibliography: p.
  Includes index.
  1. Problem-solving therapy. I. Title.
II. Series: Springer series on behavior therapy and behavioral medicine ; v.18. [DNLM: 1. Problem   Solving. 2. Psychotherapy—methods. W1 SP685NB v.18 / WM 420 D999]
  RC489.P68D98   1986   616.89'14   86-13897
  ISBN 0-8261-5680-0

Printed in the United States of America

Contents

Foreword

Life is full of problems to be solved. Selecting and purchasing an automobile, coordinating the redecoration of a kitchen, and the longer if not infinite list of the routine activities of managing a family, a business, or both. Personal and interpersonal problems arise in all aspects of life.

Even if intentions and plans are followed reasonably well, one is still inevitably faced with dilemmas. Plans made by different individuals are not typically compatible without explicit negotiations. Communications among individuals that have the best of plans are, since we are human, yet another source of problems. Murphy's Law is alive and well, and if there is an extended interpersonal interaction, there will be problems that require the attention of the parties involved. It is a problem-solving model for clinical intervention that offers the promise of teaching the skills necessary for successful adjustment to life's inevitable dilemmas.

This book is rich with information and recommendations. The wealth of research and clinical materials on problem-solving are brought together in a readable fashion by one of the leading figures in the field. The work includes a description of the problem-solving model and incorporates related research. The procedures for assessment and the strategies for application are detailed—again with proper consideration for the methods and outcomes of related research. Accounts of both case examples and related treatment programs buttress the breadth of coverage provided by D'Zurilla.

D'Zurilla's problem-solving approach to clinical intervention is integrative, seeking to wed cooperative strategies from several areas of clinical work. A select illustration of the integrative character of D'Zurilla's work is his concern with the appraisal process and its influence on problem solving. It is each individual's personal perception of situations, and therefore the importance of cognitive processing that is essential to a proper understanding of the nature of real-life problems. Treatments not only provide training in problem-solving skills, but also attend to the client as an active information processor. It is each individual's appraisal of his/her skills and of the demands of the environment, along with a comparison of skills and demands that provide the basis for determining what problems require solutions. Such an approach involves the contributions of research on stress, cognitive coping, social perception, and information processing in general.

Coping, and more specifically the cognitive and behavioral skills needed for successful coping with life's myriad of problems, remains a central theme deserving continued research study and clinical application. D'Zurilla embraces a coping framework and, quite accurately, does not propose that "success" is evidenced by an absence of problems. Rather, problems do and will exist and the procedures involved in the process of coping with life's inevitable speedbumps constitute the skills to be acquired. Correspondingly, the therapist does not behave in an all-knowing way. Instead the therapist offers methods to help clients search for and evaluate potential options and provides a manner for viewing the world that precludes exacerbation of needless stress and strain. Problem-solving interactions are flexible and pluralistic and, true to form, D'Zurilla communicates the need for the individualization of treatment. Focusing on the process of social problem-solving one needn't become locked in debate or battle over the results of a particular solution.

D'Zurilla's use of the term "intervention" in his title is most apt for the problem-solving approach that is prescribed, for it has application not only in remedial therapy but also in prevention and enhancement programs. Intervention is the appropriate umbrella term to communicate the versatility of the problem-solving approach.

Does the present problem-solving therapy provide *all* the answers? The answer is no, and no one book could do so. What D'Zurilla does provide, however, is the framework for learning and training in social problem-solving. Moreover, these methods can be applied to assist clients in the search for solutions for a variety of personal dilemmas. The present volume presents a pioneering approach in the social problem-solving literature, one that is also enhanced by the cumulative wisdom of a valued settler in the field.

PHILIP C. KENDALL, Ph.D.
Temple University

Preface

Problem-solving therapy, or the clinical application of problem-solving training (PST), had its beginnings in the late 1960s and early 1970s as part of the growing trend toward clinical interventions which focus on the facilitation of social competence (Gladwin, 1967). Since the early 1970s, there has been a rapid increase in the number of PST programs reported in the clinical literature. Focusing on both children and adults, PST has been employed as a treatment method (used alone or in combination with other techniques), a treatment maintenance strategy, and a prevention strategy (see D'Zurilla & Nezu, 1982; Durlak, 1983; Pellegrini & Urbain, 1985; Spivack & Shure, 1974; Spivack, Platt, & Shure, 1976; Urbain & Kendall, 1980). The present book focuses on PST for adult populations.

Part I of the book focuses on a discussion of the theoretical and empirical foundations of the problem-solving approach to clinical intervention and prevention. Part II deals with clinical applications, beginning with a description of various approaches to the assessment of problem-solving skills. A transactional/problem-solving model of stress and coping is then presented, which argues for the efficacy of PST as a stress-management approach. This is followed by a description of a specific program which may serve as a model for PST as a treatment method, a maintenance strategy, or a prevention program with goals of increasing social competence and reducing stress. Several variations in PST programs for different target populations and different program goals are then described. The book concludes with a review of empirical studies on the outcome of PST.

This book is intended for therapists and counselors in the mental health professions and education who are interested in improved methods for enhancing the social competence and stress-management ability of their clients. The book will also be of interest to community psychologists and social workers who are concerned with prevention programs and methods for increasing the effectiveness of individuals and groups in the community with the responsibility of solving community problems and making policy decisions. In addition, the book will be of interest to theorists and researchers in the areas of social problem solving, self-control, social competence, social cognition, decision making, social-information processing, and stress and coping. Finally, college instructors will find the book useful in their courses in psychotherapy and counseling, behavior modification, cognitive-behavioral therapy, abnormal psychology, personal adjustment, personality, self-management, stress-management, community psychology, and prevention.

Many individuals have influenced my thinking and my work on social problem solving and problem-solving therapy. Most of them are listed in the references at the end of this book. However, there are four people whom I would like to single out for special consideration. First, there is my colleague, Marvin Goldfried, who collaborated with me in the early development of the social problem-solving model on which the present approach is based (see D'Zurilla & Goldfried, 1971). Second, there is Arthur Nezu, my former research associate, who contributed much to a series of experimental studies that tested several components of the model (see D'Zurilla & Nezu, 1980; Nezu & D'Zurilla, 1979, 1981a, 1981b). The third influential individual is Richard Lazarus, whose work on stress and coping has helped me to recognize the parallels between social problem solving and the stress-and-coping process. Lazarus's work has also convinced me that social problem solving is best conceptualized within a transactional framework. Last but not least, I would like to acknowledge the important influence of Sidney Parnes's work on creative problem solving, which has contributed much to the present conceptualization of the social problem-solving process and to the PST methods described in this book.

I would also like to thank Philip C. Kendall and Michael J. Mahoney for their helpful comments and suggestions on an earlier draft of this book. Finally, I would like to express my appreciation to my typist, Sandi Cohen, for her willingness to make prompt revisions at short notice on a number of occasions.

I

Theoretical and Research Foundations

1

Introduction and Historical Development

Philosophers, educators, and psychologists down through the ages have recognized that humans are problem-solvers and that individual differences exist in problem-solving ability in the general population. These observers of human nature have generally assumed that problem-solving ability contributes to social competence, since everyday life is replete with problems that must be solved in order to maintain an adequate level of personal-social functioning. Despite the fact that the study of human problem solving has a long history in experimental psychology (see Kleinmuntz, 1966; Newell & Simon, 1972), the question of whether social competence can be increased through training in problem-solving skills has received very little research attention in psychology over the years. The question of whether such training might be useful as a clinical intervention or prevention strategy has received even less attention.

There are two possible reasons for the past failure to recognize the potential value of problem-solving training (PST) in clinical and counseling psychology. One reason has been the dominance of the "medical" or "disease" model of psychopathology throughout most of the history of clinical psychology. The second reason has been the lack of relevance of most of the laboratory research on human problem solving to "social problem solving" (i.e., real-life problem solving).

The medical model defines psychopathology primarily in terms of the *presence* of deviant or maladaptive cognitive-affective-motoric responses, which are presumed to be signs or "symptoms" of underlying intrapsychic conflicts. Normality is viewed primarily as the *absence* of abnormality. Effective functioning or social competence is something that is disrupted or interfered with by psychopathology and improved when psychopathology is reduced. Within this conceptual framework, clinical interventions have focused on the removal or reduction of psychopathology through the use of insight therapy. Direct, skill-training approaches have been viewed as "supportive" at best.

The research on human problem solving in experimental psychology has focused primarily on impersonal intellectual problems such as water-jar problems, jigsaw puzzles, mechanical problems, mathematical problems, and concept-formation tasks. The cognitive abilities required to solve these problems do not include many of the abilities that appear to be important for social problem solving (Guilford, 1967; Spivack, Platt, & Shure, 1976). Moreover, research in experimental psychology has focused on *descriptive* models of problem solving and decision making, which are concerned with the question of how individuals *typically* go about solving problems. More relevant for the development of PST programs are normative or *prescriptive* models, which attempt to describe and predict how individuals can *maximize* their problem-solving effectiveness.

The present problem-solving approach to clinical intervention had its beginnings in the late 1960s and early 1970s. Four different streams of historical development within the last 25–30 years have had a significant influence in shaping this approach: (a) the burgeoning interest in the nature and nurturance of creativity, (b) the rise of the social-competence approach to psychopathology as a challenge to the medical model, (c) the rapid development and expansion of the cognitive-behavioral approach within behavior modification, and (d) the development of the transactional theory of stress.

Creativity Research

The arousal of interest in the nature and nurturance of creativity that occurred in the 1950s led eventually to the first training and research programs in applied problem solving, which were developed in the fields of education and industry. In his APA presidential address in 1950, J. P. Guilford called for a major research

effort to study creativity, which he believed could have great practical significance for the future of our society, particularly in the
area of problem solving. Guilford (1967, 1977) saw much overlap
between creativity and problem solving. As he noted:

> In problem solving and creative thinking we find intellectual abilities
> working together, if the problem and its solution are at all complex. The
> two kinds of exercise are intimately related, for the solving of a problem
> calls for novel steps in behavior, and this means creative performance.
> [Guilford, 1977, p. 1984]

The traditional concept of general intelligence (IQ) was criticized
by Guilford for failing to include many of the abilities which are important for creative performance and "social intelligence" (i.e.,
social competence). Through his own research on creativity and
intelligence, Guilford developed a new model of intellect, called
the "Structure of Intellect," which includes important creative abilities as well as the traditional intellectual abilities. These creative
abilities include associational and ideational fluency, spon-
taneous and adaptive flexibility, originality, and a sensitivity to
problems.

Coming from a different field and perspective (industry), Alex F.
Osborn (1952, 1963) was a strong voice calling for the development
of training methods and techniques to nurture and enhance creative
performance. He was instrumental in the development of one of the
earliest and most influential PST programs, the Creative Problem-
Solving Program, now located at the State University College at
Buffalo. Beginning over 30 years ago, at the University of Buffalo,
this program focused initially on the stimulation of productive
thinking and creative performance using Osborn's "brainstorming"
techniques, which tap several of the creative abilities identified by
Guilford. Later, under the directorship of Sidney J. Parnes, who was
influenced by both Osborn and Guilford, the goals and procedures of
the program were broadened considerably and now focus on the
facilitation of *general competence,* i.e., productive thinking, creative
performance, and personal-social effectiveness (Parnes, 1962;
Parnes, Noller, & Biondi, 1977). In addition to the training program, which is conducted in academic courses and a week-long
Annual Creative Problem-Solving Institute, a comprehensive longitudinal research investigation was initiated in 1969 to study the
effectiveness of the program. PST programs based on the Osborn-
Parnes program have multiplied at a rapid rate in recent years, in

courses, seminars, workshops, conferences, and institutes in educational and industrial settings throughout the United States and abroad. The evidence for the effectiveness of the Parnes program and its relevance for clinical intervention and prevention will be discussed later.

The Social Competence Approach to Psychopathology

As PST programs were multiplying in education and industry, a challenge was mounting in clinical psychology against the medical model of psychopathology. Clinicians were becoming increasingly doubtful about the general applicability and validity of the medical model. Investigators were questioning whether understanding or "insight" concerning the underlying causes of maladaptive behavior could be useful without also teaching more adaptive alternative behaviors. Instead of viewing normality simply as the absence of psychopathology, theorists were beginning to talk about a *dimension* of normality or effective functioning, using such terms as "positive mental health" and "social competence" (e.g., Jahoda, 1953, 1958; White, 1959). This view led to the interesting hypothesis that social competence and psychopathology might be related in such a way that increases in social competence might be associated with decreases in psychopathology. Several studies by Zigler, Phillips, and their associates seemed to add strength to this hypothesis. They found that the posthospital adjustment of psychiatric patients was positively correlated with their levels of social competence prior to hospitalization. In addition, they found that greater deficits in social competence were associated with more severe symptomatology (Phillips & Zigler, 1961, 1964; Zigler & Phillips, 1961, 1962; Levine & Zigler, 1973).

These early findings on the relationship between social competence and psychopathology led to different interpretations. Social competence has been viewed as both a "buffer" against psychopathology and as a preventative factor. In addition, several investigators have argued that the concept of psychopathology should be broadened to include the view that maladaptive responses may *result* from deficiencies in the skills and abilities that contribute to social competence, including problem-solving skills (D'Zurilla & Goldfried, 1971; Phillips, 1978; Spivack et al., 1976).

A group of highly respected mental health professionals met with NIMH staff members at a conference in 1965 "to explore ways in which clinical interventions might be facilitated through placing a greater emphasis upon improving the social competence of persons who seek or need professional help in dealing with emotional or adjustment problems" (Gladwin, 1967, p. 30). Particularly significant for the present discussion is the fact that the conference participants defined social competence in terms that are very compatible with the concept of social problem solving. According to their definition, social competence had three major components:

1. The ability to use a variety of alternative pathways or behavioral responses in order to reach a given goal, which implies also the ability to choose between a range of goals, both instrumental and ultimate.
2. The ability to use a variety of social systems and resources within the society.
3. Effective reality testing, which involves not merely the lack of perceptual impairment, but also a positive, broad, and sophisticated understanding of the world.

The above-listed skills and abilities are also important components in the social problem-solving process, as we shall see later. Thus, according to this view, it would appear that training in social problem-solving skills might be useful as a clinical-intervention strategy.

The Cognitive-Behavioral Approach to Therapy

As the trend was developing within the field of clinical psychology in general toward the development of intervention programs based on the facilitation of social competence, the most promising competence-enhancement programs available were being applied and evaluated in the young field of behavior modification, namely, contingency management (operant conditioning) and social-skills training (Ullmann & Krasner, 1969). These approaches focused on the direct facilitation of performance skills in specific problematic situations by manipulating the consequences of specific target behaviors and by applying such procedures as prompting, modeling, behavior rehearsal, performance feedback, positive reinforcement, and shaping. These procedures were very effective in improving performance, but behavior changes were often limited to the specific training situations; generalized improvements in competence did not tend to occur. Thus, while these approaches were very useful for specific behavioral deficits, it was much more difficult to deal with clinical problems that involved generalized deficiencies in social competence, which may have resulted in many cases from deficits in social problem-solving skills.

The problem of limited behavior changes helped to instigate a trend in behavior modification in the late 1960s toward a greater emphasis on cognitive mediation in an attempt to facilitate self-control and, thus, broader behavior changes. According to Kendall and Hollon (1979, p. 1), the cognitive-behavioral perspective represented "a purposeful attempt to preserve the demonstrated efficiencies of behavior modification . . . and to incorporate the cognitive activities of the client in the efforts to produce therapeutic change." The cognitive activities focused on in this approach have ranged from specific thoughts or self-statements, to a broader level of underlying beliefs and assumptions, to more complex processes such as information processing and problem solving (Murphy, 1985; Turk & Salovey, 1985).

At a symposium on the role of cognitive factors in behavior modification at the 1968 APA convention, D'Zurilla and Goldfried presented a paper that argued that social-skills training programs should include training in problem-solving skills to facilitate generalized improvements in social competence. This paper was later expanded and published in 1971 under the title "Problem Solving and Behavior Modification." In 1976, Spivack et al. published their influential book, *The Problem-Solving Approach to Adjustment,* which presented evidence on the relationship between social problem-solving ability and psychopathology and described several early studies on PST with both children and adults. At about this point in time, Mahoney (1974, p. 212) described the promise of problem solving for behavior modification as follows:

> The potential relevance of problem solving to both clients and therapists needs little elaboration. In terms of adaptive versatility and the ability to cope with an ever-changing array of life problems, these cognitive skills may offer an invaluable personal paradigm for survival. Their potential contribution to therapeutic efficacy and independent self-improvement will hopefully become an issue of priority in future empirical scrutiny.

Following these early leads, the late 1970s and early 1980s saw the rapid development of a variety of programs involving the application of PST to treatment, treatment maintenance, and prevention. These programs have been applied within a variety of clinical settings, including individual therapy and counseling, group therapy, marital therapy, and family therapy. In addition, there have been applications in a variety of nonclinical settings, such as workshops, academic courses, and seminars. Target populations have ranged from hospitalized psychiatric patients with severe and profound deficits in social skills, to individuals with relatively minor maladjustments (e.g., academic underachievement or weight-control problems), to normal individuals and groups interested in maximizing their problem-solving effectiveness. Specific problems focused on in training have ranged from an individual's personal problems, to marital and family conflicts, to broader community problems. These PST programs will be described in more detail later in Part II.

The Transactional Model of Stress

While the preceding developments were occurring, Richard Lazarus and others in the field of stress research were developing the transactional theory of stress and coping (Lazarus, 1966, 1981; Lazarus & Folkman, 1984; McGrath, 1970, 1976). The transactional approach focuses on specific person-environment encounters or "transactions" in which environment variables (e.g., task demands) and person variables (e.g., cognitive appraisals, coping responses) interact and influence each other. As research on social problem solving and the transactional model of stress grew in the 1970s and early 1980s, it soon became clear that there is much overlap between these two approaches. Three important ways that the transactional view of stress and coping has influenced the present problem-solving approach are: (a) it has suggested that the nature of a real-life "problem" and the social problem-solving process can best be understood by viewing them within a transactional perspective, (b) it has pointed up the fact that life problems are often stressful and that emotional variables are likely to influence the problem-solving process significantly (Janis & Mann, 1977), and (c) it has suggested that PST might be useful as a stress-management approach. These points will be elaborated on in a later chapter.

Summary

Until recent years, the field of clinical and counseling psychology had failed to recognize the potential value of problem-solving training (PST) for clinical intervention. Two possible reasons for this neglect are (a) the dominance of the "medical" or "disease" model of psychopathology throughout most of the history of clinical psychology and (b) the lack of relevance of most of the laboratory research on human problem solving for "social problem solving" (i.e., real-life problem solving). The present problem-solving approach to clinical intervention had its beginnings in the late 1960s and early 1970s. Rapid development and expansion has occurred since 1976. Four streams of historical development have shaped this approach: (a) the arousal of research interest in the nature and nurturance of creativity, (b) the rise of the social-competence approach to psychopathology, (c) the development and expansion of the cognitive-behavioral approach within behavior modification, and (d) the development of the transactional theory of stress. The next chapter describes the skills and abilities that are involved in the social problem-solving process.

2

The Social Problem-Solving Process

Definitions

A discussion of the social problem-solving process must begin with a definition of the terms *problem solving, problem,* and *solution.* It is also important for theory, research, and practice to distinguish among the concepts of problem solving, solution implementation, and social competence. These distinctions will help to clarify the relationship between PST and social-skills training (Bellack, 1979).

In the real-life social context, *problem solving* may be defined as a cognitive-affective-behavioral process through which an individual or group identifies or discovers effective means of coping with problems encountered in everyday living (D'Zurilla & Nezu, 1982). This process includes both the generation of solution alternatives and decision-making or choice behavior (D'Zurilla & Goldfried, 1971). In the clinical and counseling psychology literature, real-life problem solving has come to be known as *social problem solving* (D'Zurilla & Nezu, 1982; Krasnor & Rubin, 1981), although the terms *interpersonal problem solving* (Shure, 1981), *interpersonal cognitive problem solving* (Spivack et al., 1976), *personal problem solving* (Heppner & Petersen, 1982), and *applied problem solving* (Heppner, Neal, & Larson, 1984) have also been used.

Social problem solving is at the same time a social-learning process, a self-management technique, and a general coping strategy. Since the solving of a problem results in a change in performance capability, it is a learning process (Gagné, 1966). Since problem solving can be applied by an individual independently (i.e., with little or no external direction or control) to a wide variety of problems in living, it is a self-management technique and an active, versatile coping strategy, which has important implications for treatment maintenance, generalization, and prevention (D'Zurilla & Goldfried, 1971; Mahoney, 1974).

A *problem* is defined here as a life situation that demands a response for effective functioning, but for which no effective response is immediately apparent or available to the individual or group confronted with the situation (D'Zurilla & Goldfried, 1971). The individual (or group) in such a situation perceives a discrepancy between "what is" (current or anticipated circumstances) and "what should be" (circumstances which are demanded or desired), under conditions where the means for reducing this discrepancy are not immediately apparent or available due to some obstacle or obstacles (e.g., ambiguity, uncertainty, skill deficit, or lack of resources). A current problem may be a time-limited event which keeps recurring, or it may be a continuous, ongoing situation, such as a chronic illness. The demands in the problematic situation may originate in the environment (e.g., objective task demands) or within the person (e.g., a personal goal, need, or committment). They are best described as *perceived demands* since an individual is likely to be influenced more by his perception of the demands in the situation when identifying problems than by the objective demands themselves. As it is defined here, a problem should *not* be viewed as a characteristic of the environment alone, nor as a characteristic of the person alone. Instead, it is best described as a person-environment encounter or "transaction" (Lazarus, 1981), involving a reciprocal relationship between environment variables and person variables which is constantly changing over time. Thus, a problem can be expected to increase or decrease in difficulty or significance over time, depending on changes in the environment (e.g., objective demand characteristics), the person (e.g., appraisal of task demands, response availability), or both.

According to transactional stress theory, stress begins with a specific person-environment transaction in which demands (external and/or internal) tax or exceed coping resources or capabilities, as perceived by the individual (Lazarus, 1981; Lazarus & Folkman, 1984). This particular type of person-environment transaction is very similar to the present concept of a problem. This view is shared by stress researcher Schönpflug (1983), who has observed that stress usually begins with concern about a problem.

Problems are likely to be stressful if they are at all difficult, because difficult problems are likely to involve conflict, uncertainty, and/or perceived uncontrollability (Epstein, 1982; Hamberger & Lohr, 1984; Janis, 1982; Phillips, 1978). If problems can be viewed as stressors, then social problem solving is an activity that is often carried out under stressful conditions (Janis, 1982; Janis & Mann, 1977). The role of stress and other emotional variables in problem solving has been a neglected topic in most laboratory-based theories of rational problem solving and decision making (Edwards, 1954; Kleinmuntz, 1966; Newell & Simon, 1972). An adequate theory of social problem solving must account for the effects of these variables, and PST programs must include methods for controlling them in order to facilitate problem-solving performance.

A *solution* is a coping response or response pattern that is effective in altering a problematic situation and/or one's own personal reactions to it so that it is no longer perceived as a problem, while at the same time maximizing other positive consequences (benefits) and minimizing negative consequences (costs) (D'Zurilla & Goldfried, 1971). The relevant benefits and costs include effects on others as well as personal consequences, and long-term implications as well as short-term effects. The *effectiveness* of any particular solution may vary for different individuals or different environments, depending on the norms, values, and goals of the problem-solver or significant others who are responsible for judging the problem-solver's performance.

A theory of social problem solving should distinguish among the concepts problem solving, solution implementation, and social competence (D'Zurilla & Goldfried, 1971; D'Zurilla & Nezu, 1982). As defined above, *problem solving* refers to the process by which an individual or group *discovers* a solution to a problem. *Solution implementation,* on the other hand, refers to the *performance* of the solution response, which is a function not only of problem-solving, but also of other factors related to the individual's learning history, such as performance skill deficits, emotional inhibitions, and motivational (reinforcement) deficits. *Social competence* is the broadest concept of the three, referring to a wide range of social skills, behavioral competencies, and coping behaviors, which enable an individual to deal effectively with the demands of everyday living (Goldfried & D'Zurilla, 1969; McFall, 1982; Wrubel, Benner, & Lazarus, 1981). Effective problem-solving performance is only one component of social competence, albeit a very significant one (Sarason, 1981).

It should now be clear that PST and social-skills training are both interventions designed to enhance social competence. In the past, social-skills training programs focused almost exclusively on social performance skills (Bellack, 1979). However, the concept of social skills has since been broadened to include cognitive skills (Kagan,

1984; McFall, 1982). A number of investigators have argued that problem solving is an important cognitive skill which should be incorporated into social-skills training programs (D'Zurilla & Goldfried, 1971; Kagan, 1984; Liberman, McCann, & Wallace, 1976; McFall, 1982; Sarason, 1981; Trower, Bryant, & Argle, 1978). One example of a social-skills training approach that includes training in some problem-solving skills is Goldstein's Structured Learning Therapy (see Goldstein, 1973; Sprafkin, Gershaw, & Goldstein, 1980).

Levels of Process Variables

Social problem solving has been defined here as a cognitive-affective-behavioral process that results in the discovery of a solution to a problem. The variables involved in this process can be described at three different levels, each reflecting increased specificity of effects on problem-solving performance. For the present discussion, these three levels of problem-solving variables will be labeled *problem-orientation cognitions, specific problem-solving skills,* and *basic problem-solving abilities.* Each level affects problem-solving performance in a different way.

Problem-Orientation
Cognitions

At the most general level is a set of cognitive variables that tend to have generalized or nonspecific effects on problem-solving performance. These cognitions do *not* include the specific skills or abilities that are required to solve a particular problem successfully. Instead, they are best described as higher-order "metacognitive" variables (Butler & Meichenbaum, 1981; Meichenbaum & Asarnow, 1979), which define an individual's *general orientation* to problems in living. This orientation describes how an individual attends to and thinks about (i.e., perceives, judges, appraises) problems in general, independent of any particular problematic situation. It reflects the person's beliefs, values, and commitments concerning real-life problems and problem solving as a means of coping with them, as well as the person's past reinforcement history related to independent problem solving (i.e., successes and failures). Important problem-orientation variables include problem perception (the recognition and labeling of problems); causal attributions; problem appraisal; beliefs about personal control; and values concerning the commitment of time and effort to independent problem solving. These variables will be described in more detail in the next chapter.

The different problem-orientation variables are constantly interacting and influencing each other. Depending on the nature of these variables, a particular set of problem-orientation cognitions may facilitate or inhibit problem-solving performance, influencing the initiation and generalization of problem-solving activity, the amount of effort expended, and persistence in the face of obstacles and emotional distress. A facilitative set of problem-orientation cognitions, which may be described as a generalized problem-solving cognitive set, contributes to a positive problem-solving coping style. An inhibitive set of problem-orientation variables, on the other hand, tends to produce a negative coping style, such as "dependency," "helplessness," or "defensive avoidance" (Janis, 1983; Janis & Mann, 1977).

Specific Problem-Solving Skills

At an intermediate level of specificity is a set of relatively specific problem-solving skills, each of which has a distinct contribution to make toward a successful outcome in a particular problem-solving situation. This set of skills can be described as a sequence of specific goal-directed tasks that must be performed in order to solve a particular problem successfully. They include the tasks of defining and formulating the problem, generating a list of alternative solutions, making a decision, implementing the solution, and evaluating the solution outcome (D'Zurilla & Goldfried, 1971). In behavioral terms, this sequence of problem-solving tasks can be conceived of as a behavioral chain, where the successful completion of each task reinforces task performance, and the reinforcing outcome for the entire series of tasks is the discovery of a solution to the problem. In the next chapter, these specific problem-solving skills will be discussed further.

Basic Problem-Solving Abilities

At the most specific level is the set of basic problem-solving abilities that underlie and affect the ability to learn and implement the problem-solving operations at the general and intermediate levels. Relatively little is known about these basic abilities at the present time, but they are likely to include the cognitive abilities described by Spivack et al. (1976) as being important for social problem solving, including: *sensitivity to problems* (ability to recognize that a problem exists); *alternative thinking* (ability to generate alternative solutions); *means-ends thinking* (ability to conceptualize relevant means to a goal); *consequential thinking* (ability to anticipate consequences); and *perspective taking* (ability to perceive a situation from another person's perspective, empathic ability).

The cognitive abilities identified by Spivack et al. (1976) and other basic abilities that might underlie the social problem-solving process are likely to be found in Guilford's (1967, 1968) Structure-of-Intellect model. This model has three dimensions: (a) *contents* (major kinds of information), (b) *products* (how information is structured or organized), and (c) *operations* (intellectual processes). In Guilford's model, there are five kinds of informational content (visual, auditory, symbolic, semantic, and behavioral), six kinds of products (units, classes, relations, systems, transformations, and implications), and five kinds of operations (memory, cognition, convergent production, divergent production, and evaluation). Each cell in the model represents a specific ability. The abilities that are measured by traditional IQ tests are included in the intellectual operations of *memory* (storage and retrieval of information), *cognition* (knowing and understanding), *convergent production* (focused search for one correct answer or conclusion), and *evaluation* (comparing and judging information). The operation of *divergent production* (broad search for alternative ideas or solutions) is not included in traditional IQ tests and is not correlated with traditional IQ measures. However, divergent-production abilities are major determinants of creativity. They include abilities such as *fluency* (ability to produce a large number of ideas), *flexibility* (ability to produce a variety of kinds of ideas), and *originality* (ability to produce unusual or novel ideas).

Guilford (1977) stresses the overlap that exists between creativity and problem solving. In his Structure-of-Intellect Problem Solving (SIPS) model, all five intellectual operations are represented, but divergent production is emphasized. Within the informational content dimension, the abilities associated with the categories labeled *semantic* (verbal, meaningful information) and *behavioral* (personal-social information) are most relevant for social problem solving. According to Guilford, the behavioral category, in particular, entails a large number of abilities that come under the general heading of "social intelligence" (e.g., social information-processing abilities, generation of alternative solutions to interpersonal problems). The operation of memory is important because it involves the storage and retrieval of information as needed during the problem-solving process. The operation of cognition focuses on two important problem-solving events: awareness that a problem exists (cognition of implications) and comprehension of the nature of the problem (cognition of relations and systems). Convergent production and divergent production both contribute to the generation of solutions, divergent production being most important because of the emphasis on fluency, flexibility, and originality. In addition, the abilities associated with the product category of *transformations* (ability to modify and improve information or ideas) are considered important for the generation of good-quality solution alternatives. Finally, the operation of evaluation is necessary for comparing and judging solutions and assessing solution outcome.

Research is badly needed to determine exactly what basic abilities account most for individual differences in social problem-solving performance. The Guilford model and many of the tests that have been developed to measure the abilities that make up the model could contribute much to this research (Guilford, 1967, 1977; Parnes & Noller, 1973). In addition, the recent work on social-information processing and its relationship to social skills and social competence seems to be a step in the right direction (McFall, 1982; McFall, McDonel, & Lipton, 1984).

Relationship Between Social Problem Solving and Intelligence

Several studies have investigated the relationship between social problem-solving ability and general intelligence, as measured by traditional IQ tests and tests of academic aptitude. These studies have consistently found low correlations (Heppner & Petersen, 1982; Spivack et al., 1976). Tests of Guilford's divergent-production operation also show low correlations with IQ tests. However, according to Guilford (1977), there is an interesting kind of relationship between divergent-production ability and IQ. Individuals with low IQs have only low scores on divergent-production tests. However, when IQs are high, divergent-production scores vary. Thus, it appears that IQ puts an upper limit on divergent-production performance, but high IQ does not ensure high divergent-production ability. According to Guilford, this relationship must be qualified in that it has been established only with divergent-production tests that focus on semantic content. If divergent production is important for social problem solving, as Guilford suggests, then there may be a similar relationship between IQ and social problem-solving ability. Such a relationship would be consistent with the observation that mentally retarded individuals are generally deficient in both general intelligence *and* adaptive social functioning, while individuals with higher IQs show greater variability in social competence.

Summary

Social problem solving is defined as a cognitive-affective-behavioral process through which an individual (or group) identifies or discovers effective means of coping with problems encountered in everyday living. Social problem solving is at the same time a social-learning process, a self-management technique, and a general coping strategy which has important implications for treatment maintenance, generalization, and prevention. A *problem* is defined as a life situation that demands a response for effective functioning, but for which no effective response is immediately available to the individual (or group) confronted with the situation. Problems are likely to be stressful if they are at all difficult because difficult problems are likely to involve conflict, uncertainty, and/or perceived uncontrollability. An adequate theory of social problem solving must account for the effects of stress and other emotional variables on problem-solving performance. A *solution* is a coping response that is effective in altering a problematic situation and/or one's own personal reactions to it so that it is no longer perceived as a problem, while at the same time maximizing other positive consequences (benefits) and minimizing negative consequences (costs). The present view of social problem solving distinguishes between the concepts of problem solving, solution implementation, and social competence. These distinctions help to clarify the relationship between problem-solving training (PST) and social-skills training.

The variables involved in the social problem-solving process can be described at three levels, each reflecting increased specificity of effects on problem-solving performance. At the most general level is a set of *problem-orientation cognitions,* which tend to have generalized or nonspecific effects on problem-solving performance. At an intermediate level is a set of *specific problem-solving skills,* which may be described as a sequence of specific goal-directed tasks that

must be performed in order to solve a particular problem successfully. At the most specific level is a set of *basic problem-solving
abilities,* which underlie and affect the ability to learn and implement the problem-solving operations at the general and intermediate levels. Most of the basic cognitive abilities that underlie
the social problem-solving process are likely to be found in Guilford's (1967, 1968) Structure-of-Intellect model. The most important
basic abilities for social problem solving might be Guilford's divergent-production abilities, which are important determinants of
creativity. Studies on the relationship between social problem-
solving ability and general intelligence as measured by traditional
IQ tests have consistently found low correlations. However, it is
possible that IQ might put an upper limit on social problem-solving
ability. Low IQs may be associated with low problem-solving ability,
but high IQs may not ensure high problem-solving ability.

3

A Prescriptive Model
of Social Problem Solving

Training in social problem-solving skills may focus on problem-solving variables at any or all of the three levels described in the previous chapter, depending on where the significant deficits are found. With most adult populations, training programs have focused on the first two levels, problem-orientation cognitions and specific problem-solving skills. There appear to be two reasons for this emphasis. One is the assumption that most adults already possess the basic problem-solving abilities; therefore, training is not required at the basic level. The second reason is the lack of information about the nature of the basic abilities and about methods for enhancing them. The first assumption, if incorrect, could be the reason for the failure or minimal success of a PST program. As more information is learned about the basic cognitive abilities underlying the social problem-solving process, it will be important to assess these abilities prior to initiating a PST program, especially with populations showing severe deficits in problem-solving performance (e.g., psychiatric patients, mentally retarded individuals).

Based on a review of the most relevant problem-solving theory and research literature from the fields of experimental psychology, education, and industry, D'Zurilla and Goldfried (1971) proposed a prescriptive model of social problem solving to guide the development of PST programs in clinical psychology. A *prescriptive* or normative model attempts to specify how individuals *should* solve problems in order to maximize their effectiveness, as compared to a *descriptive* model, which describes how individuals *typically* go about solving problems. The D'Zurilla and Goldfried model, as later revised by D'Zurilla and Nezu (1982), has five components or stages, which include skills and abilities at all three levels. These five components are: (1) problem orientation, (2) problem definition and formulation, (3) generation of alternative solutions, (4) decision making, and (5) solution implementation and verification. Individually, each component has a definite purpose or function in the problem-solving process. Together, the five components, when applied effectively to a particular problem, are expected to maximize the probability of discovering the most effective solution.

The order in which the five components of the model are presented above represents a logical and useful sequence for training and systematic, efficient application. For example, problem solving *should* begin with a positive problem orientation, since such an orientation is likely to facilitate general problem-solving performance (Butler & Meichenbaum, 1981; Heppner & Petersen, 1982; Heppner, Hibel, Neal, Weinstein, & Rabinowitz, 1982). A problem-solver *should* define and conceptualize the problem carefully before beginning the tasks of generating solution alternatives and decision making, since the conceptualization of the problem is likely to influence performance on these tasks (Nezu & D'Zurilla, 1981a, 1981b; Tversky & Kahneman, 1981). Moreover, it is *necessary* to generate solution alternatives before the decision-making task can be started, and it is *necessary* to choose a solution before the final stage, namely, solution implementation and verification, can be carried out to complete the problem-solving process.

The order in which the model's components are presented does *not* mean that problem solving should proceed in an orderly, one-directional sequence beginning with step 1 and ending with step 5. Effective problem solving is likely to involve movement back and forth from one task to another before the process is finally terminated with the discovery of a satisfactory solution. For example, questions are often raised about the problem during the generation-of-alternatives and decision-making tasks that lead to a better understanding of the problem or a reevaluation of problem-solving goals. Likewise, evaluation of solution alternatives during decision making often suggests modifications or improvements (Guilford's transformations) that make available additional, better-quality solution alternatives. Most importantly, information obtained during solution implementation and verification, which involves the evaluation of solution outcome in the actual problematic situation, often indicates that the chosen solution is ineffective, requiring the problem-solver to go back to one or more of the previous stages in an attempt to identify a better solution. The problem-solver exits from the process only when a satisfactory solution is found, or when it is determined that the problem is insoluble and must be accepted and coped with as it is. What follows is a description of the goals and basic principles associated with each component of the problem-solving model, including several modifications and additions based on recent research and theoretical developments.

Problem Orientation

This component consists of a set of facilitative cognitive variables which are associated with a generalized problem-solving coping style. As noted above, these variables are expected to have a generalized, facilitative effect on problem-solving performance throughout the problem-solving process. Specifically, the function or purpose of these problem-orientation variables is to (a) increase sensitivity to problems and set the occasion for problem-solving activity, (b) focus attention on positive problem-solving expectations and away from unproductive worries and "self-preoccupying thoughts" (Sarason, 1980), (c) maximize effort and persistence in the face of obstacles and emotional stress, and (d) minimize disruptive emotional distress while attempting to maximize the likelihood of positive, facilitative emotional states. The major problem-orientation variables are: problem perception (recognition and labeling); problem attribution; problem appraisal; personal control; and time/effort commitment.

Problem Perception

Problem perception involves the recognition and labeling of problems. Positive problem perception refers to the likelihood that an individual will attend to and monitor his transactions with the environment in such a way as to recognize problems accurately and label them appropriately. A sensitivity to problems is an important prerequisite for effective problem solving because it sets the occasion for problem-solving activity. However, problems are not always easily recognizable. They are often embedded within a social context involving many transactions that are not problem-related. They are often masked by ambiguity or unrecognizable because of unavailable or incomplete information. Since problems are often difficult, threatening, and stressful, there is a tendency to avoid or deny them, rather than recognize and be forced to cope with them directly (Janis & Mann, 1977; Lazarus, 1983). Since unsolved problems often result in maladaptive responses (Phillips, 1978; Mather, 1970), there is a tendency to focus on these responses and label them "the problem," instead of recognizing the "real" problem causing them. For example, a young, ambitious sales representative labels his anxiety a "problem" without recognizing that the real problem causing his anxiety is the conflict between job demands and his new family responsibilities. In order to recognize and label problems accurately, individuals must learn to conceive of a problem as a *situation* with which one must cope (a discrepancy between demands and response availability), and learn to use their maladaptive responses (e.g., anxiety, ineffective behavior) as cues to monitor their transactions with the environment and identify the problematic situation that is causing these responses.

In addition to the effects of inappropriate labeling, the label a person uses to identify a problem may affect problem solving in a different way. Based on a person's beliefs, values, and prior learning experiences, problem labels may have meaning and significance to the person which may affect other problem-orientation cognitions and influence whether the person will approach the problem to solve it or avoid the problem. For example, to some individuals a "sex problem" may be a problem to avoid rather than a problem to solve because the label may "mean" (signify) inadequacy, thus, threatening self-esteem. In fact, to some individuals the label "problem" itself is threatening and leads to avoidance or denial.

Problem Attribution

Problem attribution refers to a person's causal attributions concerning problems in living. A positive or facilitative problem attribution involves the readiness or tendency to attribute the cause of problems to environmental factors and/or relatively benign, transient or changeable personal factors, instead of attributing the cause to some stable personal abnormality or defect. For example, a person with a positive problem-attribution tendency might attribute the cause of a problem at work to an incongruity between difficult or complex task demands and a lack of job experience, instead of attributing the cause to "stupidity" or "inadequacy." This person is more likely: (1) to perceive problems as normal, inevitable life events with which everyone must cope; (2) to approach rather than avoid or deny problems; and (3) to initiate problem-solving activity with confidence. A negative problem attribution, on the other hand, is likely to result in negative self-evaluations, negative affect, avoidance tendencies, and inhibition of problem-solving perform-ance (Abramson, Seligman, & Teasdale, 1978; Beck, 1967; Ellis, 1977).

Problem Appraisal

Problem attribution is likely to influence problem appraisal, which refers to a person's appraisal or evaluation of the significance of a problem for personal-social well-being. This concept is basically Lazarus's concept of *primary appraisal* (Lazarus & Folkman, 1984). When confronted with a problematic situation, the person asks: "Does this problem represent potential harm or benefit to me, physi-cally, psychologically, socially, or economically?" Positive problem appraisal refers to the likelihood that a person will perceive a problem as a "challenge" or potential benefit to his well-being (e.g., opportunity for mastery, achievement, etc.), instead of viewing it as a harmful or threatening situation. A person who views a problem as a challenge or opportunity for personal growth is more likely to approach the problematic situation and initiate effortful, planful problem-solving activity (Folkman, Lazarus, Dunkel-Schetter, De-Longis, & Gruen, in press). A negative or threatening problem appraisal, on the other hand, is more likely to result in anxiety, avoidance, and a disruption in problem-solving performance (Janis & Mann, 1977; Lazarus & Folkman, 1984; Meichenbaum, Henshaw, & Himel, 1982).

Personal Control

Personal control has two components: (a) the likelihood that an individual will perceive a problem as soluble or controllable, and (b) the likelihood that an individual will believe that he is capable of solving a problem through his own efforts. These two personal-control cognitions are basically Bandura's (1977) concepts of "out-come expectancy" and "self-efficacy expectancy" applied to problem-solving behavior. According to Bandura, positive outcome ex-pectations refer to the belief that a particular coping behavior will have a favorable outcome in a problematic situation (a stress situa-tion), while self-efficacy expectations refer to the belief that one will be capable of performing that coping behavior successfully. Favorable outcome expectations not only influence the intention to perform coping behavior, but they also influence perceptions of self-efficacy (Maddux, Sherer, & Rogers, 1982). According to a study by Baumgardner, Heppner, and Arkin (1983), individuals who appraise themselves as effective problem-solvers are more likely than those who appraise themselves as ineffective problem-solvers to view common life problems as being caused by factors that are changeable or controllable. Perceived control and self-efficacy expectations have been found to reduce anxiety and facilitate adaptive coping performance in stress situations, affecting the initiation of coping behavior, as well as persistence or effort in the face of obstacles (Bandura, 1977; Bandura, 1980; Hamberger & Lohr, 1984). A perception of uncontrollability, or low self-efficacy, on the other hand, tends to increase anxiety, avoidance behavior, and other maladaptive behaviors in stressful problematic situations (see Bandura, 1980; D'Zurilla & Nezu, 1982; Hamberger & Lohr, 1984; Mather, 1970; Phillips, 1978).

Time/Effort Commitment

Time/effort commitment also has two components: (a) the likelihood that an individual will estimate accurately the time it will take to solve a particular problem successfully, and (b) the likelihood that the individual will be willing to devote the necessary time and effort to problem solving. In a study by Baumgardner, Heppner, and Arkin (1984), it was found that individuals who appraised themselves as effective problem-solvers were more likely to view *effort* as an important determinant of their performance than were those who appraised themselves as ineffective problem-solvers.

The time and effort that an individual devotes to different activities is an indication of the reinforcing value of those activities for that particular individual (Premack, 1965). If an individual recognizes that successful problem solving takes time and values or is reinforced by independent problem-solving activities, then he will be more likely to commit sufficient time and effort to problem solving than an individual who underestimates the amount of time that is required and does not value independent problem solving. The former individual is more likely to approach the problem, initiate problem-solving activity, and demonstrate persistence in the face of obstacles or disappointments. The latter individual is more likely to avoid the problem or adopt a dependent coping style.

A sense of time urgency and a lack of commitment or motivation for independent problem solving is often the result of a history of ineffective problem solving and the consequent anxiety or fear of failure in problem-solving situations. In order to overcome this motivational problem and facilitate independent problem-solving behavior, Levine (in press) has suggested that the individual must adopt the principle of *intimate engagement.* To apply this principle and overcome anxiety and avoidance tendencies, the individual must make a conscious committment to "engage" the problem "intimately," which implies not only the initiation of problem-solving *thinking,* but *active approach and exploratory behavior* in the problematic situation as well.

Problem Definition and Formulation

It may not be too much of an exaggeration to state that a well-defined problem is half-solved. A well-defined problem is likely to facilitate the generation of relevant solutions, improve decision-making effectiveness, and contribute to the accuracy of solution verification (i.e., assessment of solution outcome). In the real-life setting, problem solving usually begins with a problem that is "messy" (vague, ambiguous, irrelevant cues, inaccurate information, unclear goals). Thus, the purpose of this initial problem-solving task is to (a) gather as much relevant, factual information about the problem as possible, (b) clarify the nature of the problem, (c) set a realistic problem-solving goal, and (d) reappraise the significance of the problem for personal-social well-being.

Gathering Information

Before gathering information about the problem, the problem solver must know what kind of information to look for and what cues to attend to. In social problem solving the most relevant cues and information can be described as *task information* (included in Guilford's semantic content category) and *social-behavioral information.* Task information refers to the demands and requirements associated with the various tasks that one must perform in order to function effectively in different life roles (e.g., employee, parent, husband, friend, etc.). Social-behavioral information refers to the problem-solver's own behavioral characteristics and those of others with whom he must interact during the performance of these life tasks, including words, actions, beliefs, values, goals, and feelings.

While gathering information, the problem-solver must change vague, ambiguous, and unfamiliar concepts and information into more specific, concrete, and/or familiar terms (Bloom & Broder, 1950). This will help the problem-solver to distinguish relevant from irrelevant information, and objective facts from unverified assumptions, inferences, and interpretations. The latter information must be checked and verified before using it to define and formulate the problem. If it cannot be verified, it is probably best to ignore it or give it very little weight in determining the nature and significance of the problem. The aim is to arrive at an accurate understanding of the problem and avoid having to deal with a biased or distorted perception of the problem. However, even when an individual is reasonably certain that all the concrete facts are accurate, there is still the possibility of distortion because the person must "process" (evaluate, judge, interpret) this information in order to make it meaningful. Subjective factors may influence this process and result in distortions.

When the definition or formulation of a problem is based on distorted information, the problem-solver is actually dealing with a pseudo-problem rather than a real problem. This pseudo-problem cannot be solved because the solution chosen to deal with it is likely to be inappropriate for the problematic situation as it exists in reality. For example, if a person thinks a friend is ignoring him because the friend does not like him anymore (distorted perception), when in reality the friend has just been very busy, the person may choose an inappropriate solution, such as demanding more time with the friend in an attempt to be more "likeable."

In connection with his cognitive theory of depression, Aaron Beck (1967, 1970) has identified several common distortions that occur during social-information processing that could result in pseudo-problems. Knowledge of these distortions may help problem-solvers to avoid creating them.

1. *Arbitrary Inference.* This distortion is illustrated in the example described above. A person draws a conclusion, usually about the motives, intentions, or feelings of others without sufficient facts to support it or rule out alternative interpretations.

2. *Selective Abstraction.* This distortion has also been referred to as "cognitive deficiency" (Beck, 1970). A person attends to certain

selected information or cues in a situation and makes an assumption or draws a conclusion based on this information, while ignoring other important information that may contradict this assumption or conclusion. For example, a baseball player focuses on his own errors in a ball game and assumes that the loss was his fault when, in fact, several other players made more costly errors. A problem-solver often makes this type of error when attempting to judge the relevancy of information in a problematic situation.

3. *Overgeneralization.* A problem-solver often makes assumptions about the general characteristics of people or situations within a given class when defining a problem. A serious mistake would be to draw general conclusions on the basis of insufficient information, such as a single, often trivial event. For example, a salesman forgets one sales meeting and the sales manager concludes that the person is not dependable.

4. *Magnification and Minimization.* Magnification occurs when an individual exaggerates the value, intensity, or significance of an event. A man who gets rejected by one woman considers the rejection a "catastrophe" which "proves" that he is inadequate. Minimization, on the other hand, refers to the opposite mistake of inappropriately devaluing or reducing the significance of an event. A woman minimizes the danger of walking down a particular lonely street at night, or a worker fails to recognize the significance of his habit of coming to work late.

In addition to the above cognitive distortions, there is another type of mistake individuals often make in defining problems, which is related to causal and consequential thinking (Guilford's cognition of implications). This error involves overestimation or underestimation of the probability that a particular effect will follow a certain antecedent event, or that particular consequences will follow certain behaviors. When this error occurs, pseudo-problems may again be created. For example, consider a student who greatly overestimates the likelihood of failing an exam following a given amount of study time. If the student does not have any more study time available, he may perceive a problem where none exists in reality. Another example is an employee who greatly underestimates his chances of getting a raise if he were to ask the boss for one. He may try to figure out what more he can do to impress the boss, when it is not really necessary to do so. It should also be emphasized at this point, however, that when an individual responds in a given situation on the basis of misinformation or misconceptions, he may indeed create a *real* problem for himself because his behavior may turn out to be inappropriate or maladaptive.

Understanding the Problem

At the same time that he is gathering information, the problemsolver attempts to organize this information so as to comprehend or understand the nature of the problem. Earlier, a "problem" was defined as an imbalance or discrepancy between demands and response availability. From the problem-solver's viewpoint, such a situation can be understood as a perceived discrepancy or incongruity between "what is" (present conditions) and "what should be" (what is demanded or desired), with the presence of some obstacle or obstacles preventing the identification and/or performance of an effective response for reducing this discrepancy. In order to comprehend the problem in these terms, the problem-solver must specify: (a) what present conditions are unacceptable (task characteristics and/or social-behavioral characteristics); (b) what changes or additions are demanded or desired; and (c) what obstacle or obstacles are preventing him from meeting these demands (e.g., emotional obstacles, informational deficit, ability deficit, skill deficit, ambiguity, uncertainty, conflicting demands). The problem-solver cannot always *know* what the obstacles are (for example, whether or not he has an ability deficit), but he can generate alternative hypotheses (a divergent-production skill) and check them out when possible.

Setting Goals

Goal setting is an important part of problem formulation because it provides direction for the generation of alternative solutions as well as performance standards for the evaluation of solutions. The two important rules in goal-setting are: (a) state the goals in specific, concrete terms and (b) avoid stating unrealistic or unattainable goals. Stating the goals in specific, concrete terms helps the problem-solver to identify relevant, appropriate solutions and facilitates decision-making effectiveness. Unrealistic goals would change the problem from a soluble one to an insoluble one, for which it would be impossible to find a satisfactory solution. This would result in perceived uncontrollability, which is likely to have disruptive emotional effects (Abramson et al., 1978; Ellis, 1977). The problem-solving goal is stated in the form of a "How" or "What" question: "How can I meet more people?" or "What do I have to do to get an A on the next exam?" The goal may focus on (a) meeting the task demands ("How can I increase my sales this month by 50%?"), (b) overcoming a specific obstacle or obstacles to meeting these demands ("How can I make available more time so that I can increase my sales?"), (c) reducing or changing the task demands ("How can I reduce my boss's unreasonable demands?"), or (d) some combination of the above. The demands in question may be *external,* for example the boss's orders, or they may be *internal,* such as an individual's personal goals and commitments. In keeping with the transactional perspective, the demands in most cases can be expected to involve *both* external requirements and the person's own interpretations and appraisals of these requirements, reflecting his personal goals, values, and commitments.

Getting at the "Real" Problem

The problem-solver must be aware that there are different ways to state or formulate a problem, and that the way a problem is stated will affect problem-solving outcomes such as the preference for particular solutions and the satisfaction with solution outcomes (Tversky & Kahneman, 1981). Therefore, it is important for the problem-solver to generate alternative problem formulations.

In some cases, a solution may prove to be unsatisfactory because the problem as stated is not the "real" problem, meaning that it is not the primary, basic, or most important problem. The basic problem in some instances might be the first problem in a cause-effect problem chain, where problem A causes problem B, which in turn causes problem C. Instead of focusing on problem C, it might be better to identify problem A and solve it first, since it is possible that the solution to problem A will eliminate the remaining problems as well.

In an attempt to identify whether a problem might be a consequence of a more important antecedent problem, it is helpful to state the problem and then ask "What caused or led up to this problem?"

In some cases, an antecedent problem that no longer exists may have initiated a cause-effect sequence resulting in the present problem. If the problem no longer exists, it cannot be solved; only the current problems can be solved. Therefore, the problem-solver need not look far into the past for primary or basic problems; he should focus only on antecedent problems that are present in his current life situation.

In other cases, a solution may prove to be unsatisfactory because the specific problem that the problem-solver has focused on may be only one part of a broader, more important problem that has not been recognized (Parnes et al., 1977). It may be more efficient and effective to work on the broader problem instead of focusing only on the one specific problem. Parnes et al. (1977) recommend the use of a "Why" question to get at more general problems. For example, the sales representative might ask: "*Why* do I want to increase my sales?" The answer might be: "So that I can get my boss off my back," which would suggest the more general and possibly more important problem: "How can I reduce my boss's frequent unreasonable demands?" Identifying a more general problem allows the problem-solver to make available more alternatives for dealing with an important immediate concern. For example, an individual who is concerned about his general physical condition might be focusing on the specific problem: "How can I get more exercise?" Instead, he might deal more effectively with his immediate concern if he would state the more general problem: "What can I do to improve my physical condition?"

Dealing with Complex Problems

Instead of beginning with a specific problem and then trying to find a more important, *general* problem, there are times when a problem-solver begins with a broad problem and tries to break it down into more *specific* subproblems; a broad, complex problem can often be better understood and dealt with more effectively by breaking it down in that way (Parnes et al., 1977). For example, a business executive might initially state his problem in the following general way: "How can I avoid wasting time?" This problem might be dealt with most effectively by breaking it down into the following subproblems: (a) too many telephone interruptions, (b) too many drop-in visitors, (c) too much "junk" mail and too many business publications to read, and (d) too much time spent traveling.

In cases where the initial problem focused on is a specific problem, an effective strategy might be to first ask "Why" to determine if there is a more important general problem, and then if the general problem is too complex to deal with as a whole, to break it down into more manageable subproblems and deal with them one at a time. If any subproblems are causally related to each other, the primary problem should be solved first.

Reappraising the Problem

When the nature of the problem is clarified and the goals are stated, the problem-solver completes the problem-definition and formulation task by reappraising the significance of the problem for his personal-social well-being. Because the problem was initially vague, ambiguous, and undefined, the first problem appraisals are often influenced more by the person's past experiences with problems than by present facts and circumstances. This problem ambiguity, together with negative past experiences with problems, often result in a distorted and threatening initial problem appraisal. Later, with a concrete, well-defined problem confronting him, the problem-solver can appraise the significance of the problem more accurately.

The significance of the problem is reappraised by considering the likely benefits and costs (long-term as well as short-term) of solving the problem vs. not solving the problem. A problem is considered "significant" or important if there are likely to be more benefits and/or fewer costs associated with solving the problem than not solving the problem. Taking reappraisal a step further, the problem-solver then appraises the problem as *benign*, a *threat*, or a *challenge*. A benign appraisal means that little or no costs are expected whether or not the problem is solved successfully. A threatening appraisal emphasizes the possible *costs* of solving the problem and/ or not solving the problem. A challenging appraisal emphasizes the possible *benefits* of solving the problem. It is possible for a problem to be appraised as both a threat and a challenge at the same time when the possible benefits and costs are given equal emphasis or significance. In this case, an attempt to concentrate on the challenging aspects of the problem will have more positive emotional consequences and a more beneficial effect on problem-solving performance (Folkman et al., in press). According to Parnes et al. (1977), if individuals would think of problems as "challenges" or "opportunities" more often, they would be less inclined to ignore or avoid so many problems.

Generation of Alternative Solutions

The purpose of this task is to make available as many solution alternatives as possible, in such a way as to maximize the likelihood that the "best" (most preferred) solution will be among them. This task focuses on the operation of divergent-production, which is the major operation in Guilford's Structure-of-Intellect Problem-Solving model.

The major obstacles to the creative generation of alternative solutions are *habit and convention* (Parnes et al., 1977). Many habits are adaptive and necessary in many everyday social situations (e.g., dressing appropriately, table manners, etc.). Habits can also be useful in social problem solving when effective responses learned in past problem-solving situations can be generalized to new but similar problematic situations. However, habits can also hinder effective problem solving when individuals respond "automatically" to new problematic situations with previously learned habits without stopping to think and question their applicability or appropriateness. In order to maximize *effectiveness* in problem solving, an individual cannot rely entirely on old habits; he must consider *different* approaches. In order to maximize *creativity* in problem solving, an individual cannot limit his thinking to conventional ideas; he must consider *novel* or original ideas.

The present model emphasizes three basic principles or rules for generating alternative solutions, which are based on Guilford's (1967) divergent-production operation and Osborn's (1963) method of "brainstorming." These principles are: (a) the quantity principle, (b) the deferment-of-judgment principle, and (c) the variety principle. The *quantity principle* suggests that the more solution alternatives that are produced, the more good quality ideas will be made available, thus, increasing the likelihood that the "best" solution will be discovered. According to the *deferment-of-judgment principle,* more good-quality solution ideas will be generated when a person suspends evaluation of ideas until later on in the problem-solving sequence (during the decision-making task). According to

Parnes et al. (1977), judgment tends to inhibit imagination when both are used at the same time. Imagination and judgment are both important abilities for problem solving, but each should be used for a different purpose at a different point in the problem-solving process. Imagination is used to *create* alternative solutions; judgment is used later to sort out and *evaluate* these solutions.

The *variety principle* states that the greater the range or variety of solution ideas, the more good-quality ideas will be discovered. When generating alternative solutions, the problem-solver may fall into a "set" to produce ideas that reflect only one possible "strategy" or general approach to the problem. This narrow set may occur even though the quantity and deferment-of-judgment rules are being followed adequately. One way to avoid this set is to look over the list of solutions that were generated by following the quantity and deferment-of-judgment principles, and then group the solutions into categories representing different strategies or approaches. Then the problem-solver can proceed to (a) generate more specific solution ideas for strategies that are underrepresented, (b) generate additional new strategies that are not represented, and (c) generate specific alternative solutions for the new strategies.

Following the generation of a list of alternative solutions using the above rules, the quantity and variety of available solutions can be increased further by generating *combinations, modifications,* and *elaborations.* To produce combinations, the problem-solver looks over the list of solutions and determines what responses can be combined to produce new solutions. To generate modifications and elaborations, the problem-solver considers changes and/or additions that might improve existing solutions or produce new ones (Guilford's divergent production of transformations and implications). Following these procedures, the problem-solver is ready to begin evaluating the solution alternatives.

Decision Making

The purpose of this task is to evaluate (compare and judge) the available solution alternatives and to select the "best" one(s) for implementation in the problematic situation. The present decision-making approach is based on two theoretical decision models: (a) *expected utility theory,* where choice behavior is based on a rational benefit/cost analysis (Beach & Mitchell, 1978; Edwards, 1961), and (b) *prospect theory,* which takes into account the effects of perceptual and subjective factors on choice behavior (Kahneman & Tversky, 1979; Tversky & Kahneman, 1981). Both theoretical frameworks have strong empirical support (Payne, 1982).

In the expected utility model, a judgment as to the utility or effectiveness of a given solution alternative is based on a joint consideration of the *value* and *likelihood* of anticipated consequences. In social problem solving, most of the costs and benefits associated with particular alternatives are not certain; they can only be estimated. Before estimating the likely benefits and costs associated with each solution alternative, the decision-maker can simplify the task considerably by first screening the list of solution alternatives and eliminating all those that are obviously (a) *not feasible* because of a lack of ability or resources to implement them appropriately, or (b) *unacceptable* because of the high likelihood of serious negative consequences. Information seeking regarding the availability of requisite abilities or resources might be appropriate at this point if there are any doubts about what alternatives should be eliminated, since this information is not always immediately available to the problem-solver.

After anticipating the likely benefits and costs (short-term and long-term) of each solution alternative, the decision-maker *judges* the expected outcome or utility of each alternative, and then *compares* alternatives, to select the solution or solution combination with the best expected utility. In the present approach, judgments of expected utility are based primarily on four benefit/cost criteria: (a) problem resolution (likelihood of achieving the problem-solving goal); (b) emotional well-being (quality of expected emotional outcome); (c) time/effort (amount of time and effort expected to be required), and (d) overall personal-social well-being (total expected benefit/cost ratio).

Problem resolution is emphasized most because other benefits would lose much of their significance if the problem were not solved satisfactorily. *Emotional well-being* is given special consideration because emotional pleasure and pain are benefits and costs of major significance in most people's lives. *Time and effort* are emphasized because these are highly valued resources to most people. Other things being equal, individuals are likely to choose the alternative which requires the least amount of time and effort. Indeed, for some decision-makers, the desire to minimize time and effort is a stronger motive than the desire to maximize problem-resolution effectiveness (Payne, 1982). *Overall personal-social well-being* takes into account the balance between total expected benefits and total expected costs, long-term as well as short-term. The question which the decision-maker asks here is: "How favorable (benefits outweigh costs) or unfavorable (costs outweigh benefits) is the likely total benefit/cost ratio?" This question is important because a solution which is judged favorably according to the first three criteria may still be rejected as a poor solution because the *total* expected costs are perceived as far outweighing the expected benefits, especially when taking possible long-term consequences into account. This set of outcome criteria applies to problems and decision-makers in general. Any particular decision-maker can use *any* set of outcome criteria he considers important for judging solution alternatives for *any* particular problem.

Even when common outcome criteria are being used, decision-makers will still vary in their evaluations of solution outcomes because of differences in personal norms, values, and commitments. Therefore, the best procedure is for each decision-maker to rate the degree of his satisfaction with the expected outcome for each solution (vis-à-vis the outcome criteria) on a scale from "very satisfied" to "very dissatisfied." On the basis of these ratings, the expected utility of each solution alternative can be established (see Chapter 8 for a further description of this procedure).

In prospect theory, there are two phases in the choice process: (a) an initial phase in which solution alternatives, solution outcomes, and contingencies (conditional probabilities relating solutions to outcomes) are "framed" (i.e., conceived or formulated) and (b) a subsequent phase of evaluation involving a generalized expected-utility process. According to Tversky and Kahneman (1981), the frame or conception that a decision-maker adopts for different solutions is determined partly by the formulation of the problem (e.g., the statement of goals) and partly by the personal-social characteristics of the decision-maker (e.g., beliefs, values, commitments, emotions). These investigators have found that the way a decision problem is framed significantly influences the preference for solution alternatives. For example, when making decisions, people tend to be influenced more by potential losses than by possible gains. The greater the loss, the stronger this effect will be. Thus, a solution that is framed in such a way that potential losses are emphasized will tend to be less preferred than one that is framed in a way which emphasizes possible gains. Most importantly, Tversky and Kahneman report that people are normally unaware of alternative frames for the same solution, and of the frames' potential effects on the relative attractiveness of solution alternatives. This tends to reduce the quality or effectiveness of decision making and may result in a lack of commitment to the chosen solution, thus reducing the likelihood of effective implementation.

There are several procedures that the decision-maker can use to facilitate awareness of alternative decision frames, as well as the beliefs, values, and emotions that might influence his preference for solution alternatives. First, the decision-maker can go over his list of solution alternatives and change any vague or ambiguously stated solutions into more concrete, behavioral terms. If possible, the decision-maker might even "try out" different solution alternatives using behavior rehearsal (role-playing) or covert rehearsal (imaginal role-playing) (Janis & Mann, 1977). These procedures force the decision-maker to deal with a concrete, behavioral representation of the solution idea, which increases the likelihood that he will become aware of relevant feelings and beliefs associated with the particular solution. Second, the decision-maker can attempt to view the problem from a different perspective and generate alternative problem formulations (a return to the problem-definition and formulation task). For example, the person might consider alternative ways to restate the problem-solving goal or goals, which is likely to change the preference for different solutions.

A third procedure for facilitating awareness of different decision frames is to generate as many solutions as possible and consider alternative solution conceptions; that is, the person can consider different ways to state or express the same solution, which might change the "meaning" of the solution and, hence, its significance or attractiveness. Finally, and most importantly, the decision-maker can consider all possible solution outcomes by anticipating as many different gains and losses as possible for each solution alternative. These gains and losses should include not only the direct objective outcomes but also the immediate and long-term effects of the solution on personal and social well-being (e.g., subjective feelings, self-esteem, vocational-economic security, social evaluations, interpersonal relations). According to Tversky and Kahneman (1981), people generally evaluate solution options in terms of a "minimal account," which includes only the direct consequences of the action (e.g., efficacy and time/effort). In order to improve the quality of decisions, they recommend that people apply the "predictive criterion" of rationality. This criterion encourages the decision-maker to anticipate future implications for emotional well-being and to ask "What will I feel then?" instead of focusing only on "What do I want now?"

Based on his evaluation of the estimated outcomes of the available solution alternatives, the decision-maker then answers three questions: (a) Is the problematic situation changeable or unchangeable? (b) Do I need more information before I can decide on a course of action? and (c) What solution or solution combination should I choose to implement? The answer to the first two questions will have a significant influence on the answer to the third question, namely, the choice of a solution plan (Folkman et al., in press). If the problem is appraised as changeable, then instrumental actions aimed at changing the situation will be emphasized. If the problem is appraised as unchangeable, the problem must then be reformulated and solutions that emphasize acceptance, changing perspective, and emotional control will be preferred. If it is decided that more information is needed, the latter approaches might be considered as a temporary solution until more information can be obtained.

After questions a and b have been answered, the decision-maker then decides on the solution plan that appears to have the best chance of maximizing expected utility. This plan may be *simple* or *complex*. A simple plan involves the selection of a single course of action. There are two types of complex plans: a solution combination and a contingency plan. A *solution combination* involves the choice of a combination of solution alternatives to be implemented concurrently. A *contingency plan* involves the choice of a combination of solution alternatives to be implemented contingently: implement solution A; if that does not work, implement solution B, etc.

Solution Implementation and Verification

The purpose of this task is to assess the solution outcome and verify the "effectiveness" of the chosen solution strategy in the real-life problematic situation. Up to this point in the problem-solving process, the problem has been solved symbolically, but the effectiveness of the solution in coping with the real-life problem has not yet been established. The only way to accomplish this is to implement the solution strategy in the real-life setting and evaluate the outcome objectively.

The conceptual framework for the solution-implementation and verification task is based on control theory or cybernetics (Carver & Scheier, 1982; Miller, Galanter, & Pribram, 1960) and the cognitive-behavioral conception of self-control (Bandura, 1971; Kanfer, 1970). The basic concept in control theory is the negative feedback loop, termed *negative* because its function is to negate or reduce perceived discrepancies from a comparison value. Applying this concept to self-control, an individual's performance on a given task is influenced or guided by the degree of congruence between his performance and a given standard or reference value. When the discrepancy between task performance and the reference standard is "unsatisfactory," the individual continues to "operate" or perform on the task until a satisfactory match is achieved, at which time the individual terminates the particular activity and task performance is considered "successful."

The cognitive-behavioral conception of self-control consists of four components: (a) performance, (b) self-monitoring, (c) self-evaluation, and (d) self-reinforcement.

Performance, as applied to social problem solving, refers to solution implementation. It is important to recognize that the performance of the chosen solution plan in the real-life setting may be influenced significantly by factors other than problem-solving ability. For example, solution performance might be inhibited or disrupted because of other ability deficits (academic aptitude), performance skill deficits (social skills), emotional distress, or motivational (reinforcement) deficits. If the problem-solver discovers immediately that effective solution performance is not possible because of obstacles such as these, it will be necessary at that time to return to previous problem-solving tasks in order to select an alternative solution, or to reformulate the problem to include overcoming the obstacle or obstacles to effective solution performance.

Self-monitoring involves observation of one's own solution behavior and/or its products (outcomes). In order to accomplish an accurate and objective assessment of the solution, it is necessary to record or measure solution performance in some objective way. For example, if the individual's solution involves the preparation of a strict budget to save money, he might keep a careful record of the amount of money spent each day. A person who is attempting to reduce tardiness at work might keep a careful record of the number of days he arrives at work on time each week. The most relevant measure of solution outcome will be determined by the formulation of the problem, particularly the statement of the problem-solving goal or goals.

Self-evaluation involves the feedback loop concept. The problem-solver compares the observed solution outcome with the predicted or expected outcome for that solution, based on the decision-making process. If the match is "satisfactory," then the problem-solver moves to the final step, namely, *self-reinforcement,* where he rewards himself for "a job well done." This reward may simply be a positive self-statement (for example, "I'm proud of myself, I handled that very well"), or it might be some more tangible reward, such as purchasing some desired object or engaging in some enjoyable activity. In addition to self-reward, perhaps the most powerful reinforcement of all is likely to come from the positive solution outcome itself, which might involve events such as the reduction of aversive stimulation, the occurrence of positive social reinforcement, the removal of an obstacle to a desired goal, or the resolution of a conflict. This reinforcement step is critical for social problem solving not only because it reinforces effective problem-solving performance, but also because it strengthens perceived control and self-efficacy expectations, which are so very important for future problem-solving efforts.

If the discrepancy between the observed solution outcome and the expected outcome is "unsatisfactory," the problem-solver must "troubleshoot" or attempt to determine whether the source of the difficulty is somewhere in the problem-solving process or in solution performance (e.g., skills deficit, emotional inhibition). At this point, the problem-solver may decide to go back to one or more of the problem-solving tasks in an attempt to find a more effective solution, or he may try to work out a solution plan for overcoming the obstacle or obstacles to effective solution performance. If the individual cannot succeed after attempting these various corrective strategies, then the best solution at that point might be to seek help or advice, or accept the problem as insoluble and focus on palliative or emotion-focused coping techniques (Folkman et al., in press; Meichenbaum & Cameron, 1983).

Earlier it was pointed out that the setting of unrealistic goals during the problem-definition and formulation task could have negative consequences for the other stages in the problem-solving process. These negative consequences are nowhere more serious than during the solution-implementation and verification task. If an individual's goals or standards are unrealistically high or strict, it may be impossible for him to achieve a satisfactory match between the observed outcome of his solution behavior and his performance standards. Instead of terminating the problem-solving process and getting help or advice, some problem-solvers may feel "compelled" to continue the problem-solving activity despite the lack of success. In order to avoid this "vicious circle" of unsuccessful problem solving, the problem-solver must be careful to set realistic goals initially, and then avoid an overly strict adherence to these standards or an insistence on finding the "perfect match" when evaluating the solution outcome. In direct support of this position, behavior therapists have warned about the negative consequences of unrealistic and overly strict performance standards in the application of self-control procedures (Rimm & Masters, 1979). Cognitive therapists have long argued that perfectionistic goals and expectations can have serious negative emotional consequences (Ellis, 1962; Ellis & Grieger, 1977). Moreover, perfectionism in problem solving, and the inability to accept the fact that some problems may not be soluble, at least not in their present formulation, are consistent with many of the characteristics of the Type A personality, which appears to be prone to the development of stress-related disorders (Grimm & Yarnold, 1984; Jenkins, 1975).

Empirical Evaluation of Model Components

Several experimental studies have investigated the efficacy of training in individual problem-solving component skills or in different combinations of components. The dependent measure in most studies was performance on hypothetical socially-oriented problem-solving or decision-making tasks. A few studies on the generation-of-alternatives components used creative problem-solving tasks as the dependent measure. The subjects in most studies were normal college students. However, one study included both depressed and nondepressed college student subjects, one study focused on after-care psychiatric patients; and another focused on alcoholic inpatients.

The *problem-orientation* component was evaluated in a study by Cormier, Otani, and Cormier (1986). Subjects who received instruction in the content of problem orientation performed significantly better than control-group subjects on a problem-solving task in which they were asked to select the best alternative from a list of solution alternatives to several socially oriented problems. In addition, there is much experimental support for the effects of one particular problem-orientation variable on coping performance—namely, perceived self-efficacy (Bandura, 1977, 1980). According to Bandura (1980), people avoid tasks they believe exceed their coping capabilities, but they willingly undertake activities they judge themselves capable of managing successfully. In addition to these studies, Heppner and his associates have reported studies suggesting that such problem-orientation variables as problem-solving confidence and a perception of control have a positive influence on problem-solving performance (Heppner & Petersen, 1982; Heppner, et al., 1982).

Several studies have provided evidence supporting the efficacy of training in *problem definition and formulation* (PDF). In one study, subjects who were given specific training in PDF did significantly better on a decision-making task than subjects who received no training (Nezu & D'Zurilla, 1981a). In another study, subjects who were trained in PDF produced more effective solution alternatives on a problem-solving task than did a control group which did not receive training (Nezu & D'Zurilla, 1981b). Results supporting the important role of PDF in problem solving were also found by Cormier et al. (1986). In this study, subjects trained in problem-solving skills which included PDF supporting the important role of problem definition and formulation selected significantly better solution alternatives after a one-month follow-up than did subjects whose training did not include PDF. These results are consistent with those reported by Nezu and D'Zurilla (1981b) while providing additional evidence for the durability of training effects.

Several studies have investigated the efficacy of principles involved in the *generation-of-alternative solutions* component of the model. Brilhart and Jochem (1964) found that "brainstorming" instructions (quantity principle, deferment-of-judgment principle, and variety principle) resulted in more good-quality solution ideas than instructions requesting subjects to produce only *good* ideas. D'Zurilla and Nezu (1980) found that subjects who received training in the use of the quantity principle produced significantly more effective solutions than control subjects who received no training. These results were later replicated by Nezu and D'Zurilla (1981b) and by Nezu and Ronan (in press). The latter study found significant training effects with depressed as well as nondepressed college students. Several studies have focused on creative problems, such as finding new uses for an ordinary broom or wire coat hanger and inventing brand names for new products. Results supporting brainstorming instructions have been found by Meadow, Parnes, and Reese (1959), Parnes and Meadow (1959), and Weisskopf-Joelson and Eliseo (1961). Evidence for the deferment-of-judgment principle has been provided by Bayless (1967) and Parloff and Handlon (1964).

Four studies have been reported which provide support for the model's *decision-making* component. Nezu and D'Zurilla (1979) investigated the effects of training in decision making on the ability of subjects to make effective decisions when asked to choose the best solution from among a list of alternative solutions to socially-oriented test problems. The results showed that subjects who received specific training in the decision-making component made more effective choices than control subjects who received no training or who were provided only with a general definition of the expected-utility model of decision making. These results were later replicated in studies by Nezu and D'Zurilla (1981a) and Nezu and Ronan (in press). The latter study found significant results for both depressed and nondepressed college students. Results supporting the role of the decision-making component were also reported by Cormier et al. (1986). Focusing on a task in which subjects were required to describe in detail the behaviors they used to solve problems, Cormier et al. found that subjects trained with the decision-making component described significantly more problem-solving behaviors at a one-month follow-up assessment than did subjects trained without the decision-making component.

In addition to providing evidence supporting the individual contributions of problem orientation, problem definition and formulation, and decision making to problem-solving effectiveness, the study by Cormier et al. (1986) also assessed the effects of training in all three of these components together *plus* the generation-of-alternative-solutions component. Compared to an untrained control group, they found that the trained subjects selected significantly better solution alternatives and described significantly more problem-solving behaviors at posttesting and at the one-month follow-up.

In a study which focused on seven chronic psychiatric patients enrolled in an aftercare program, Hansen, St. Lawrence, and Christoff (1985) used a multiple-baseline design to evaluate the effectiveness of training in the following problem-solving component skills: (a) problem identification (specific statement of a problem); (b) goal definition (specific statement of a desired end); (c) solution evaluation (specific benefit or cost statement regarding a solution); (d) evaluation of alternatives (specific benefit and/or cost statement regarding at least two solutions); and (e) selection of a best solution (explicit choice of one of the proposed solutions as the best course of action).

A group training format was used, with sessions conducted twice weekly. Training focused on the first skill component until the subjects demonstrated skill acquisition, and then the next component was trained, and so on. Following each training session, skill acquisition and the effectiveness of solutions were assessed with four of the problematic situations used in training and four unfamiliar generalization situations. A social validation assessment was also conducted by comparing the patients' problem-solving effectiveness with that of 20 "normal," nonpsychiatric persons living in the community. All of the problematic situations used for training and assessment approximated actual situations that the patients were likely to encounter in the community and that were reported as problematic by the patients and the program staff.

The results showed that each component skill was rapidly improved with the introduction of training for that particular skill, with the improvement generalizing to the untrained problematic situations. Moreover, problem-solving effectiveness (i.e., the effectiveness of solutions as rated by independent judges) improved significantly over time, with the largest increase occurring during the solution evaluation phase of training. With regard to the social validation assessment, prior to training the patient sample showed a significant deficit in problem-solving effectiveness compared to the criterion nonpsychiatric sample. By the evaluation-of-alternatives phase of training, however, the patients' problem-solving effectiveness had improved to the point where it was equivalent to that of the criterion sample.

In a similar multiple-baseline study focusing on five alcoholic inpatients, Kelly, Scott, Prue, and Rychtarik (1985) provided training in problem-solving component skills related to problem definition, the generation of alternative solutions, and decision making. Training resulted in significant improvement in all three component skills; however, no concurrent improvement was found in problem-solving effectiveness using personally relevant problematic situations related to alcohol.

The negative results for the problem-solving performance test in the Kelly et al. study conflict with the positive results found with college student subjects in the Nezu and D'Zurilla studies and the Nezu and Ronan studies, and with the chronic aftercare psychiatric patients in the Hansen et al. study. An informal observation reported by Kelly et al. suggests a possible explanation for their negative findings. On the problem-solving test, subjects were asked to generate alternative solutions and then choose the "best" one. According to the investigators, their alcoholic subjects often *generated* more effective solutions but rejected them, either because of negative beliefs about the solution or because of a desire to avoid a stressful encounter, such as an assertive confrontation. This observation supports the view that negative cognitive and emotional factors can have a detrimental effect on problem-solving performance, especially in a clinical population, and that PST programs must include procedures to assess and control these disruptive factors. Since the problem-orientation component of the present problem-solving model is designed for this purpose, it would appear to be a very important component for PST programs with clinical populations (Heppner & Anderson, 1985).

There have been no experimental studies specifically investigating the *solution-implementation-and-verification* component of the model. However, it is an undisputed fact that an objective assessment of outcome is necessary to establish clearly the success of any behavior-modification procedure. Thus, the evidence supporting the use of self-monitoring and self-evaluation in behavioral assessment *in general* can be used to support the efficacy of solution implementation and verification (see Cone & Hawkins, 1977; Barlow, 1981; Barlow, Haynes, & Nelson, 1984).

In conclusion, there is empirical support for the efficacy of all five components of the present problem-solving model. All components contribute significantly to problem-solving effectiveness. The strongest evidence appears to favor the problem definition and formulation component. These results argue for a careful definition and formulation of the problem before proceeding to the tasks of generating alternative solutions and decision making.

Summary

A prescriptive model of social problem solving is presented which consists of five components: (a) problem orientation, (b) problem definition and formulation, (c) generation of alternative solutions, (d) decision making, and (e) solution implementation and verification. The goal of *problem orientation* is to develop a facilitative, problem-solving cognitive set. The objective in *problem definition and formulation* is to gather relevant factual information about the problem, clarify the nature of the problem, set a realistic problem-solving goal, and reappraise the significance of the problem for personal-social well-being. The purpose of the model's third component, *generation of alternative solutions,* is to make available as many solution alternatives as possible in such a way as to maximize the likelihood that the "best" solution will be among them. The objective of *decision making* is to evaluate the available solution alternatives and to select the "best" one(s) to implement in the actual problematic situation. Finally, the purpose of the fifth component of the model, *solution-implementation and verification,* is to assess the solution outcome and verify the "effectiveness" of the chosen solution in the real-life problematic situation.

Experimental evidence is presented which supports the efficacy of individual components of the model. The strongest evidence seems to favor problem definition and formulation. Problem-solvers are advised to carefully define and formulate a problem before moving on to the tasks of generating solutions and making a decision.

4

Role of Emotions in
Social Problem Solving

Unlike human problem solving in the laboratory setting, emotional factors play a major role in problem solving within the real-life social setting. Although several investigators have discussed the effects of stress and other emotional variables on social problem-solving performance (George, 1974; Janis, 1982; Janis & Mann, 1977; Mandler, 1982; Mechanic, 1970, 1974; Snyder, Bruck, & Sapin, 1962; Staats, 1975), the subject has received very little empirical attention to date. It is hoped that the present analysis will help to provide some suggestions and guidelines for future research.

There are three possible sources of emotional arousal in social problem solving: (a) the objective problematic situation, (b) the problem-orientation cognitions (problem perception, problem appraisal, etc.), and (c) the specific problem-solving tasks (problem definition and formulation, decision making, etc.). Emotions from all three sources may facilitate or inhibit problem-solving performance, depending on such variables as the subjective quality of the emotional response (pleasure vs. pain) and the intensity of emotional arousal (autonomic nervous system activity). The effects may be specific (e.g., effects on solution preference) or generalized (e.g., effects on performance efficiency). Awareness and control of these emotions is essential for effective social problem solving.

The Objective Problematic
Situation

The objective problematic situation may produce "conditioned" and/or "unconditioned" emotional responses. Conditioned emotional responses result from prior emotional conditioning or associative learning experiences involving the particular problematic situation or stimulus elements associated with it. These emotional responses will vary in nature and intensity across situations and individuals, depending on each person's past associative learning experiences.

> Mary is having a problem with her roommate, Beth. Beth criticizes her frequently and the criticism is often unfair and unjust. Criticism provokes very strong conditioned anxiety in Mary because, in her past, criticism was frequently associated with harsh physical punishment. Because of her anxiety, Mary is having much difficulty coping with this problem and usually tries to avoid Beth as much as possible.

Unconditioned emotional responses are the result of stimulus conditions which produce emotional arousal independent of any prior associative learning experiences involving those particular conditions, although other learning experiences (e.g., perceptual development, conceptual learning) may contribute to the capacity of these conditions to produce arousal. For example, after a period of cognitive learning whereby a child learns to perceive environmental events as familiar, a novel event, such as the appearance of a stranger, may provoke a fear response (Hunt, 1963). These emotionally arousing conditions tend to produce similar autonomic effects across individuals, although the subjective quality of the emotional responses may vary depending on individual differences in the perception (interpretation) and appraisal of the autonomic activity and the stimulus conditions producing it. Some of these stimulus conditions are problematic because they tend to be perceived as "aversive" or stressful, thus, instigating efforts to remove or reduce them, but an effective response is not always readily apparent or available. They include the following conditions:

- Harmful or painful stimuli which threaten the homeostatic balance of the body, including various pathogens and any intense physical stimulus (e.g., noise, heat, cold, pressure, etc.) (Selye, 1983)
- Conflict (e.g., competing stimulus demands, conceptual conflict, decisional conflict) (Epstein, 1982; Janis & Mann, 1977; Phillips, 1978)
- Frustration (i.e., an obstacle preventing a goal response) (Mather, 1970)
- Loss or deprivation of customary reinforcers (Mowrer, 1960a, 1960b)

- Unpredictability (uncertainty) or uncontrollability of aversive events (Hamberger & Lohr, 1984)
- Ambiguity (Wrubel, et al. 1981)
- Complexity or novelty that cannot be assimilated successfully with stored information or prior experience (McClelland & Clark, 1966; Hunt, 1963).

Jane loves her pet parakeet. She likes to feed it, listen to it chirp, and walk around the apartment with it on her shoulder. One morning Jane woke up and went to feed her pet, but she found that it was dead. She felt very upset (loss of customary reinforcers). After a few days, she was feeling even more upset because she could not do anything to keep the picture of the dead bird out of her mind (uncontrollability of an aversive event).

Jim graduated from college with a degree in banking and finance. He took a job as an office worker with a small financial company. Since Jim is very ambitious and would like to advance rapidly in his career, he applied after six months for a well-paid job with much more responsibility with a major financial corporation. During the job interview, Jim became increasingly anxious because he was being asked questions he could not adequately answer due to his lack of experience in the field (complexity or novelty that cannot be assimilated successfully with stored information or prior experience). He became even more anxious when he realized that the interview was going poorly and that it might be a major obstacle to getting the job (obstacle preventing a goal response). Later, after learning that he did not get the job, he was anxious because he was unsure as to whether he should continue to look for a better job, or stay with his present job for a longer period of time (conflict).

Maintaining a transactional perspective with regard to the nature of a problem, emotional arousal generated by the problematic situation is likely to interact with problem-orientation cognitions in such a way that the two sets of variables are likely to influence each other. Problem-produced emotional responses may influence the nature of problem-orientation cognitions (problem-perception, problem appraisal) and these cognitions may, in turn, affect the nature and intensity of the original emotional responses. For example, an anxiety response generated by a conflict between different job demands may be the first sign to an individual that a problem exists, thus facilitating problem recognition. However, if the person focuses on his internal anxiety response instead of attending to the external conditions producing it (i.e., the job conflict), he might label the problem an "emotional problem" instead of a "job problem," which might increase his anxiety. A strong anxiety response might also affect other problem-orientation cognitions adversely, possibly influencing the individual to: (a) attribute the cause of the problem to an internal defect or abnormality (emotional hypersensitivity, psychological "weakness"); (b) appraise the problem as a significant threat to well-being (self-esteem); (c) doubt his ability to cope with the problem successfully; and/or (d) experience a sense of time urgency, resulting in the failure to devote a sufficient amount of time and effort to problem solving. These negative problem-orientation cognitions may, in turn, affect the original anxiety response, possibly exacerbating it or changing it into a feeling of inadequacy or anxious depression.

Problem-Orientation Cognitions

In addition to their effect on problem-produced emotions, problem-orientation cognitions may also produce *new* emotional responses. These emotional responses may include (a) conditioned emotional responses to the verbal labels used to identify problems and (b) emotions associated with the perceptual characteristics (i.e., meaning, significance) of the problem-orientation cognitions (Lazarus, 1982; Lazarus, Kanner, & Folkman, 1980).

The nature of conditioned emotional responses to problem labels may vary in accordance with each individual's past associative learning experiences and present interpretations and appraisals. For example, the label "illness" or "health problem" may provoke a conditioned anxiety response if the person had a serious illness in the past, or if a close friend had recently died during an illness. Emotions associated with the perceptual characteristics of problem-orientation cognitions may vary in nature depending on whether the meaning or significance of these cognitions contain expectations of *benefit* (personal growth, achievement) or expectations of *harm or loss* (failure, loss of control). Cognitions that contain positive expectations are likely to produce positive affect (hope, relief, feeling of confidence) and those that contain negative expectations are likely to produce negative affect (fear, disappointment, depression). Since the different problem-orientation cognitions interact with one another, the meaning, significance, and emotional quality of one will influence the nature and feeling tone of the others, resulting in the possibility of a generalized problem-solving cognitive set, which produces positive affect and approach behavior, or a generalized negative cognitive set, which produces negative affect and avoidance behavior.

The sales manager has just informed John that he wants him to increase his sales performance next month by 50%. Although John is not immediately aware of how he can accomplish this goal, he approaches the problem with a feeling of hope and confidence. These feelings are the result of the way John *thinks* about the problem. First, he realizes that a problem such as this is a normal, inevitable part of life. He does not blame himself for the problem or think that it means he is incompetent or inadequate. He believes, instead, that the problem could happen to anyone. Second, he views the problem as a challenge or opportunity to learn something and improve himself. He believes in the philosophy that it is better to take on a challenge and fail than to avoid the problem and not try to solve it at all. Third, John believes that there is a solution to the problem and that he is capable of finding it if he tries. Fourth, he realizes that solving the problem might take time and effort. However, he values independent problem solving and is willing to commit time and effort to the problem.

Bob has also been informed by the sales manager that he is expected to increase his sales performance next month by 50%. Like John, Bob is also unsure of how he can accomplish this goal but, unlike John, he approaches the problem with much anxiety, fear, and self-doubt. These feelings are a result of the way *Bob thinks* about the problem. First, Bob blames himself for the problem, thinking that he is an incompetent salesman and probably not suited for the job. Second, he views the problem not as a challenge, but as a threat to his well-being psychologically (self-esteem), socially (reputation), and economically (job security). As a result, he would like to avoid the problem if he can. Third, Bob does not believe that he is capable of finding a satisfactory solution to the problem on his own. He believes that his only alternatives are to get help from someone else or to quit the job and try some other kind of work. Fourth, he thinks that a competent person would be able to find a solution to the problem without much time and effort. His failure to do so confirms his view that he is incompetent. Moreover, Bob does not value independent problem solving enough to commit much time and effort to this activity. He prefers to get others to solve his problems for him.

Specific Problem-Solving Tasks

The specific problem-solving tasks may produce four types of emotional responses: (a) conditioned emotional responses to the verbal labels used to define and formulate the problem and to identify solutions and outcomes; (b) emotions associated with the perceptual characteristics of particular problem formulations, solution frames, and outcome frames (Tversky & Kahneman, 1981); (c) emotions associated with the outcomes or consequences of problem-solving task performance (i.e., reinforcement and punishment) (Mowrer, 1960a, 1960b), and (d) unconditioned emotional responses produced by conditions inherent in information processing and decision making (i.e., ambiguity, uncertainty, decisional conflict (Janis, 1982; Janis & Mann, 1977).

The verbal labels used to define problems and describe solutions and outcomes may produce conditioned emotional responses based on past emotional conditioning experiences. In an earlier example, the label "health problem" provoked conditioned anxiety because of a person's previous serious illness or his friend's terminal illness. The further clarification and definition of the health problem may provoke even more anxiety if the medical details are similar to the person's previous illness or the friend's illness. Moreover, possible solutions and outcomes, such as taking a certain kind of medication with undesirable side effects, may provoke more anxiety because of past aversive experiences with similar medication, or the friend's negative experiences with that type of medication. During this experience, the conditioned anxiety is likely to influence the person's reappraisal of the health problem, possibly causing the person to exaggerate the threat to well-being, which is likely to increase anxiety even further.

Emotions associated with the perceptual characteristics of problem formulations (including problem reappraisal), solution frames, and outcome frames will be positive or negative depending on whether their meaning or significance contains expectations of *benefit* (e.g., hope, relief) or expectations of *harm or loss* (e.g., fear, disappointment, depression). The emotional effects of problem formulations can contribute to cognitive distortions and influence the selection of problem-solving goals.

For example, consider a psychiatrist whose formulation of a clinical problem includes the possibility of suicide. Reappraising the problem following this formulation, he perceives the problem as a significant threat (expectation of harm or loss), which provokes anxiety. This anxiety might cause the psychiatrist to magnify the significance of certain information about the problem or to ignore, deny, or minimize its importance. On the other hand, the anxiety might serve a useful purpose if it alerts the psychiatrist to important information which he might have otherwise ignored. The psychiatrist's anxiety might also influence his selection of a problem-solving goal. He might try to find a way to refer the patient to another psychiatrist instead of trying to determine the best treatment strategy. On the other hand, he might set a goal of trying to reduce his own anxiety about treating patients with suicidal tendencies.

Emotions associated with the formulation of alternative solutions and outcomes are likely to have a significant effect on the preference for different solutions (Tversky & Kahneman, 1981). As noted in an earlier chapter, the potential harm or loss (negative affect) associated with different solutions appears to have a greater influence on solution preference than the potential benefits (positive affect). Moreover, the probability of significant harm or loss is more likely to be overestimated, possibly because such events are pictured more vividly in the mind, due to the strong affect associated with them. During the generation of alternative solutions, the problem-solver attempts to disregard these emotional outcomes. However, during decision making, it is important for the problem-solver to be aware of these emotions and to take them into account when evaluating solution alternatives.

> Bill is a middle-aged divorced man who would like to develop a close relationship with a woman. He has recently met two women and he would like to ask one of them out for a date. Helen is a very attractive woman with whom Bill has much in common (benefits/positive affect). However, he is unsure of how she feels about him and he believes that the likelihood of rejection from her is high (harm or loss/negative affect). Susan is much less attractive and her interests are less similar to Bill's (harm or loss/negative affect). However, Bill knows that Susan likes him and would probably accept a date with him (benefits/positive affect). Because Bill is extremely sensitive to rejection, he exaggerates the threat to his well-being if Helen were to reject him and he overestimates the probability of its occurrence. As a result, he decides to ask Susan for a date instead of Helen. Bill's oversensitivity to rejection is recognized during his therapy and cognitive restructuring is conducted in an attempt to reduce it.

Each specific problem-solving task has a definite purpose or goal in the problem-solving process. Positive reinforcement is likely to occur when task performance has a successful outcome or when signs of progress are perceived, whereas punishment is likely to occur when the outcome is unsuccessful or when obstacles are encountered. Positive reinforcement produces positive affect (hope, relief), which tends to strengthen performance, while punishment produces negative affect (fear, disappointment), which tends to weaken performance (Mowrer, 1960a, 1960b). In addition to strengthening performance on one problem-solving task, reinforcement-produced positive affect will also provide approach motivation for the next task. On the other hand, punishment-produced negative affect may motivate avoidance behavior. These emotional variables are particularly important during the final problem-solving task,

namely, solution implementation and verification. Emotions associated with past and present solution outcomes may facilitate or
inhibit solution performance, depending on the quality and intensity of emotional arousal. They are also likely to have a significant
direct influence on the individual's satisfaction with particular solutions. Thus, the quality and intensity of emotional outcomes are
important criteria to consider in evaluating solution effectiveness
during this task. During PST, an attempt is made to maximize
positive reinforcement and, thus, positive affect, using the principle
of shaping or successive approximations—i.e., presenting exercises
and homework assignments in progressive steps of increasing difficulty and complexity so as to maximize the probability of success.

Emotional arousal will also be generated by the conditions of
ambiguity, uncertainty, and conflict, which are inherent in information processing and decision making. Ambiguity and uncertainty
are usually present during problem solving because most problems
are initially vague and poorly defined. If the problem is at all
difficult or complex, there will also be uncertainty and conflict
regarding the choice of the "best" solution. According to Janis and
Mann (1977), such "decisional conflict" is likely to be most stressful
when there are simultaneous tendencies to accept and to reject a
given course of action under conditions where there are significant
risks associated with all the available alternatives.

The Effect of Emotions
on Performance Efficiency

Emotional arousal from all three sources described above, the objective problematic situation, problem-orientation cognitions, and
specific problem-solving tasks, can combine to have a significant
generalized effect on performance efficiency throughout the problem-solving process. The variables that influence the relationship
between emotional arousal and performance efficiency during problem solving have not yet been clearly established, but they are
likely to include the subjective quality of emotional responses, the
intensity of emotional arousal (autonomic activity), and the duration of emotional stress. In general, positive emotions may be expected to facilitate problem-solving performance; negative emotions
may be expected to inhibit performance. In addition, however, the
effects of emotional arousal may also depend to a considerable extent on the intensity of emotional arousal. If we apply the Yerkes-

Dodson Law (Yerkes & Dodson, 1908) to social problem solving, we might expect an inverted U relationship between emotional arousal and performance efficiency. When emotional arousal is low, performance efficiency should be poor, but as arousal increases, performance should also increase to an optimal level, after which a further increase in arousal should result in a deterioration in performance. The intensity of arousal is also likely to influence the subjective quality of the emotional experience. Arousal levels above the optimal point are likely to be experienced (perceived) as negative affect, while arousal below the optimal level may be experienced as either positive or negative affect, depending on the nature of the specific cues in the situation and the person's interpretation and appraisal of these cues as well as his autonomic activity.

While the inverted U model has a great deal of common-sense appeal, its generality has been seriously questioned (Hockey & Hamilton, 1983; Mandler, 1982). According to Hockey & Hamilton (1983), there is general support for the positive part of the curve, but less unambiguous direct support for the detrimental effects of "excessive" arousal. Studies have produced conflicting results. One possible reason for the conflicting results is that the measures of arousal have varied widely. In fact, Lacey (1967) has argued that there is no single unitary and useful concept of arousal. Another explanation more relevant here is related to the cue utilization hypothesis of Easterbrook (1959). According to this hypothesis, as emotional arousal increases, a narrowing or restriction in attention occurs, reducing the number of cues attended to. Easterbrook points out that in some cases a narrowing of attention may result in an improvement in performance. For example, when the excluded cues are irrelevant to the task, performance might improve because of the activating effects of arousal. However, on complex tasks, which require attention to a wide range of cues, as is often the case in problem solving, a narrowing of attention is more likely to reduce performance efficiency.

It has often been observed that individuals attempting to perform under stress frequently focus their attention on task-irrelevant cues, such as their own autonomic activity and their own threatening interpretations and appraisals (Mandler, 1982; Sarason, 1980). Sarason calls the latter cognitions "self-preoccupying thoughts," which include catastrophizing, blaming oneself, unproductive worries, and thoughts of helplessness. After reviewing several studies on the narrowing of attention under stress, Mandler (1982) concluded that stress reduces attentional capacity and narrows it to *central* cues—i.e., the cues that are initially maximally attended to in the stress situation. The task-irrelevant cues described above are often central for a problem-solver under stress, because they are threatening and thus considered to be highly significant for well-being (Baddeley, 1972). However, if a problem-solver perceives the target problem-solving task as central, then problem-solving performance could very well improve under stress.

The problem-solving deficiencies that may result from high stress have been discussed by Janis (1982, 1983) and Mandler (1982). According to Mandler (1982), the narrowing of thought processes under high stress affects the generation of alternatives and decision making in such a way that only obvious solution alternatives and outcomes are considered, thus severely limiting the range of available solutions and the range of outcomes affecting solution choice. In a similar vein, Janis (1982) points out that high stress is likely to result in cognitive deficiencies, which include narrowing the range of perceived alternatives, overlooking long-term consequences, inefficient information-seeking, erroneously evaluating expected outcomes, and using oversimplified decision rules that fail to take into account the full range of values relevant to the choice.

Janis and Mann (1977) have identified two types of maladaptive decision-making patterns that may result from a high degree of stress: (a) defensive avoidance and (b) hypervigilance. Defensive avoidance is characterized by procrastination and by attempts to shift responsibility for decision making to someone else. Hypervigilance is a paniclike state in which the decision-maker searches frantically for a solution, rapidly shifting back and forth between alternatives, and impulsively seizing upon a hastily contrived solution that seems to promise immediate relief.

Thus far, our discussion has focused on the effects of the intensity and subjective quality of emotional arousal on performance efficiency. Another variable which may influence these effects is the *duration* of emotional stress. Prolonged emotional stress may result from frequent exposure to difficult life problems, emotional oversensitivity to problems, and/or inability to solve problems effectively, resulting in frequent "punishment" (i.e., aversive consequences, loss of reinforcement) and a perception of uncontrollability.

What are the possible effects of repeated or prolonged exposure to stressful problems on performance efficiency? Although this question has not yet been adequately studied, stress research by Hans Selye (1983) has provided some clues. Working with both animals and human subjects, Selye found that a nonspecific pattern of biochemical responses occurs when an organism is continuously exposed to any "stressor" or strong demand for adjustment. This nonspecific response pattern, called the *general adaptation syndrome,* evolves over time through three stages: (a) the alarm reaction, (b) the stage of resistance, and (c) the stage of exhaustion. The alarm reaction is the organism's initial reaction to the occurrence of a strong demand for adjustment. This reaction has two phases: shock and countershock. In the shock phase, there are physical symptoms such as tachycardia, loss of muscle tone, decreased temperature, and decreased blood pressure. In the countershock phase, there is a rebound reaction marked by a mobilization of the body's defenses, involving an increase in blood pressure, enlargement of the adrenal cortex, and secretion of corticoid hormones.

According to Selye, most of the acute stress diseases correspond to the two phases of the alarm reaction. It appears that this reaction is associated with high levels of autonomic arousal and negative affect, which are likely to reduce performance efficiency and increase vulnerability to additional problems or stressors, as well as contribute to or exacerbate negative physical symptoms.

With continued exposure to the stressor, the body's hormonal defenses allow the alarm reaction to give way to the stage of resistance, when full adaptation to the stressor occurs, including an improvement in or disappearance of the physical symptoms. During this stage, autonomic arousal seems to decrease somewhat, but it still remains relatively high. The affective experience is still likely to be negative, but less unpleasant. Therefore, performance efficiency is likely to improve during this stage, but this improvement is very tenuous, since the person still remains more vulnerable to an increase in the intensity of the stressor or the occurrence of new problems.

If the stressor is intense and prolonged enough, the hormonal reserves eventually become depleted and the organism enters the stage of exhaustion, when physical symptoms reappear and there is decreased ability to resist either the original stressor or other new stressors. During this stage, arousal level drops and the individual is likely to experience a sensation of fatigue and an affective experience of "apathy" or "depression," with a consequent reduction in performance efficiency. The clinical implications of this stage are clear: When a depressed client has a history of ineffective problem solving, the depression may not simply be a result of lack of reinforcement or negative self-evaluations. Instead, a major contributing factor may be prolonged emotional stress, which may or may not involve a deficit in stress-resisting hormones.

On the basis of the above discussion, it is clear that in order to understand the relationship between emotional arousal and performance efficiency during problem solving, it is necessary to have knowledge not only of the subjective quality and intensity of emotional arousal, but also of specific stressors or task demands, the duration of stress, and the person's interpretations and appraisals of all of these variables. When excessive or prolonged emotional arousal and its negative effects appear to be a significant factor, PST programs should include training in various stress- and anxiety-management techniques. Useful techniques might include: *cognitive restructuring techniques,* e.g., reappraisal of threat, correcting misconceptions (Ellis & Greiger, 1977; Goldfried, Decenteceo & Weinberg, 1974); *self-instruction,* e.g., coping self-statements, positive self-talk (Janis, 1983; Meichenbaum & Cameron, 1983); and *relaxation/desensitization techniques* (Bernstein & Borkovec, 1973; Woolfolk & Lehrer, 1984). Cognitive restructuring techniques, especially rational reappraisal of threat, help to reduce anxiety resulting from irrational beliefs and exaggerated threatening appraisals. Self-instructional training helps the problem-solver learn to focus on task-relevant cues and on beliefs and expectations that are likely to facilitate problem-solving performance. Finally, relaxation and desensitization techniques help the problem-solver maintain an optimal level of arousal for effective problem solving. These techniques might include progressive muscle relaxation, meditation, the use of "relaxation breaks" during difficult or extended problem solving, and the use of covert (imaginal) rehearsal, where problem solving under emotional conditions is practiced in the imagination. The latter procedure may be used to "desensitize" an individual to problem-solving situations, or to provide practice in the use of relaxation as an active coping skill in such situations.

Summary

Unlike human problem solving in the laboratory setting, emotional factors play a major role in problem solving in the real-life setting. There are three possible sources of emotional arousal in social problem solving: (a) the objective problematic situation, (b) the problem-orientation cognitions (problem perception, problem attribution, etc.), and (c) the specific problem-solving tasks (problem definition and formulation, generation of alternative solutions, etc.) The types of emotions produced during problem solving may include unconditioned and conditioned emotional responses, emotions associated with the perceptual characteristics of problem-solving variables such as problem appraisals and problem formulations, and emotions produced by reinforcement and punishment occurring as a consequence of problem-solving task performance.

Emotional responses may facilitate or inhibit problem-solving performance, depending on such variables as the subjective quality or value of the emotional response (pleasure vs. pain), the intensity of emotional arousal (autonomic nervous system activity), and the duration of emotional stress. Emotional variables may also play a role in problem recognition, the setting of problem-solving goals, the evaluation of solution alternatives and the evaluation of solution performance.

Awareness and control of emotional responses is important for efficient and effective problem-solving performance. When excessive emotional distress appears to be a significant factor in problem solving, the PST program should include training in various stress and anxiety management techniques. Important techniques include *cognitive restructuring* (reappraisal of threat, correcting misconceptions) *self instruction* (coping self-directions, positive self-talk) and *relaxation/desensitization* techniques.

5

Social Problem Solving and Adjustment

The basic assumption underlying the problem-solving approach to clinical intervention and prevention is that social problem solving is positively related to social competence (positive adjustment) and inversely related to psychopathology or maladaptive behavior. About 30 years ago, Jahoda (1953, 1958) argued that problem-solving ability is an important criterion to consider in defining positive mental health, suggesting that deficiencies in problem-solving ability might be associated with maladjustment or psychopathology. This viewpoint has been elaborated and extended in recent years by several investigators (D'Zurilla & Goldfried, 1971; Mechanic, 1968, 1970; Phillips, 1978; Spivack et al., 1976). For example, Phillips has proposed a "functional definition of psychopathology," which includes the following components:

1. The organism is unable to solve a problem, reach a goal.
2. The organism persists in attempting to solve the problem.
3. The organism lacks the immediate skills or means with which to solve the problem or reach the goal.
4. The persistent or redundant efforts to reach the goal are not adaptive, resourceful, inventive, or effective.
5. The redundant and maladaptive efforts to reach the goal, bring out, or are associated with, maladaptive and unsuccessful behaviors in other respects, or in other aspects of the organism's repertoire, or in other goal-seeking.
6. The organism is temporarily unable (under the conditions under which the above definitional terms are observed, or are observable), in terms of the existing repertoire, to make the adaptive shifts needed to solve the problem and

therefore requires some means that will increase its adaptability, such as utilizing previously unutilized behaviors, learning new behaviors sufficient to reach the goal, restructuring goal efforts (e.g., redefining or relinquishing the goal), or gaining the aid of a prosthetic environment in order to attain the goal. [Phillips, pp. 101–102]

Experimental Studies

Phillips' functional view of psychopathology is based on a number of experimental studies in which laboratory animals were placed in aversive problematic situations where the availability of a solution was impossible or highly unlikely (for example, Masserman, 1943; Maier, 1949; Solomon, 1964; Seligman, 1975; Seligman & Maier, 1967). In such situations, the animals showed a number of "neurotic" or maladaptive behaviors, including perplexity, loss of control, rigidity, stereotyped behavior, and "bizarre" or unusual behavior. Similar studies have been done with humans; subjects are placed in problematic situations where the ability of the subject to predict or control an aversive or rewarding outcome is manipulated. Under conditions of unpredictability or uncontrollability, subjects have shown a variety of maladaptive responses, including "learned helplessness" (Hiroto & Seligman, 1975); anxiety or discomfort (Corah & Boffa, 1970; Geer, Davison, & Gatchel, 1970); obsessive-compulsive behavior (Marquart & Arnold, 1952; Jones, 1954); and high blood pressure (Hokanson, DeGood, Forrest, & Brittain, 1971).

Several studies have shown that when predictability, control, or the *perception* of control (whether veridical or nonveridical) is introduced into the situation, stress effects are ameliorated (Badia, Suter, & Lewis, 1967; Corah & Boffa, 1970; Geer et al., 1970). Studies by Weiss (1968, 1970) suggest that the reduction in uncertainty is the effective mechanism in diminishing stress effects when control, or the *perception* of control, is introduced in the experimental situation. According to Miller and Weiss (1969), the reduction in uncertainty allows the subject to concentrate more on the relevant cues and tasks in the situation. It has also been suggested that beliefs or expectations of control are likely to produce lasting stress-reduction effects only if they are confirmed by some external criterion of effective coping performance (Hamberger & Lohr, 1984). This view suggests that any attempt to develop positive personal-control expectations in PST must be followed by training in the specific skills required for effective problem-solving, so that these expectations can be reinforced and maintained by effective coping performance.

One must use caution in drawing conclusions from the results of the above experimental studies. Since they are all laboratory-analogue studies, the external validity of the results can be questioned. The differences in relevant variables between laboratory and real-life problem-solving situations may be too great to permit any meaningful conclusions regarding the determinants of psychopathology. However, these studies do at least strengthen the hypothesis that problem-solving deficiencies might contribute to psychological stress and maladaptive behavior.

Correlational Studies

The relationship between social problem solving and either positive adjustment or psychopathology has also been investigated in a number of correlational studies. Heppner and his associates and others have reported a number of studies which have focused on Heppner and Petersen's (1982) Problem-Solving Inventory (PSI). The PSI has been described as a measure of self-appraisal of problem-solving ability (Heppner, Neal, & Larson, 1984) and as a measure of problem-solving style (Sherry, Keitel, & Tracey, 1984). It is a 35-item self-report instrument which focuses on problem-orientation cognitions as well as specific problem-solving skills. Primarily using college student subjects, a number of studies have found significant differences between self-appraised effective problem-solvers and self-appraised ineffective problem-solvers on a variety of measures of social competence, positive adjustment, maladjustment, and psychopathology.

Specifically, the results show that self-appraised effective problem-solvers are more motivated to solve problems, have higher expectations of success, are less impulsive and avoidant, more systematic and persistent, and have a clearer understanding of problems (Heppner et al., 1982). They have a more positive self-concept, a greater need to understand their experiential world, fewer dysfunctional thoughts, and fewer irrational beliefs (Heppner, Reeder, & Larson, 1983). In addition, these individuals are more interpersonally assertive and less anxious (Neal & Heppner, 1982).

They also tend to employ more rational decision-making strategies (Phillips, Pazienza, & Ferrin, 1984) and are less intuitive and less dependent in their decision making (Neal & Heppner, 1982). In the area of vocational planning and decision making, these individuals are more confident about their career decision-making ability and occupational potential, and they tend to utilize career planning resources more often (Heppner & Krieshok, 1983; Larson & Heppner, 1985).

Self-appraised ineffective problem-solvers, on the other hand, report more current life problems (Heppner et al., 1982; Nezu, 1985; more health and physical symptoms (Sherry et al., 1984); more anxiety (Sherry et al., 1984; Neal & Heppner, 1982; Nezu, 1985; more depression (Heppner, Baumgardner, & Jackson, 1985; Heppner, Kampa, & Brunning, 1984; Nezu, 1985; Nezu & Ronan, 1985; Nezu, Kalmar, Ronan, & Clavijo, 1986); more psychological distress as measured by the SCL-90 (Heppner, Kampa, & Brunning, 1984); and more psychological maladjustment as measured by the MMPI (Heppner & Anderson, 1985).

The above results show a strong relationship between self-appraised problem solving and maladjustment. It can be hypothesized that self-appraisal of problem-solving ability might affect adjustment in two ways. First, it can affect adjustment directly by influencing a person's self-esteem and feelings of well-being. Second, it can affect adjustment by influencing actual problem-solving performance which, in turn, affects adaptive functioning (Heppner et al., 1982). From a transactional perspective, it would be expected that the positive consequences of effective performance on the environment would then reinforce and maintain positive self-appraisal. However, positive self-appraisal cannot facilitate effective problem-solving performance unless the individual also possesses the specific problem-solving skills required to solve problems effectively. Therefore, it is expected that the more specific problem-solving skills and abilities should also be related to adjustment or psychopathology.

The relationship between more specific social problem-solving abilities and maladjustment or psychopathology has been investigated in a series of studies conducted by Spivack, Platt, Shure, and their associates at the Hahnemann Community Mental Health/ Mental Retardation Center in Philadelphia (see Spivack et al., 1976). Most of the Hahnemann group's studies have focused on the "means-ends ability" in social problem solving: "the ability to orient oneself to and conceptualize the step-by-step means of moving toward a goal" (Spivack et al., 1976, p. 83). This ability is described by Spivack et al. as incorporating the recognition of obstacles that must be overcome, the provision of alternative strategies to prevent or overcome these obstacles, and a sensitivity to the idea that a solution may take time to carry out and may at times be a complicated process.

In order to assess the means-end ability, the Hahnemann group developed a method they have called Means-Ends Problem Solving (MEPS) (Platt & Spivack, 1975). The MEPS involves the written or verbal presentation of a series of story stems, which depict situations in which a need is aroused in a protagonist at the onset of the story, and is satisfied by him at the conclusion. The means by which the protagonist achieves the goal is left out. The subject is required to complete the story by filling in those events that might have enabled the protagonist to achieve his goal of satisfying the need. The dependent measures include: relevant means, enumerations, obstacles, time, and relevancy scores. *Relevant means* are the discrete, effective steps that allow the hero of the story to achieve his goal. *Enumerations* are elaborations or specific examples of a more basic means. *Obstacles* measure the recognition of possible obstacles blocking the attainment of the goal. *Time* is a measure of the recognition of a time element in reaching the goal. The *relevancy score* is obtained by calculating the ratio of total relevant means to total irrelevant means plus no means. *Irrelevant means* are those judged to be ineffective for the particular situation in question. *No means* are responses that are merely repetitions of the story, value judgments, or "accidental" solutions.

Using the MEPS as their main dependent measure, the Hahnemann investigators compared the performance of various disturbed and maladjusted groups of subjects to that of supposedly normal matched controls. They found deficits in MEPS performance in adolescent psychiatric patients (Platt, Spivack, Altman, Altman, & Peizer, 1974); heroin addicts (Platt, Scura, & Hannon, 1973); and adult psychiatric patients (Platt & Spivack, 1972a, 1973). In addition to these studies, the Hahnemann group conducted two studies relating MEPS performance to adjustment level *within* patient groups. In one study with psychiatric patients, a higher level of premorbid social competence was found to be associated with a greater number of means and higher relevancy scores (Platt & Spivack, 1972b). In the second study, it was found that male psychiatric patients who obtained low scores on the MEPS also had MMPI profiles that were more clearly psychotic than those of patients who obtained high MEPS scores (Platt & Siegel, 1976). In all of the above studies, the significant results were based primarily on the relevant-means and relevancy scores.

Several investigators outside of the Hahnemann group have done similar studies using the MEPS with noninstitutionalized subjects; the results generally support the findings reported above. Appel and Kaestner (1979) found significant differences in MEPS performance between a group of narcotic drug abusers judged to be in "poor" standing in an outpatient rehabilitation program and a group judged to be in "good" standing. Gotlib and Asarnow (1979) found highly significant differences on several MEPS measures between depressed and nondepressed college students. In the same study, these investigators also found significant correlations between MEPS measures and scores on the Beck Depression Inventory, or BDI (Beck, 1967), which provides another test of the relationship between MEPS performance and degree of psychopathology.

Despite the apparently strong findings of the Gotlib and Asarnow study (1979), there also have been some conflicting results regarding the MEPS. Recently, Doerfler, Mullins, Griffin, Siegel, and Richards (1984) failed to find a significant difference between depressed and nondepressed college students on the MEPS, using the same measure of depression employed by Gotlib and Asarnow (the BDI). Two possible reasons discussed by Doerfler et al. for the inconsistent results are: (a) differences in sample characteristics and (b) the questionable external validity of the MEPS (see also Butler & Meichenbaum, 1981; D'Zurilla & Nezu, 1982). Regarding sample characteristics, the depressed subjects in the Gotlib and Asarnow study sought help for depression at a college counseling center, whereas the depressed subjects in the Doerfler et al. study were individuals who were coping with depression on their own and had volunteered to be interviewed about their coping efforts. It is possible that the latter group of depressed subjects is an exceptional group with relatively good problem-solving skills who are coping effectively with their depressive problems. Some suggestive evidence for this viewpoint comes from a study by Doerfler and Richards (1981), who interviewed severely depressed women who had made a concerted effort to cope on their own with their depression. They found that about half of these individuals were successful in reducing their depression significantly. These successful individuals reported using effective self-control strategies, including positive self-instruction and problem-solving procedures, such as defining problems in specific, concrete terms.

Regarding the issue of the validity of the MEPS, since there is some question as to the relationship between this measure and actual problem-solving performance, it is important to look at the relationship between problem solving and depression using other problem-solving measures. Several studies have focused on Heppner and Petersen's (1982) PSI. As reported earlier, these studies have found that self-appraised ineffective problem-solvers are significantly more depressed (BDI, SCL-90) than self-appraised effective problem-solvers (Heppner et al., 1985; Heppner, Kampa, & Brunning, 1984; Nezu, 1985; Nezu & Ronan, 1985; Nezu et al. (1986). In the Nezu et al. (1986) study, self-appraised problem-solving ability was significantly related to depressive symptomatology even after the effects of negative attributional style (internality, stability, and globality) were accounted for.

Two other studies on depression have used specific problem-solving performance tasks. Nezu and Ronan (in press) found deficits in depressed as compared to nondepressed subjects on a generation-of-alternatives task and a decision-making task. The nondepressed subjects generated better quality solutions and chose more effective solution alternatives than the depressed subjects. The mean BDI scores of the depressed subjects in this study were similar to that of the group in the Gotlib and Asarnow study. In another study using conceptual problems, Dobson and Dobson (1981) found results implicating a problem-solving deficit and a conservative problem-solving style in depression.

Several other studies using specific problem-solving tasks have focused on other forms of maladjustment. Using a family-oriented problem-solving task, Claerhout, Elder, and Janes (1982) found significantly greater problem-solving deficits in battered rural women as compared to nonbattered women. Nonbattered women produced more total solution alternatives and more effective alternatives. They also *chose* more effective solutions. Battered women produced more avoidance and dependent solution alternatives. Getter and Nowinski (1981) found that psychotherapy clients generated less effective solutions and more avoidance solutions than control subjects on a socially oriented problem-solving task. In a study by Freedman, Rosenthal, Donahoe, Schlundt, and McFall (1978), delinquent teenagers produced solution responses rated less competent than those produced by nondelinquents on a socially oriented problem-solving task relevant to teenagers.

In a study focusing on abusing and neglectful mothers, Azar, Robinson, Hekimian, and Twentyman (1984) found that both groups of maltreating mothers showed significantly poorer problem-solving skills on a parent problem-solving test than did matched nonabusing mothers. Finally, several studies have found deficits in psychiatric patients, as compared to normal controls, on measures of basic problem-solving abilities, including: alternative thinking (ability to generate alternative solutions, Platt et al., 1974); consequential thinking (ability to anticipate consequences, Platt & Spivack, 1973); causal thinking (ability to think in terms of cause-effect relationships, Platt & Spivack, 1973); and perspective taking (ability to appreciate the point of view of others, Platt et al., 1974).

Caution is needed in interpreting the results of the above studies because of the lack of clear-cut evidence for the ecological validity of the verbal measures of social problem solving used in these studies (see Butler & Meichenbaum, 1981; Kendall & Fischler, 1984). This issue will be discussed further in the next chapter. Another problem in interpreting the above results is that the data are correlational and thus no definite conclusions are possible concerning cause-effect relationships. It is possible that deficiencies in problem solving cause or contribute to psychopathology, but it is also possible that factors associated with psychopathology might cause deficiencies in problem-solving performance (for example, high levels of emotional arousal, distractibility, or the effects of psychiatric drugs).

The possibility that emotional arousal might disrupt problem-solving performance must be considered a strong hypothesis in view of the evidence on the negative effects of stress-induced arousal on complex task performance (see Chapter 4). In addition, the findings of a recent study by Mitchell and Madigan (1984) suggest that dysphoria associated with depression may also contribute to deficiencies in social problem-solving performance. Mitchell and Madigan investigated the effects of induced elation and depression on MEPS performance. Subjects who were exposed to the depression-inducing procedure showed significant deficits on several MEPS measures compared to subjects who were exposed to the elation-inducing procedure. Taken together, these findings and the results of other studies on the relationship between problem solving and depression are interpreted by Mitchell and Madigan as suggesting a reciprocal relationship between cognitive activities such as problem solving and depressive affect: Problem-solving deficits influence depression which, in turn, affects problem-solving performance. This view is consistent with the transactional perspective of Coyne, Aldwin, and Lazarus (1981) regarding problem solving and depression.

Effects of PST
on Adjustment

The next step in evaluating the relationship between social problem solving and adjustment is to train individuals in problem-solving skills and observe the effects of training on positive adjustment (social competence) and maladjustment. The problem-solving approach offers the following hypotheses:

- Training in problem-solving skills will increase social competence and contribute to the *reduction in maladaptive behavior* in certain patients who are receiving therapy (patients with deficits in problem-solving ability and/or performance).
- Training in problem-solving skills will increase social competence and help to *prevent the recurrence of maladaptive behavior* in certain patients, following therapy (patients with deficits in problem-solving ability and/or performance).
- Training in problem-solving skills will increase social competence and help to *prevent the development of new maladaptive behavior* in certain vulnerable or at-risk populations (people who are experiencing an increase in the number and/or complexity of stressful problems with which they must cope, such as the recently divorced, the elderly, adolescents, for example).

If problem-solving ability contributes to social competence, and if problem-solving deficits contribute to maladaptive behavior, then the above hypotheses should receive strong support in outcome studies on PST. However, even if the causal relationship between problem solving and psychopathology is reversed (psychopathology causes or is associated with problem-solving deficits), PST might still be useful as part of a treatment package by facilitating problem-solving efficiency and/or effectiveness and thus minimizing the negative effects of psychopathology on personal-social functioning. For example, in the study by Nezu and Ronan (in press), problem-solving effectiveness (generation of alternative solutions, decision making) was increased significantly in subjects who met the criteria for "clinical depression," even without the concurrent application of any other treatment procedure. In addition, if PST is successful in increasing problem-solving efficiency and/or effectiveness, it might also help to maintain treatment gains and prevent the future development of maladaptive behavior. The outcome studies on PST that test these hypotheses will be reviewed in a later chapter.

Summary

A major assumption in the problem-solving approach to clinical intervention is that social problem solving is positively related to social competence (positive adjustment) and inversely related to psychopathology or maladaptive behavior. Experimental and correlational studies are reported that support this assumption. In the experimental studies, subjects who were placed in problematic situations where the availability of a solution was impossible or highly unlikely showed a variety of maladaptive stress responses. When control, or the perception of control, was introduced into the experimental situation, stress effects were reduced. In the correlational studies, significant relationships were found between various measures of social problem solving and a variety of measures of positive adjustment and maladjustment.

Caution is needed in drawing conclusions from these studies. The external validity of the experimental studies can be questioned because they are all laboratory-analogue studies. The differences in relevant variables between laboratory and real-life problem-solving situations may be too great to permit definite conclusions regarding the determinants of psychopathology or maladaptive behavior. However, the results do at least strengthen the hypothesis that problem-solving deficiencies contribute to maladaptive behavior.

Most of the correlational studies must be interpreted with caution because of the lack of clear-cut evidence on the relationship between verbal measures of social problem solving and problem-solving performance in the real-life setting. Moreover, since the data are correlational, no definite conclusions are possible regarding cause-effect relationships between problem-solving deficits and adjustment. Deficits in problem solving may contribute to psychopathology, but it is also possible that factors associated with psychopathology might produce deficits in problem-solving performance. A third possibility is that a reciprocal cause-effect relationship exists, in which the two variables influence each other. Regardless of the nature of the relationship, PST is likely to be useful as a treatment method, maintenance technique, and/or prevention strategy. Evidence for the efficacy of PST will be presented in a later chapter.

II

Clinical Applications

6

Assessment

Assessment for PST occurs as part of a general cognitive-behavioral assessment of a client's clinical problems (Ciminero, Calhoun, & Adams, 1977; Cone & Hawkins, 1977). During this assessment, it is important to determine not only whether a problem-solving deficiency exists, but also whether this deficiency is generalized or specific, so that the most appropriate problem-solving measures can be selected to evaluate treatment progress and outcome. The present chapter will focus on a discussion of various methods and measuring instruments for assessing social problem-solving skills. Before describing specific methods, however, it is important to discuss the distinction between problem-solving ability and problem-solving performance.

Problem-Solving Ability vs. Performance

The assessment of problem-solving ability focuses on the problem-solving *process*—i.e., the discovery process. Assessment techniques measure the extent of an individual's *knowledge or possession* of the important problem-solving process variables, including problem-orientation cognitions, specific problem-solving skills, and basic problem-solving abilities. Measures of problem-solving ability are important for identifying specific skill deficits and planning an appropriate training program, as well as assessing training progress and outcome.

Problem-solving performance refers to the *application* of the skills to solve particular problems. The assessment of problem-solving performance focuses, therefore, on the *product* or outcome of the problem-solving process—the chosen solution. A measure of social problem-solving performance can be viewed as one measure of social competence. Measures of problem-solving performance are particularly important for assessing treatment progress and outcome. Improvements in problem-solving ability do not have practical significance without concomitant improvements in problem-solving performance.

There are two general ways of assessing problem-solving ability and performance: (a) self-report or verbal assessment and (b) observational assessment. Verbal assessment employs such methods as questionnaires, pencil-and-paper scales and inventories, interviews, and verbal problem-solving tests, using real and hypothetical problems. Observational assessment involves the direct observation of an individual's performance in problematic situations in the natural environment or in simulated problematic situations (e.g., role playing) in an experimental or clinical setting.

Verbal Assessment

Several investigators have used questionnaires, inventories, or structured interviews to assess problem-solving ability. The Problem-Solving Inventory (PSI) (Heppner & Petersen, 1982) has been described as a measure of self-appraisal of problem-solving ability. It uses 35 Likert-type items to assess problem-orientation cognitions and several specific problem-solving skills, with an emphasis on the former. Although there is only limited evidence suggesting that the PSI is related to actual problem-solving performance (Heppner et al., 1982; Heppner & Petersen, 1982), studies have shown that the measure has good reliability (Heppner & Petersen, 1982); it is correlated with a wide range of measures of positive adjustment and maladjustment (see Chapter 5); and it distinguishes between individuals who have received PST and those who have not (Dixon, Heppner, Petersen, & Ronning, 1979; Heppner, Baumgardner, Larson, & Petty, 1983). Because the PSI is also brief and easy to administer and score, it is very useful as a research instrument, a treatment outcome measure, and a rough screening device to identify clients who might benefit from PST. (See Appendix A, PSI, for information concerning inventory items, instructions, and scoring.)

The Problem Solving Knowledge and Information Test (PKIT) (Bedell, Archer, & Marlowe, 1980) is a multiple-choice test, used in one outcome study to assess knowledge about the problem-solving process. The Problem Solving Self-Evaluation Test (PSET) is a

Likert-type questionnaire used in the same study to obtain self-ratings of the frequency of actually performing various problem-solving behaviors in real-life problematic situations. In another study, Heppner et al. (1982) used a one-hour structured interview to question subjects about how they solved real-life problems. Following the session, interviewers rated the subjects on several cognitive and behavioral variables related to problem solving.

Another verbal method for assessing problem-solving ability is one which requires subjects to demonstrate their problem-solving skills or abilities by performing specific tasks designed to test these skills and abilities. For example, the popular Means-Ends Problem Solving (MEPS) method (Platt & Spivack, 1975) attempts to assess means-ends ability by asking subjects to conceptualize the possible means by which a person might achieve a specific goal in a particular life situation. Other specific problem-solving skills have been tested in studies on social problem solving, including: (a) the generation of alternative solutions and decision-making (D'Zurilla & Nezu, 1980; Nezu & D'Zurilla, 1981a, 1981b; Nezu & Ronan, in press); (b) consequential thinking and perspective-taking (Spivack et al., 1976); and (c) the basic cognitive abilities that make up Guilford's Structure-of-Intellect Problem-Solving (SIPS) model (Guilford, 1967, 1977; Parnes & Noller, 1973). The advantage of these specific problem-solving tasks over questionnaires and inventories for assessing problem-solving skills and abilities is that they assess not only the subject's knowledge of the content of the problem-solving process, but also the ability to apply this knowledge to specific problematic tasks. Thus, they are likely to have greater external validity.

There is a need for a reliable and valid test of general problem-solving ability, consisting of subtests that assess the full range of problem-solving abilities, including problem-orientation abilities, specific problem-solving skills, and basic problem-solving abilities. The tests that are currently being used to assess problem-solving skills focus on only a limited number of component abilities. Thus, it should not be surprising that these specific measures often fail to show a strong relationship with real-life problem-solving performance (Butler & Meichenbaum, 1981; D'Zurilla & Nezu, 1982), or that negative results are sometimes found in studying the relationship between these measures and psychopathology. For example, in the Doerfler et al. (1984) study, the failure to find a deficiency in MEPS performance in the depressed population in that study does not necessarily mean that no deficiency exists in problem-solving ability in that particular population. Since the MEPS measures only one component problem-solving ability—means-ends ability—the results indicate only that the depressed subjects in that study may not be deficient in that particular ability. They may still be deficient in other problem-solving abilities, such as problem definition or decision making.

The verbal approach to assessing problem-solving performance (the product of problem solving) requires subjects to solve particular test problems, which may be the real problems of the subjects' or hypothetical problems, and report their solutions. Specific measures may use a pencil-and-paper format, a structured interview, or a dyadic or group discussion format in the case of interpersonal or group problem-solving. This approach can also be used to assess problem-solving *ability* at the same time by incorporating the "think-aloud" method, which requires subjects to verbalize or provide a written description of their problem-solving thoughts as they solve the problem (Meichenbaum, Henshaw, & Himel, 1982). The think-aloud method can also be used to confirm that the subject's response is, in fact, the product of an antecedent problem-solving process and not a direct, previously learned response to the test problematic situation based upon past experience with similar problems. To avoid the latter possibility, it is important to present the test as a problem-solving task and to give instructions to the subjects telling them to engage in careful problem-solving thinking before responding.

A verbal problem-solving performance measure can be viewed as a *sign* or indirect measure of problem-solving ability; however, it must be recognized that a verbal problem-solving performance test does not reflect the abilities and skills involved in the final step of the problem-solving process, namely, solution implementation and verification.

Goldfried and D'Zurilla (1969) have provided a set of guidelines for the construction of verbal problem-solving performance tests for particular subject populations or environments (e.g., college freshmen). Tests based on this "behavior-analytic" approach may be viewed as specific measures of social competence. Their guidelines include the following steps: (a) *situational analysis* (identifying significant problematic situations); (b) *response enumeration* (determining a range of possible responses or solutions for each situation); (c) *response evaluation* (judging the solutions); (d) *development of a measuring instrument format* (e.g., pencil-and-paper, structured interview, free response, multiple-choice); and (e) *evalua-*

tion of the measure (reliability and validity studies). Depending on the nature of the measuring instrument format, a variety of different measures can be derived from this method, including solution effectiveness, solution productivity (number of solutions), and coping style (e.g., approach, avoidance, dependency).

Measures based specifically on the above approach include the Adolescent Problem Inventory (API) (Freedman et al., 1978), used to assess competence in delinquent adolescents, and the Family Problem Questionnaire (Claerhout et al., 1982), used to assess problem-solving performance of rural battered women. Other similar problem-solving tests include the Interpersonal Problem Solving Assessment Technique (IPSAT), College Form (Getter & Nowinski, 1981); the Situational Competence Test (SCT) for assessing problematic situations involving alcohol (Chaney, O'Leary, & Marlatt, 1978); the Hypothetical Problem Situations (HPS) test, which focuses on eating and exercise-related problems (Black, in press); and the Problem Solving Performance Evaluation Test (PSPET), used to assess the effects of PST with psychiatric patients (Bedell et al., 1980).

As noted earlier, a major problem with verbal measures of social problem solving is the lack of clear-cut evidence on the relationship between these measures and actual problem-solving behavior in the real-life setting (Butler & Meichenbaum, 1981; Kendall & Fischler, 1984). Some of the factors which may reduce the ecological validity of these measures are methodological—factors related to test construction and administration. For example, the instructions for the MEPS presents the task as a "test of imagination" instead of a test of problem solving. These instructions are likely to encourage subjects to be as creative and imaginative as possible in their responses, which may not reflect their characteristic way of responding in real-life problem-solving situations. In addition, as noted previously, the validity of a test of problem-solving ability may also be reduced if it fails to measure all of the component abilities required for effective problem solving. Suggestions for test construction and administration to maximize the reliability and validity of self-report measures are discussed by Bellack and Hersen (1977).

Another set of factors that may reduce the ecological validity of verbal measures of social problem solving are the possible differences in reinforcement contingencies and other relevant variables between a verbal test situation and a real-life problem-solving situation. Some people may be rewarded for reporting good problem-solving skills in the verbal test situation but punished for demonstrating these skills in the real-life situation, or vice versa. For example, a child may get approval from teachers and parents for performing well on a verbal test of social problem solving, but the same teachers and parents may punish independent problem solving in the real-life setting if they do not approve of the child's solutions or his "independence." In addition, emotional inhibitions that may disrupt problem-solving performance in the real-life setting may not operate to affect performance significantly in the verbal test situation. In view of these critical differences between a verbal test situation and the real-life problem-solving situation, it is probably best to view a verbal problem-solving measure in most cases as an indication of a person's problem-solving potential, which may not necessarily correlate highly with that person's current problem-solving behavior in the real-life setting.

Observational Assessment

The second approach to problem-solving assessment is the observational assessment of overt problem-solving performance in the natural environment or in simulated problem-solving situations in the experimental or clinical setting. This approach has limited utility for directly assessing problem-solving *ability,* or the *process* of problem solving, since overt behavioral activities play a relatively minor role in the problem-solving process as compared to cognitive activities. The observational approach is more useful for assessing problem-solving *performance,* or the *product* of the problem-solving process. The major advantage of this approach is its potential for a higher degree of validity.

An observational problem-solving performance measure may be viewed as a sign or indirect measure of problem-solving ability. However, the validity of this measure as a sign of problem-solving ability may be limited because a person's performance in a problematic situation may be influenced significantly by factors other than problem-solving ability, including deficits in specific instrumental skills, emotional inhibitions, and motivational (reinforcement) deficits. Furthermore, with an observational approach alone it is not always possible to establish with certainty that a person's performance is, in fact, the product of an antecedent problem-solving process. It may be a performance prompted directly by cues in the situation, resulting from some other learning process, such as instrumental learning, modeling, or it may result from direct verbal instruction (e.g., suggestion or advice-giving). It might be possible to ensure, prior to assessment, that the test situations are, in fact, problematic (i.e., that no effective response is immediately available to the person), but this would require experimental control over the test situations and thus the use of simulated situations rather than naturally occurring situations. Even under these controlled conditions, however, the validity of the performance measure could not be established unambiguously without at least asking subjects to report whether or not problem solving prompted their performance in the test situation.

The most useful approach to the assessment of problem-solving ability and performance might be one that combines the advantages of verbal and observational methods. One example of this approach is the problem-solving discussion method, which is useful for assessing the problem-solving behavior of couples or groups such as families (see Kendall & Fischler, 1984). In the problem-solving discussion method, subjects are asked to solve either hypothetical or real problems through group discussion. These verbal discussions are either directly observed or tape-recorded and then later coded and analyzed for specific problem-solving skills and solutions. With this method, the problem-solving *process* and *product* can both be observed directly in a controlled test situation that closely approximates the subjects' real-life problem solving.

Another example of an approach combining the advantages of verbal assessment and observational assessment is self-observation or self-monitoring. Using this approach, subjects can be asked to keep careful records daily of significant problematic situations as they occur in the natural environment. One promising method of this type is the Problem-Solving Self-Monitoring (PSSM) method (see Appendix B), which uses the following A-B-C-D-E format:

A: *Problem Information.* The subject describes all the relevant facts about the problematic situation (Who was involved? What happened? Where and when did it happen? Why was the problem important? What was your problem-solving goal?)

B: *Emotions.* The subject describes all the feelings and emotions experienced when the problem occurred. The subject also rates the intensity of emotional distress on a 9-point rating scale.

C: *Alternative Solutions Considered.* The subject describes all the possible "solutions," or ways of coping with the problematic situation that were considered before deciding on a particular course of action.

D: *Solution Choice.* The subject identifies the solution or coping method he chose to implement and describes the reasons he chose this particular solution.

E: *Solution Implementation and Outcome.* The subject describes what happened when he implemented his solution, including the specific steps that were involved in implementing the solution, the obstacles that may have been encountered, and the consequences or results of the solution. The subject also rates the degree of his satisfaction with the overall outcome of the solution on a 10-point scale from "extremely unsatisfactory" to "extremely satisfactory."

Since it would be impractical to self-record all problematic situations, the subject might be asked to record the two or three most stressful or significant problems that occurred during the previous week. This method can be used to assess: (a) deficiencies in problem-solving ability and performance; (b) progress during training; and (c) outcome of PST, including a follow-up evaluation. However, to obtain complete and accurate data, careful training and feedback are required.

Summary

A major goal during the assessment phase of therapy is to decide whether PST might be a useful intervention and, if so, how it might be used most effectively. Although the obvious case for the use of PST is when there are significant deficiencies in problem-solving skills, it can be argued that most clients are likely to benefit from including PST in their therapy because it teaches clients how to solve problems independently, which is likely to maximize their general effectiveness and adaptability.

In the assessment of social problem-solving skills, it is important to distinguish between problem-solving ability and problem-solving performance. The former refers to the possession of requisite problem-solving skills and abilities, while the latter refers to the application of these skills and abilities to particular problems. Two general approaches to the assessment of problem-solving ability and performance are verbal (self-report) assessment and observational assessment. Each method has its own advantages and disadvantages. Verbal assessment is important because it is the only means of assessing the problem-solving process directly. The observational approach is most useful for assessing problem-solving performance or the product of problem solving. A promising approach is one that combines the advantages of verbal assessment and observational assessment. One example of this approach is the problem-solving discussion method, which is used to study the problem-solving behavior of couples and groups. Another example is the Problem-Solving Self-Monitoring (PSSM) method, which focuses on real-life problem-solving behavior.

7

A Problem-Solving Approach to Stress Management

Rationale

The use of PST for competence enhancement has already been emphasized. Its application as a stress-management approach is suggested by the degree of overlap between the present problem-solving model and the transactional theory of stress and coping (Lazarus, 1981; Lazarus & Folkman, 1984; McGrath, 1976, 1982).

The two approaches are similar in that they both employ the transactional perspective, which emphasizes a reciprocal relationship between environmental variables (e.g., task demands) and person variables (e.g., response availability, appraisals). Both approaches are based on a view of man as an active, thinking, problem-solving organism that *interacts* with his environment, as opposed to the behavioristic conception of man as an organism that *reacts* passively to environmental stimuli.

The definition of a "problem" in the present problem-solving approach is very similar to the conception of a stress situation in transactional stress theory. Difficult problems often result in a perception or threat of uncontrollability, which appears to be a major factor contributing to stress (Hamberger & Lohr, 1984). Social problem solving is an important strategy by which an individual can achieve and maintain personal control. Indeed, many investigators in the field of stress research have recognized problem solving as an important technique for coping with stress (see Beech, Burns, & Sheffield, 1982; Hamberger & Lohr, 1984; Holroyd, Appel,

& Andrasik, 1983; Janis & Mann, 1977; Leventhal & Nerenz, 1983; Mechanic, 1968, 1970, 1974; Meichenbaum & Cameron, 1983; Meichenbaum et al., 1982; Miller & Pfohl, 1982; Nezu, in press; Nezu & Ronan, 1985; Novaco, 1979).

Several studies have been reported recently supporting the view that problem solving is important for effective stress management and prevention. Studies by Lazarus and his associates have found that serious negative stress effects (psychological and somatic symptomatology) are more closely associated with the frequency of "daily hassles" (everyday problems, conflicts, and frustrations) than with major stressful life events such as divorce, death of a loved one, or loss of job (Delongis, Coyne, Dakof, Folkman, & Lazarus, 1982; Kanner, Coyne, Schaefer, & Lazarus, 1981). Nezu and Ronan (1985) have hypothesized that major negative life events are often associated with adverse stress reactions because they usually result in an increase in the number of daily problems with which a person must cope. These investigators have hypothesized further that the relationship between stressful life events and psychological symptomatology is moderated by problem-solving ability (see also Nezu, in press). In a recent correlational study (Nezu & Ronan, 1985) they found a strong relationship between major negative life events and the frequency of current daily problems in a large group of undergraduate college students. Moreover, they found that major negative life events, current daily problems, and problem-solving ability were all significantly related to depressive symptomatology. Together, these three variables accounted for 42% of the variance in depression in this group of subjects.

In two other correlational studies, Nezu and his associates found additional results suggesting that problem solving serves as a moderator between stressful life events and adverse psychological effects. Using a multiple regression analysis, Nezu, Nezu, Saraydarian, Kalmar, and Ronan (in press) found that ineffective problemsolvers under high levels of life stress reported significantly more depression than did effective problem-solvers under similar levels of life stress. In another study using the same type of analysis, Nezu (1986b) found similar results for both state and trait anxiety.

A recent study on stress and coping by Folkman, Lazarus, Dunkel-Schetter, DeLongis, & Gruen (in press) also supports the view that problem solving is an effective coping strategy. These investigators interviewed 170 community-residing individuals once each month for six months about their most stressful encounters during the previous week. Included among the measures obtained at the time of the interviews were measures of coping and perceived coping outcomes. Coping was assessed using the Ways of Coping Checklist (Folkman & Lazarus, 1984). A factor analysis of the responses to this instrument produced eight coping types: confrontive coping, distancing, self-controlling, seeking social support, accepting responsibility, escape-avoidance, effortful/planful problem solving, and perceived growth. Outcomes were evaluated by assessing the degree to which the stressful encounters (current problems) were perceived as being resolved satisfactorily, as well as the quality of the emotional outcome.

The results showed that positive coping outcomes were significantly related to only two coping types: (a) effortful/planful problem solving; and (b) perceived growth (positive reappraisal with a focus on personal growth or challenge). In the Folkman et al. study, as well as in previous studies on coping by Lazarus and his associates (e.g., Folkman & Lazarus, 1984), it was found that perceived growth and problem-focused forms of coping (attempts to alter the stressful person-environment relationship) appeared in combination consistently in encounters that were appraised as changeable. On the basis of this observation, the investigators suggested that perceived growth may facilitate cool, rational problem-solving-oriented coping. This view is consistent with the role of positive problem appraisal and reappraisal in the present problem-solving model (see Chapter 3).

Instead of viewing problem solving as one of many possible coping techniques, as Lazarus and other stress theorists do, our present approach to stress management distinguishes between *problem solving* and *coping performance*. Problem solving is viewed here as the general strategy or *process* by which an individual approaches life's stressful problems and attempts to identify or discover effective coping responses or "solutions." These coping responses may include attempts to change the stressful problematic situation and/ or one's own personal reactions to it, depending on what the problem-solving goals are. The *performance* of these coping responses is the equivalent of *solution implementation* in the present problem-solving model. Thus, a stress-coping transaction is viewed here as a problem-solving transaction, albeit an inefficient or ineffective one at times, particularly when the level of stress is high and problem-solving ability is low (see Janis, 1982; Mandler, 1982). The outcome of an individual's problem-solving attempts is also likely to vary in effectiveness or adaptability depending on the adequacy of specific coping performance skills and the nature of other person and environment variables (e.g., specific emotional reactions, values and commitments, and specific stressors or task demands).

Within the present problem-solving approach, training in specific coping performance skills (e.g., instrumental skills, anxiety-management skills) is provided, as needed, in the same manner that such training occurs in other stress-management approaches (see Meichenbaum & Jaremko, 1983). However, although the goals of the present approach are similar to the self-management goals of approaches such as Meichenbaum's stress-inoculation method (see Meichenbaum & Cameron, 1983), the general framework and the specific instructional strategies differ, particularly in the emphasis on the *process* of problem solving versus the *content* of specific coping techniques. Before describing the problem-solving method in more detail, the model of stress and coping on which our approach is based will be discussed.

The Transactional Model of Stress

The model of stress from which the present problem-solving approach to stress management evolved integrates the transactional views of Richard Lazarus (Lazarus, 1966, 1981; Lazarus & Folkman, 1984), Joseph McGrath (1970, 1976, 1982), and Wolfgang Schönpflug and Peter Schulz (Schönpflug, 1983; Schulz & Schönpflug, 1982). In the transactional approach, stress is defined as a particular type of person-environment relationship or "transaction" in which demands (external and/or internal) tax or exceed coping resources or capabilities, as appraised by the individual (Lazarus, 1981). According to Lazarus, stressful person-environment transactions and their immediate and long-range outcomes are mediated by two critical processes: (a) cognitive appraisal and (b) coping.

Cognitive appraisal refers to the process by which an individual evaluates the significance of an encounter for his well-being. In *primary appraisal,* the individual evaluates the potential harm or benefit of a particular encounter. Three possible stressful primary appraisals are: (a) harm/loss; (b) threat (anticipated harm or loss); and (c) challenge (opportunity for personal growth or mastery). In *secondary appraisal,* the person evaluates his coping resources and options. McGrath calls this procedure the "decision-making process." The term *coping* refers to the responses or activities by which a person attempts to reduce, minimize, control, or prevent stress. Two forms of coping are identified by Lazarus: (a) *emotion-focused coping,* which is aimed at regulating distressing emotions, and (b) *problem-focused coping,* which is aimed at altering the troubled person-environment relationship that is causing the distress.

According to Schönpflug and Schulz, stress occurs when there is concern with a problem. The concern with a problem can be terminated by solving the problem in question or by recognizing the futility of problem-solving attempts (accepting the problem). In the latter case, the individual can still cope by reformulating the problem and setting a goal of reducing distressing emotions or viewing the problem from a different perspective, such as seeing it as an opportunity for personal growth or self-enhancement (Folkman et al., in press). For example, a person with a problem of an incurable disease might decide to maximize the quality of the time that remains, or to participate in a program to help others adjust to the disease. The "problem" in a stressful situation is an imbalance between perceived task demands and perceived coping capacity, such that demands tax or exceed capacity. Coping is viewed as a problem-solving activity that may be directed toward increasing capacity (coping response availability) or reducing demands. The utility of coping is thus evaluated as a function of the ratio between task demands and coping capacity. According to McGrath, the effects of coping responses on the objective problematic situation, which he calls the *outcome process,* is an important process influencing stress, which has often been ignored in stress theory.

A Transactional/Problem-Solving Model of Stress

The present transactional/problem-solving model consists of four critical factors: (a) problem, (b) emotion, (c) coping, and (d) problem solving. The *problem* or problematic situation is a person-environment transaction in which there is a perceived imbalance or discrepancy between task demands and response availability. The individual in this situation perceives a discrepancy between "what is" (the transaction as it exists) and "what should be" (the transaction that is demanded or desired), under conditions where the means or resources for reducing the discrepancy are not immediately apparent or available. *Emotion* or emotional arousal refers to perceived autonomic activity, along with the subjective affective experience that accompanies it. According to Mandler (1982), it is meaningful to talk about stress only when there is "perceptible internal change," referring to the perception of autonomic nervous system activity. The present concept of autonomic arousal should not be confused with the concept of *generalized* autonomic arousal from general arousal theory, which assumes a common pattern of autonomic arousal in all stressful situations. There has been growing evidence in recent years that the nature of the autonomic activity in stressful situations is likely to vary, depending on such factors as the specific stressors involved, the nature of perceptual and appraisal variables, and the type of coping responses used (see Lazarus & Folkman, 1984).

In the present model, the term *coping* has several meanings. In the most general sense, coping refers to the general strategy or process by which a person attempts to deal with life's stressful problems. According to the present model, the most effective and adaptive general coping strategy may be called *problem-solving-oriented coping,* or a problem-solving coping style. The individual who employs this coping strategy approaches the problem, assesses it, and attempts to find a "solution" or effective coping response. Examples of alternative coping styles that are less likely to be adaptive are "avoidance," "helplessness," and "dependency," where the individual tends to avoid or deny his problems, or attempts to get others to solve them for him (Heppner et al., 1984; Janis & Mann, 1977).

Within the problem-solving-oriented coping strategy, two more specific forms of coping can be identified: (a) goal-oriented coping and (b) facilitative coping. *Goal-oriented coping* includes all coping responses aimed at achieving the problem-solving goal(s). These coping responses make up the relevant alternative solutions to the problem. These solutions may include attempts to change the problematic situation (Lazarus's *problem-focused coping*) and/or one's own disturbing personal reactions to it (Lazarus's *emotion-focused coping*). When a problematic situation is appraised accurately as changeable, then problem-solving goals aimed at changing the situation and changing one's own personal reactions both may be adaptive. However, when the problematic situation is relatively stable or unchangeable, the only adaptive goal may be one that focuses on one's own personal reactions to the problem (e.g., emotional responses, self-evaluations, future expectations) (see Lazarus & Folkman, 1984). *Facilitative coping* includes all coping responses aimed at removing cognitive/emotional obstacles to effective and efficient problem-solving performance. Two categories of facilitative coping responses are cognition-oriented coping and emotion-oriented coping. *Cognition-oriented coping* is aimed at correcting cognitive distortions (e.g., exaggerated threatening appraisals, unrealistic goals or performance standards) and facilitating positive self-instructions (e.g., self-efficacy statements, task instructions). *Emotion-oriented coping* is aimed at directly reducing excessive autonomic activity and the negative affective experience that usually accompanies it. Both of these coping strategies may become goal-oriented solution strategies when the problem-solving goals include the modification of cognitions (e.g., beliefs about the self, expectations about the future) and/or the control of emotions (e.g., anxiety level). As noted above, these problem-solving goals may be necessary for effective coping when a stressful situation is stable or cannot be changed through one's own personal efforts.

Cognition-oriented coping and emotion-oriented coping are both included under the label of *emotion-focused coping* in Lazarus's stress and coping model. Although both types of coping strategies can be viewed as attempts to reduce or control emotional distress, they are separated in the present model because they are seen as having different functions in facilitating problem-solving performance. Cognition-oriented coping focuses on the threatening appraisals, beliefs, and expectations that cause emotional distress and disrupt problem-solving thinking, whereas emotion-oriented coping focuses *directly* on the excessive autonomic arousal and negative affect that narrow attention to task-irrelevant cues and reduce performance efficiency.

Consistent with the transactional perspective, the relationships between a problem, emotional arousal, and coping are conceived as reciprocal. Problem solving is the process that mediates these reciprocal relationships. Negative stress effects are viewed as a function of these relationships, as mediated by the problem-solving process. The adequacy or effectiveness of the problem-solving process is expected to vary considerably from person to person and situation to situation. At one extreme, a person may show little or no deliberate problem-solving activity when faced with a stressful situation and the coping response may be a more or less "automatic" response to cues in the situation, based on past learning and conditioning experiences involving those cues or similar ones. At the other extreme, a person may engage in a significant amount of thoughtful problem-solving activity and, in this case, the coping response would represent the outcome of a deliberate, effortful problem-solving process.

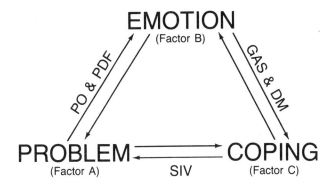

Figure 7.1 Reciprocal relationships between problem, emotion, and coping. PO = problem orientation; PDF = problem definition and formulation; GAS = generation of alternative solutions; DM = decision making; SIV = solution implementation and verification.

The reciprocal relationships between a problem, emotional arousal, and coping are illustrated in Figure 7.1. The links between factor A (problem), factor B (emotion), and factor C (coping) are mediated by different components of the problem-solving process, as described previously in Chapter 3. The link between factor A and factor B is mediated by problem orientation (PO) and problem definition and formulation (PDF). As discussed earlier, the emotional effects at B may be influenced by variables associated with the objective problematic situation (e.g., specific stressors, task demands), the nature of specific PO variables (e.g., problem appraisal, personal-control expectations), and/or the adequacy of PDF skills. In turn, these emotional effects may influence the perception of the problem, depending on how these effects are interpreted and appraised.

The link between factor B and factor C is mediated by the generation of alternative solutions (GAS) and decision making (DM). The outcome of this process is the selection of a coping response or responses at point C. The efficiency and effectiveness of this process will depend on several factors, including the difficulty and complexity of the problem, the nature of PO variables, the effectiveness of

PDF, the quality, intensity, and duration of emotional arousal, and the adequacy of GAS and DM skills. If these variables are less than optimal, inefficient or maladaptive GAS and/or DM performance may result, such as defensive avoidance or hypervigilance described by Janis and Mann (1977). As in the case of the relationship between factors A and B, the relationship between factors B and C is also reciprocal. For example, emotional arousal at B might disrupt decision making and influence the choice of a coping response at C. On the other hand, the selection of a coping response at C might reduce arousal by reducing decisional conflict or uncertainty.

The link between factor C and factor A is mediated by solution-implementation and verification (SIV). This process involves the performance of the solution or coping responses and the evaluation of coping outcome. In discussing the influence of coping outcome on stress, McGrath focuses on the effects of coping behavior on the objective situation. However, the way the person *evaluates* coping outcome can also have a significant influence on stress. For example, unrealistically high performance standards may result in perceived uncontrollability and, consequently, anxiety and/or feelings of helplessness. Another example is the stress produced when a person fails to recognize that a problem is insoluble when evaluating outcome, and continues to try out one solution after another, resulting in repeated failures and frustrations, instead of reappraising and/or reformulating the problem so that it becomes soluble, i.e., setting a goal of reducing distressing emotions or enhancing personal growth.

In the present model, coping outcome is evaluated by considering four criteria: (a) perceived problem resolution (i.e., effectiveness of the coping solution in achieving the problem-solving goal); (b) quality of the emotional outcome; (c) amount of time and effort expended; and (d) effects on overall personal-social well-being (i.e., total benefit/cost ratio). The efficiency and effectiveness of this performance and evaluation process will depend on a number of variables, including the difficulty or complexity of the problem, the nature of PO variables, the effectiveness of PDF, GAS, and DM, the quality, intensity, and duration of emotional arousal, the availability of coping responses (e.g., possession of performance skills, availability of environmental resources), the adequacy of self-monitoring and performance evaluation skills, and other person and environmental variables (e.g., values, commitments, and obstacles).

Using the above model to conceptualize the stress and coping process and assess a particular client's stress problem, PST may focus on any one or all of the above links between factors A, B, and C, depending on where the most significant deficits are. In addition, training in facilitative coping skills may be provided, as needed, to help the client overcome any emotional and cognitive obstacles to effective problem solving at any of these points. The specific problem-solving skills and instructional procedures involved in PST are described in the next chapter.

Summary

The overlap between the present model of social problem solving and the transactional theory of stress is discussed. Empirical results are presented supporting the view that problem solving is likely to be effective as a stress management strategy. The transactional model of stress is described and a modification and extension of this model is presented, which incorporates problem-solving principles. This modified model is called a transactional/problem-solving model of stress.

The transactional/problem-solving model of stress recognizes four critical factors: (a) problem, (b) emotion, (c) coping, and (d) problem solving. In this model, stress is viewed as a function of the reciprocal relationships between a problem, emotional arousal, and coping behavior, as mediated by the problem-solving process. The most effective general coping strategy is problem-solving-oriented coping, which includes goal-oriented coping and facilitative coping. Goal-oriented coping refers to coping responses aimed at achieving a problem-solving goal (potential problem solutions). Facilitative coping responses are coping responses aimed at removing cognitive and emotional obstacles to effective problem solving. The transactional/problem-solving model of stress can be used as an assessment model to develop an appropriate problem-solving-oriented stress management program.

8

Problem-Solving Training (PST)

Following a thorough assessment of a particular client's clinical problems, a decision is made as to whether PST might be a useful intervention strategy and, if so, how it might be used most effectively. As noted above, the most appropriate cases for PST are those in which maladaptive behavior or negative stress effects, such as anxiety, depression, or psychophysiological symptoms (e.g., headache pain), are associated with deficits in problem-solving ability and/or performance. Then, depending on the nature and severity of the maladaptive behavior and negative stress effects, PST might be used as the sole treatment, as part of a broader treatment program, or as a treatment maintenance/prevention strategy.

The goal of PST is to help the client identify and resolve current life problems that are *antecedents* of maladaptive responses, while at the same time teaching the client general skills that will enable him to deal more effectively and independently with future problems. In addition to solving these antecedent problems, PST might also contribute to a therapy program by focusing *directly* on maladaptive responses, such as anxiety, depression, pain, overeating, or problem drinking, and viewing them as "problems-to-be-solved." For example, a problem statement for depression might be: "I am sitting at home trying to relax on a Friday evening, but I am feeling very depressed. I cannot figure out why I feel this way. What can I do to make myself feel better?" For tension-induced pain, a possible problem statement is: "My date and I have just arrived at a restaurant for dinner. Although I like this person very much, I am not enjoying myself because I have a terrible headache. I have tried taking aspirin but it has not worked. What can I do to relieve my headache pain?" An example of a problem statement for problem drinking is: "I am sitting in a bar with a friend drinking my second Black Russian. One more drink and I will not be able to drive safely. What can I do to make sure that I do not have another drink after this one?"

While it is often useful to treat maladaptive responses as problems-to-be-solved, the emphasis in PST should always be on the identification and resolution of the *current antecedent problems* that are causally related to these responses, since this strategy is more likely to produce durable and generalized reductions in maladaptive behavior. However, in cases where antecedent problematic situations are difficult to identify, define, and/or resolve satisfactorily, then both problem-solving strategies might be emphasized equally in therapy. Indeed, for stressful situations that are appraised as stable or unchangeable, a problem-solving strategy aimed at minimizing distressing emotions and maintaining self-esteem and a positive outlook may provide the only possible "solutions" (Lazarus & Folkman, 1984).

When PST is used with other treatment methods as part of a broader therapy program, it should not be applied apart from these other methods as a separate, distinct intervention. Instead, it is the viewpoint here that therapy is best conducted *within a general PST framework,* where the other treatment procedures are applied at the appropriate points during training, as needed, either to facilitate problem-solving performance, or to deal directly with some particularly difficult problematic situation or disruptive maladaptive response. For example, cognitive restructuring might be needed to correct serious cognitive distortions when focusing on the identification and definition of current life problems. Anxiety-management training might be required when stress and anxiety are disrupting problem-solving thinking or when fear or anxiety is inhibiting adaptive instrumental performance. Social-skills training might also be required to facilitate instrumental coping performance when there are significant deficits in instrumental skills.

Although deficits in problem-solving skills are used to identify the most appropriate cases for PST, the social competence approach to clinical intervention is concerned with higher-level functioning, not merely the correction of skill deficits below the "normal" or average level of performance. The goal is to maximize social competence, which in turn will help to maximize generalization, maintenance, and prevention. Therefore, it can be argued from this point of view that most clients are likely to benefit from conducting therapy within a general PST framework, even though they might not show significant deficits in problem-solving skills. The amount of time devoted to training in problem-solving skills can vary, depending on the needs of the particular client.

In addition to its application within a broader, open-ended therapy structure, PST may also be applied as a time-limited, competence-enhancement/stress-management "package," which is designed to be carried out in approximately 14 to 16 two-hour weekly sessions. This training program may be used as a treatment, maintenance, or prevention approach, depending on the target population and the program goals. It may be adapted to an individual (one-to-one) setting, a small group setting with six to eight group members, or a larger group setting, such as a course or workshop. The advantages of individual training are privacy, more individual attention, and greater flexibility to tailor the program to a particular individual's needs. The advantages of a group program are the motivating effects of group discussion, the sharing of ideas and experiences, modeling, social support, social reinforcement, and the efficient use of trained therapists or instructors. The program described below is designed as a small-group training program. It may be conducted by one group leader or co-leaders, preferably a male-female team.

Methods of Instruction

PST employs direct didactic methods, such as verbal instructions and written materials, while also making use of the Socratic approach to instruction, which emphasizes questions and discussions that encourage group members to think for themselves and formulate their own conclusions, deductions, and elaborations. Such instruction is consistent with the PST goal of facilitating independent productive thinking. Other important training methods include coaching, modeling, rehearsal, performance feedback, positive reinforcement, and shaping. *Coaching* primarily involves verbal prompting, such as leading questions, suggestions, and instructions. *Modeling* includes written and verbal problem-solving examples and demonstrations, using hypothetical problems as well as the real problems presented by the group members. *Rehearsal* involves problem-solving practice exercises and homework assignments. In addition to written exercises and assignments, rehearsal may involve role-playing, practice in imagination (covert rehearsal), and practice in real-life problematic situations. *Performance feedback* is provided by the group leader and other members of the group, and also by self-monitoring and self-evaluation using the Problem-Solving Self-Monitoring (PSSM) method (see Chapter 6 and Appendix B). Positive reinforcement includes the group leader's praise and approval and the natural reinforcement of successful problem-solving performance in the real-life setting. Shaping involves specific training in the problem-solving process in progressive steps, with each new step being contingent on successful performance in the previous step.[1]

Program Schedule

Unit 1. Initial structuring (one session)
Unit 2. Problem orientation (one session)
Unit 3. Use and control of emotions in problem solving (two sessions)
Unit 4. Problem definition and formulation (two sessions)
Unit 5. Generation of alternative solutions (two sessions)
Unit 6. Decision making (two sessions)
Unit 7. Solution implementation and verification (two sessions)
Unit 8. Maintenance and generalization (two to four sessions)

Unit 1. Initial Structuring

Objectives: (a) To discuss the goals, rationale, and general format of the training program; (b) to begin training in problem perception (recognition and labeling of problems); (c) to provide training in the use of the PSSM method; and (d) to discuss the limited capacity of the conscious mind during problem solving.

Goals, Rationale, and General Format

The initial structuring begins with a didactic presentation of the goals, rationale, and general format of the training program. The major goal is to help group members learn how to increase their general personal-social competence and reduce, minimize, control, and prevent stress in daily living. This goal is accomplished by training members to apply a problem-solving strategy which is

---

[1]Please note that much of the material in this chapter is directed to the clients or group members. This material can be quoted verbally during PST and some of it may also be presented in the form of written handouts to facillitate learning and retention.

designed to increase their ability to cope effectively and independently with everyday problematic situations that cause stress. The following major concepts are defined: *stress, problem, problem solving, solution, coping,* and *emotion* (see Table 8.1). This is followed by a presentation and discussion focusing on an overview of the problem-solving process (see Table 8.2) and the transactional/ problem-solving model of stress and coping (see Figure 7.1). A major assumption underlying the problem-solving approach is that stress and maladaptive behavior are often caused and/or exacerbated

Table 8.1 Definitions of major concepts

Concept	Definitions
Stress	A person-environment transaction in which perceived demands (external or internal) tax or exceed perceived coping resources.
Problem	A person–environment transaction in which there is a perceived imbalance or discrepancy between demands and response availability. The individual in such a situation perceives a discrepancy between "what is" and "what should be," under conditions where the means for reducing the discrepancy are not immediately apparent or available.
Problem solving	A cognitive-affective-behavioral process by which an individual attempts to identify or discover a solution or effective coping response for a particular problem.
Solution	A coping response or response pattern which is effective in altering a problematic situation and/or one's own personal reactions to it so that it is no longer perceived as a problem, while at the same time maximizing other benefits and minimizing costs.
Coping	The responses or activities by which a person attempts to reduce, minimize, control, or prevent stress. Goal-oriented coping refers to a person's attempts to reduce stress by achieving a problem-solving goal. Facilitative coping refers to a person's attempts to remove cognitive and emotional obstacles to effective problem solving.
Emotion	A response pattern which includes physiological responses (e.g., autonomic nervous system activity), cognitive responses (e.g., threatening appraisals), and motoric responses (e.g., avoidance responses). Emotions vary in subjective quality (pleasure vs. pain) and intensity (degree of autonomic arousal).

Table 8.2 Overview of problem-solving process

   I.   Problem Orientation (PO)
       A. Problem perception
       B. Problem attribution
       C. Problem appraisal
       D. Personal control
       E. Time/effort commitment

  II.   Problem Definition and Formulation (PDF)
       A. Gathering relevant, factual information
       B. Understanding the problem
       C. Setting a realistic problem-solving goal
       D. Re-appraising the problem

 III.   Generation of Alternative Solutions (GAS)
       A. Quantity principle
       B. Deferment-of-judgment principle
       C. Variety principle

  IV.   Decision Making (DM)
       A. Anticipating solution outcomes
       B. Evaluating (judging and comparing) solution outcomes
       C. Preparing a solution plan

   V.   Solution Implementation and Verification (SIV)
       A. Carrying out the solution plan
       B. Self-monitoring
       C. Self-evaluation
       D. Self-reinforcement
       E. Troubleshooting and recycling

---

by personal factors such as perceived uncontrollability (i.e., low personal-control expectations), inadequate problem solving, and ineffective coping performance. The problem-solving approach is designed to strengthen personal-control expectations, improve problem-solving ability and performance, and increase coping effectiveness. Following this didactic presentation, the program schedule is described and explained. The training program is organized into eight content units which are covered in 14 to 16 two-hour weekly sessions. Approximately one half of the program time is devoted to instruction in specific problem-solving skills and coping techniques, and the other half is spent solving the group members' real-life current problems, with direction and guidance from the group leader.

At this point in the program, the group members are asked to introduce themselves and tell the group something about themselves. Before beginning these introductions, however, the group is asked first to treat this request as a problem-to-be-solved, involving the problem statement: "What should I tell the group about myself at this time?" They are asked to close their eyes and imagine alternative self-introductions. Following the actual self-introductions, the members are asked to describe their thoughts and feelings when the request was first made, while they were imagining alternative self-introductions and trying to decide what to say about themselves, and during their actual self-introductions. Regardless of whether or not the group members reveal all their true thoughts and feelings at this time, this experience can be used by the group leader as a concrete example to help illustrate some important points about problem perception, other problem-orientation variables (e.g., problem attribution, problem appraisal), the nature of stress, the role of emotions in problem solving, and the use of specific problem-solving skills or principles (e.g., problem definition and formulation, generation of alternative solutions, etc.).

Problem Perception

Training in problem perception (one component of problem orientation) begins by asking the group members to generate common real-life problems, beginning with group and societal problems (e.g., community problems, world problems) and later asking for individual problems (e.g., personal problems, interpersonal problems). The latter problems may be the real problems of the members or hypothetical problems at this point. In a group setting, individuals are often more comfortable generating group problems and hypothetical problems initially. During the process of generating problems, the group leader or one of the members should write down the problems for future reference, or the session can be tape recorded. If necessary the group leader can facilitate the process of generating problems by providing some examples of his own, either real or hypothetical. The following are a few examples of common group and individual problems which can be presented.

1. *Campus crime problem:* A university community is concerned about the frequency of crime on campus and would like to reduce or eliminate crime, but they are hesitant to commit financial resources to deal with the problem because they are not sure what would be effective.

2. *Nuclear weapons problems:* The world community is concerned because there are too many nuclear weapons ready to be used. The nations possessing these weapons would like to reduce or eliminate them but they cannot agree about how this can be accomplished.
3. *Dating problem:* A college student who is dissatisfied with his current dating relationships would like to meet and date an attractive girl whom he has seen frequently on campus, but he does not know how to approach her and ask for a date without a high risk of rejection.
4. *Curfew problem:* A parent has set a curfew for his teenaged daughter of 9 P.M. on weekdays and 11 P.M. on weekends. However, the daughter has been consistently one to two hours late despite repeated threats of punishment.

The PSSM Method

After spending several minutes of the session generating common problems, the group then receives instruction in the use of the PSSM method, focusing on one or two of the problems which have just been generated. The following is an incomplete and inadequate PSSM record (excluding the ratings) that was produced early in training by a 40-year-old woman with a problem involving the loss of a relationship through divorce:

1. *Problem information:* I have not been able to meet any stable, respectable single men who are interested in a serious, long-term relationship. Most interesting men that I meet are either married or they are just interested in a "one-night stand." I am beginning to believe that I will never have an intimate long-term relationship with a man again and that I will be alone for the rest of my life.
2. *Emotions:* I have been feeling lonely and depressed most of the time. I am losing my self-confidence and feeling very inadequate as a woman. I am feeling increasingly anxious and fearful about the future.
3. *Alternative solutions considered:*
   a. Go to singles bars.
   b. Join Parents Without Partners (a social support group).
   c. Apply to a dating service.
   d. Put a personal ad in the newspaper.

4. *Solution choice:* I decided to join Parents Without Partners. I thought that this choice would make me feel the least uncomfortable and would involve the least financial cost.
5. *Solution implementation and outcome:* I went to several Parents Without Partners meetings and social activities. I felt only slightly uncomfortable initially. However, I did not meet any interesting or likeable men. I was bored most of the time. This experience has made me feel even more discouraged and depressed.

As the training program progresses, it is expected that improvements in problem-solving ability and coping performance will be reflected in the PSSM records, with members producing more adequate and complete records as well as reporting more successful solution outcomes. In addition to the instruction provided in the session, training in the use of the PSSM method also includes a homework assignment to (a) list problems which occur in daily living during the week and (b) record two or three of the most difficult and significant problems using the PSSM framework. Feedback is provided in the next session and then this assignment is repeated on a regular weekly basis throughout the training program. These assignments provide the major real-life problem-solving tasks for training purposes and outcome assessment.

Limited Capacity of the Conscious Mind

At this point during the initial structuring part of the program, information is presented about the limitations of the conscious mind which tend to reduce problem-solving efficiency and effectiveness. Several rules or principles are then suggested which can help the problem solver overcome these limitations so as to maximize his problem-solving performance.

Research in cognitive psychology over the last 25 years has shown that the conscious mind is remarkably limited in the amount of activity that it can perform efficiently at any one time. According to Marvin Levine (in press), a researcher in human problem solving for over 20 years, the conscious mind engages in three important activities during problem solving: (a) it receives information from the environment (external and internal) and interprets it; (b) it "displays" information when you need it (remembering); and (c) it manipulates information that you are remembering and attempting to comprehend (e.g., combines information, adds and subtracts information). However, the capacity of the conscious mind is limited in that it cannot perform all three activities efficiently at the same time, especially when the quantity and/or complexity of the information is great. Often, one activity interferes with another. For example, attempting to remember all the important information about a problem may, under certain conditions, interfere with the manipulation of information that is involved in the comprehension or understanding of the problem. Fortunately, according to Levine, research on problem solving has suggested several rules or principles which can help you to overcome these natural limitations and maximize your problem-solving effectiveness. Three rules which are particularly useful for social problem solving are "externalize," "visualize," and "simplify."

Externalization involves the display of information externally as often as possible (e.g., writing it down, drawing diagrams to show relationships, etc.), including information about the nature of the problem, alternative solutions, and solution outcomes. This procedure relieves the conscious mind from having to actively display information being remembered, which allows you to concentrate more on other activities, such as interpretation and comprehension of information. *Visualization* emphasizes the use of vision and visual imagery whenever possible during the problem-solving process. To apply this rule, you should directly observe all aspects of the problematic situation, rehearse alternative solutions using role-playing, and actively test different solution options in the real problematic situation. When these procedures are not feasible or practical, you can use your imagination to visualize the problematic situation and "test" or "rehearse" solution alternatives. Experimental research has demonstrated convincingly that visualization is a powerful tool which facilitates remembering as well as the comprehension of verbal information (i.e., grasping the logic, perceiving relationships between bits of information). The *simplification* rule involves various attempts to simplify the problem in order to make it more manageable. To apply this rule, you should attempt to focus only on the most relevant information, break down complex problems into more manageable sub-problems, and translate complex, vague, and abstract concepts into more simple, specific, and concrete terms. These three rules will be emphasized throughout the training program.

Example: Externalize, Visualize, Simplify

Bill is a 38-year-old divorced male who was having difficulty establishing relationships with women. In particular, he was concerned that when he approached women in singles bars to try to meet them, he was frequently rejected. In attempting to understand and solve this problem, Bill used the rules of *externalization, visualization,* and *simplification.* He wrote down as much specific, concrete information as possible about the places he went to in order to meet women, the types of women he approached, his own behavior, and the behavior of the women. He tried to *look at* the problem from all angles. He observed his own behavior and the behavior of the women he approached in the actual situation. He also observed the interactions of other men and women who were meeting for the first time. In addition, following encounters with women, he reconstructed the situations in his imagination and imagined them from his own perspective, the perspective of the woman, and the perspective of an observer or spectator.

The above procedures helped Bill to recognize that he was primarily approaching tall, statuesque, beautiful women, and that he was generally monopolizing the conversation, talking about his own accomplishments and trying to impress the woman. Bill is a short, average-looking man who is a good school teacher but not a famous person with great accomplishments or talents. In attempting to solve the problem, Bill thought of different ways to approach women and wrote them down, specifying as much detail as possible (e.g., type of woman, introductory remarks, questions to ask, topics of conversation to introduce, etc.). He also wrote down the "pros" and "cons" of each approach. He then selected several approaches which he thought were most likely to be successful, which included approaching shorter, less beautiful women and asking a lot of questions to show more of an interest in the woman and less in himself. This problem-solving process was facilitated by watching other successful men approach and interact with women, rehearsing different approaches in imagination, and experimenting with different approaches in the actual situation. Before long, Bill was meeting more women and dating often.

At this point, the initial structuring ends and training begins to focus on the five components of the problem-solving process. Each unit begins with a statement of the training objectives for that unit, followed by a didactic presentation and discussion of the relevant problem-solving principles and coping techniques, interspersed with examples, demonstrations, and problem-solving exercises, using both hypothetical problems and the real problems of the group members. In addition to the problem examples and exercises described in this chapter, another rich source for this information is Parnes et al. (1977) and Noller, Parnes, and Biondi (1976).

Unit 2. Problem Orientation

Objectives: (a) To increase sensitivity to problems and set the occasion for problem-solving activity (vs. avoidance); (b) to focus attention on positive problem-solving thoughts and activities and away from unproductive, inhibitive worries and "self-preoccupying thoughts" (Sarason, 1980); (c) to maximize effort and persistence when obstacles and emotional distress are encountered; and (d) to minimize emotional distress/maximize positive emotional states.

The first part of this unit extends and completes the training in problem perception ("How to Recognize Problems"). The second part focuses on a motivational presentation or "pep talk" emphasizing the adoption of a positive problem-solving cognitive set, which involves the problem orientation variables of problem attribution, problem appraisal, personal-control expectations, and time/effort committment. If time remains in the session, it may be devoted to *guided problem solving,* where the group leader directs and guides the group through the problem-solving process for one of the real problems recorded by group members as a homework assignment during the previous week.

How to Recognize Problems

Problems are not always easy to recognize. They are often embedded within a social context which contains many problem-irrelevant events. The relevant problem information is often vague, ambiguous, or not immediately available. In addition, since many problems are stressful, we often tend to avoid them to protect ourselves from threat and anxiety. This is often self-defeating because we experience the negative consequences of the unsolved problem (i.e., emotional distress, ineffective performance) and tend to label them as "the problem" without recognizing what the real problem is. Here are some suggestions for increasing your sensitivity to problems:

1. *Use your feelings as a cue for problem recognition.* Instead of labeling your negative feelings as "the problem," use these feelings as a cue for observing your environment and monitoring your behavior in an attempt to recognize the real problem which is causing these feelings. Common emotional consequences of everyday problems are anxiety, uncertainty, depression, anger, dissatisfaction, disappointment, confusion, guilt, feelings of inadequacy, and feelings of helplessness.

2. *Use your ineffective behavior as a cue for problem recognition.* At times, your feelings may not be sufficient cues for accurate problem recognition. It may be only after you keep making mistakes and failing to respond effectively that you will realize that a problem exists. Instead of focusing on your ineffective behavior and labeling it as "the problem", you should use it as a cue for seeking out and identifying the problematic situation (both personal factors and environmental factors) which you are not coping with effectively.

3. *Using a problem checklist.* Once your negative feelings and/or ineffective behavior prompt a search for problem recognition and labeling, a problem checklist can often help you to pinpoint the problem or problems.

Examples of a work-related problem checklist and a general problem checklist are presented in Tables 8.3 and 8.4. A comprehensive problem checklist for use in problem-recognition training is the Mooney Problem Checklist (Mooney & Gordon, 1950). This instrument is also useful as an assessment measure for evaluating the outcome of PST (for example, Heppner, Baumgardner, Larson, & Petty, 1983).

Importance of a Problem-Solving
Coping Style

An individual's general beliefs, assumptions, and expectations concerning life's daily problems and his ability to solve them greatly influences the way he actually copes with everyday problems and the amount of stress he experiences in the process. This cognitive "set," together with the person's coping dispositions, can be referred

Table 8.3 Work-Related problem checklist

Job-finding problem?	Not enough job autonomy?
Job-interview problem?	Limited opportunity for advance-
Inadequate job performance?	ment?
Absenteeism or tardiness?	
Unsafe practices?	Poor communication with
Too much work?	superiors?
Too little work?	
Work not challenging enough?	Poor communication with
Work too difficult or complex?	subordinates?
Ambiguous job demands?	Poor relationships with peers?
Ambiguous job goals?	Interpersonal disputes?
Conflicting job demands?	Ineffective delegation or lack of
Too much responsibility?	assertiveness?
Too little responsibility?	Lack of recognition?
Lack of opportunity to participate	Aversive or unhealthy work
in decision-making which	environment?
affects my job?	Inadequate pay or benefits?
Procrastination?	Poor job security?
Unproductive meetings?	Commuting problems?
Wasting time?	Too much traveling in the job?

to as his "coping style." An example of a maladaptive coping style is the avoidant or dependent coping style. A more effective and adaptive coping style is the problem-solving coping style.

Avoidant/Dependent Coping Style

1. The individual blames himself for the problem and thinks that it means that there is something wrong with him (e.g., he is abnormal, incompetent, stupid, bad, or unlucky).
2. The individual perceives the problem as a significant threat to his well-being (physical, emotional, self-esteem, social, economic). He minimizes the benefits of solving the problem and maximizes and exaggerates the harm or losses which might result from failure to solve the problem successfully.
3. The individual has little real hope of coping with the problem effectively, either because he perceives the problem as insoluble, or because he does not believe that he is capable of solving the problem successfully through his own efforts. As a result, he avoids the problem or tries to get someone else to solve it for him.

Table 8.4 General problem checklist

Job or career problem?	Drug problem?
Marriage problem?	Time-management problem?
Problem with children or adolescents?	Self-discipline problem?
Academic problem?	Low self-esteem?
Conflict between job and family responsibilities?	Emotional problem?
	Moral conflict?
Conflict between academic and family responsibilities?	Religious problem?
	Legal problem?
Housekeeping or home maintenance problem?	Lack of recreation or leisure activities?
Problem with parents or other relatives?	Transportation problem?
	Concern about the neighborhood?
Lack of social relationships?	Concern about the community?
Interpersonal conflicts?	Concern about the environment?
Sexual problem?	Problems with business products or services?
Sleep problem?	
Financial problem?	Problem with professional services?
Illness or disability problem?	
Lack of exercise?	Problem with social or government services?
Weight problem?	
Drinking problem?	Concern about world problems?

4. The individual believes that a competent person should be able to solve the problem quickly, without much effort. He believes that his failure to do so means that he is inadequate or incompetent. In addition, he does not place a high value on independent, effortful, problem-solving activity. He would *prefer* to have someone else solve the problem for him.

Problem-Solving Coping Style

1. The individual perceives the problem as a normal, ordinary, inevitable event in life. He realizes that the problem is *not* necessarily an indication that something is wrong with him. He recognizes when a problem is caused by environmental circumstances and/or relatively benign, changeable or transient personal factors (e.g., lack of experience, uncertainty),

rather than by global and stable personal defects or abnormalities. He believes that when a problem *is* a result of some personal deficit or inadequacy, this means only that he is human and not perfect; the important thing is to learn from your problems and mistakes and try to prevent them from happening again.

2. Instead of appraising the problem primarily as a threat-to-be-avoided, the individual sees the problem as a "challenge" or opportunity for personal growth or self-improvement (e.g., learning something new, changing one's life for the better, feeling better about oneself). The individual does not view failure as a catastrophe, but instead, views it as a corrective learning experience. He believes in the philosophy that it is better to take on a problem or a challenge and fail, than not to try to solve it at all.

3. The individual believes that there is a solution to the problem and that he is capable of finding this solution on his own and implementing it successfully. He understands that the more a person *believes* that he can cope with problems successfully, the better he *will* be able to cope with them.

4. The individual realizes that solving the problem is likely to take time and effort. He resists the temptation to respond to the problem on the basis of the first impulse or idea to come to mind. He understands that the first impulses and ideas are not usually the best because they tend to be influenced more by feelings than by reasoning. He values independent, effortful, problem solving and is prepared to be persistent and not give up too easily if a solution is not quickly discovered. He realizes that even the best problem solvers need time to think in order to solve difficult problems effectively. However, he also understands that if he has tried his very best and still cannot succeed, *then* he must either accept the problem as unchangeable in its present form and try to view it from a different perspective (e.g., reducing personal distress, seeking a compromise), or go get help with it.

Following the above presentation of the two coping styles, a discussion is held about the important differences between the two approaches with an emphasis on the reasons why the problem-solving coping style is likely to be more generally effective and adaptive.

Exercise: Viewing Ordinary Problems
as Challenges

In order to adopt a positive problem-solving coping style, you must learn to recognize the many "normal" or ordinary problems which occur in everyday living, and to view these problems as "challenges," or opportunities for personal growth, mastery, or achievement, instead of thinking of them only in negative terms, such as threats, conflicts, frustrations, hassles, etc. The following exercises might be helpful:

1. Think of all the "normal" or ordinary problems you have experienced recently (problems that do *not* signify abnormality or deviance).
2. Think of all the problems you have experienced recently that can be viewed as challenges or opportunities to learn something worthwhile or to improve yourself in some way.

If the group members are having trouble generating ordinary problems and challenges, the group leader can act as a model and present examples from his own life experiences or from the group members' own problem lists and PSSM records. This exercise can also be modified by asking members to *recognize* the ordinary problems and challenges from a list of problems presented to them. At the conclusion of this session, group members are asked to practice applying positive problem-solving self-talk during their everyday problem-solving activities. To facilitate this process, they can be asked to write positive problem-solving self-statements on small 5" × 3" cards and keep them in a shirt pocket or purse. They can then take out the cards and read the self-statements whenever they are confronted with a problem during their daily activities.

After focusing on positive problem-solving expectations throughout the session, there is a danger that some members might become overly optimistic and develop unrealistic expectations that problem solving will be easy, which might lead to discouragement when difficulties are encountered. To put things in proper perspective, the group members should be cautioned about "Murphy's Laws" (Douglass & Douglass, 1980):

1. Nothing is as simple as it seems.
2. Everything takes longer than it should.
3. If anything can go wrong, it will. [p. 94]

Unit 3. Use and Control of Emotions in Problem Solving

Objectives: (a) To discuss the role of emotions in social problem solving; (b) to discuss how emotions can be used to facilitate problem-solving effectiveness; and (c) to provide instruction in the use of facilitative-coping methods to control disruptive emotions.

Role of Emotions in Problem Solving

Your emotions play an important role in real-life problem solving. There are three sources of emotional arousal during problem solving: (a) the objective problematic situation; (b) your beliefs, appraisals, and expectations regarding the problem and your ability to solve it successfully (problem-orientation cognitions); and (c) the specific problem-solving tasks (defining the problem, generating alternative solutions, making a decision, implementing the chosen solution and evaluating the outcome).

Most problematic situations are stressful because they usually involve such circumstances as harm or pain, loss of something valued, frustration, conflict, unpredictability, uncertainty, ambiguity, complexity, or novelty. Your beliefs, appraisals, and expectations may produce emotions in a problem-solving situation because they often involve the anticipation of significant personal growth or mastery (a "challenge") or the anticipation of significant harm or loss (a "threat"). If you view the problem as an important challenge, you are likely to experience positive affect, such as a feeling of exhilaration or positive excitement. On the other hand, if you view the problem mainly as a significant threat to your well-being, you are likely to experience negative affect, such as fear or anxiety. The specific problem-solving tasks, such as problem definition and decision making, may produce emotional responses because they often involve the conditions of ambiguity, uncertainty, and conflict, which tend to be stressful, and also because they may involve a number of successes, failures, frustrations, or disappointments before a satisfactory solution is finally discovered.

Emotional arousal which is produced before and during problem-solving activities may facilitate or inhibit problem-solving performance, depending on its subjective quality (pleasure vs. pain), intensity, and duration. In general, positive affect (e.g., "hope," "relief") is likely to facilitate performance, while negative affect (e.g., "fear," "disappointment") is likely to inhibit performance. Low and moderate levels of emotional arousal tend to facilitate problem-solving performance by increasing motivation and alertness. However, high levels of arousal are likely to reduce performance efficiency by causing a narrowing of attention to task-irrelevant cues, such as unproductive worries, negative self-judgments, threatening problem appraisals, and your own disturbing physiological responses. A high level of emotional stress may also cause you to avoid the problem instead of trying to solve it, or to give up too easily when you encounter obstacles. In addition, high levels of emotional arousal of long duration may result eventually in psychological and physiological exhaustion or fatigue, with concomitant depressive affect which is likely to reduce motivation and performance efficiency further. In addition to the possible effects of emotional arousal on performance efficiency, your emotions may also play a role in problem solving by influencing your recognition and labeling of problems, the problem-solving goals that you set, your preferences for different solutions, and your evaluation of the outcome after you implement your solution in the real-life problematic situation.

How to Use Your Emotions
to Facilitate Problem-Solving Effectiveness

When attempting to solve real-life problems, you may increase your problem-solving effectiveness by using your emotional responses in the following ways:

1. *As a cue for problem recognition.* When you experience a negative emotional response, look for the antecedent problematic situation which may be producing it.
2. *To facilitate motivation for problem solving.* This can be done by adopting the positive problem-solving cognitive set or "coping style" which was discussed earlier (e.g., viewing a problem as a "challenge" rather than a "threat").
3. *As a problem-solving goal.* It is often adaptive to set a problem-solving goal of increasing positive affect (e.g., feelings of self-worth, sexual pleasure) or reducing negative affect (e.g., anxiety, anger). For example, when a stressful situation is relatively stable or unchangeable, the only realistic problem-solving goals may be to minimize emotional distress and/or maintain or increase feelings of self-worth.

4. *As a possible consequence to consider when anticipating solution outcomes during decision making.* We will emphasize later that the possible effects of a solution alternative on feelings of emotional well-being is an important criterion to consider when evaluating solution alternatives.

5. *As a criterion for evaluating the solution outcome following solution implementation.* The actual emotional outcome is an important criterion to consider when evaluating the effectiveness or adaptiveness of the solution in the actual problematic situation.

6. *To reinforce effective problem-solving behavior.* The careful application of effective problem-solving rules and principles, including the rules of externalization, visualization, and simplification, will facilitate successful problem-solving task performance which, in turn, will produce positive emotional consequences (positive reinforcement).

How to Control Disruptive Emotions

Following the above presentation and discussion, instruction and training is provided, as needed, in *facilitative coping,* which is aimed at controlling or overcoming cognitive-emotional obstacles to effective and efficient problem-solving performance. The group members are taught to distinguish between *cognition-oriented* facilitative coping and *emotion-oriented* facilitative coping. Cognition-oriented coping focuses on disruptive, stress-producing cognitions. Relevant coping techniques include *cognitive restructuring* (e.g., correcting irrational beliefs, exaggerated threatening appraisals, unrealistic goals, and other cognitive distortions) and *self-instruction* (e.g., positive self-talk, coping self-statements, directing attention to task-relevant cues). Emotion-oriented coping focuses *directly* on disruptive emotional arousal. Important techniques include a variety of *relaxation* and *desensitization* methods, such as progressive muscle relaxation, meditation, positive imagery, autogenic methods, and applied relaxation or self-desensitization (Goldfried, 1979; Woolfolk & Lehrer, 1984). Specific examples should be used to illustrate some of these facilitative coping techniques. If there is time in the session, an introductory muscle relaxation or meditation session can be conducted as a demonstration of these skills.

To supplement the instruction in facilitative coping provided in this unit of the program, a self-help book on stress and anxiety management should be required reading as a homework assignment at this point in order to provide further home-based instruction and practice in facilitative coping techniques (e.g., McKay, Davis, & Fanning, 1981; Davis, Robbins Eshelman, & McKay, 1982). Further training can also be provided in later sessions, if needed. However, the viewpoint here is that most individuals already have a variety of resources available to them for reducing or controlling the cognitive-emotional effects of stress (e.g., music, hobbies, pleasant imagery, distraction, social support, exercise, etc.). Instead of specialized emotion-focused coping techniques, they may only need training in how to (a) recognize potentially disruptive emotions and cognitions; (b) identify the various resources they already have available for coping with these negative effects; and (c) use these resources when needed to minimize, control, and prevent these effects so that problem-solving performance will not be disrupted.

At the conclusion of Unit 3 or the beginning of Unit 4, group members are told that Units 4 through 7 will each involve two sessions. The first session for each unit will involve didactic instruction in a specific problem-solving task or skill (e.g., problem definition and formulation, decision making), using a variety of examples and exercises related to that task. Handouts will be distributed during the session which summarize the major points of the didactic presentation. Group members will be asked to study these handouts as a homework assignment during the week and to apply the principles in their everyday problem solving. The PSSM method will provide a means for monitoring and measuring these applications.

The second session for each unit will focus on *guided problem solving,* with an emphasis on the specific problem-solving task or principles taught in the previous session. The problems focused on will be the current real-life problems of the group members, taken from the lists and PSSM records completed as a weekly homework assignment. For each problem presented, the group leader will direct and guide the group through the complete problem-solving process from problem definition and formulation through the development of a solution-implementation plan. This process will include attempts to identify and correct negative problem-orientation cognitions (e.g., threatening problem appraisals, low personal-control expectations) as well as attempts to identify and overcome obstacles to effective solution implementation (e.g., emotional inhibitions, skill deficits). As each unit of training is completed, the group leader will provide less *direct* instruction and guidance for the problem-solving skills which have already been taught in previous sessions. Once a solution plan is completed for a particular problem, the group member who presented the problem will be asked to implement the solution during the next week and report back to the group about the outcome in the next session. At that time, feedback will be provided by the leader and other group members and any necessary corrections or modifications in the solution plan will be made.

Unit 4. Problem Definition and Formulation

Objectives: (a) To gather as much relevant, factual information about the problem as possible; (b) to clarify the nature of the problem; (c) to set a realistic problem-solving goal; and (d) to re-appraise the significance of the problem for personal-social well-being.

Gathering Information

In order to understand the problem, you must first gather as much relevant, factual information about the problematic situation as possible. To facilitate this task, the following who, what, where, when, and why questions can be helpful:

1. Who is involved?
2. What happens (or does not happen) that bothers you?
3. Where does it happen?
4. When does it happen?
5. Why does it happen? (i.e., known causes or reasons for the problem)
6. What is your response to the situation? (i.e., actions, thoughts, and feelings)

In keeping with the simplification rule, it is important to describe the above information in *specific, concrete* terms. This will help you to distinguish more easily between relevant and irrelevant information, and between objective facts and unsubstantiated assumptions, inferences, and interpretations. For example, if the relevant information you are seeking is about the behavior of another person, be sure that the information describes what that person actually *said* or *did*. The description, "John is too lazy," is too general and vague. Instead, "John does not start working until an hour after he punches in," is a more concrete description of John's problem behavior that is likely to result in a better understanding of the problem. In order to facilitate this process further, use the externalization rule and write down as much of this information as possible.

Relevant information about the problem may include information about environmental events (e.g., task requirements, the behavior and expectations of other people), personal events, i.e., your own thoughts, goals, feelings, physical sensations, and behavior, and relationships or interactions between the two. A useful visualization technique to facilitate the identification of relevant information in these categories is the *imaginal replay technique*. To use this procedure, close your eyes and reconstruct in your imagination a recent experience which was an instance of a recurring problem or part of a current, ongoing problematic situation. First, imagine that you are *in* the situation (not viewing it as an observer) and experience it imaginally as it actually happened. As you are experiencing the situation, ask yourself: "What am I thinking and feeling?" Next, repeat the experience, but this time as an observer, as if watching a movie or video tape of the situation. Play it in slow motion and ask yourself: "What is happening? What is the other person(s) saying, doing, and feeling? What am I saying, doing, and feeling?" This technique can also be used to *anticipate* and pinpoint possible future problems. For example, a recently divorced woman used this technique to anticipate sexually-related problems which might occur when attempting to develop new relationships with men.

Correcting Distortions and Misconceptions

After obtaining as many relevant facts as possible about the problem, you must then structure or "process" (interpret, appraise) this information in order to make it meaningful. Subjective factors, such as feelings and values, can influence this process and result in distortions. Distorted information may result in a distorted understanding of the problem which will lead to ineffective problem solving. The following are some common types of distortions which occur when processing social information. When you are defining and formulating problems, you should try to recognize these distortions and correct them.

1. *Arbitrary inference.* A person draws a conclusion without sufficient facts to support it or rule out alternative interpretations. For example, a woman turns down a request for a date and the man concludes that the woman does not like him.

2. *Selective abstraction.* A person attends to certain selected information or cues in a situation and makes an assumption or draws a conclusion based on this information while ignoring other important information which contradicts this assumption or conclusion. For example, a person participating as a member of a team in an athletic contest concludes that his mistake cost the team a victory, while ignoring the fact that several other team members made more serious errors.

3. *Overgeneralization.* A person makes assumptions about the *general* characteristics of people or situations within a given class on the basis of a single event. For example, a worker makes a single mistake and the boss concludes that he is "incompetent."

4. *Magnification or minimization.* Magnification occurs when an individual exaggerates the value, intensity, or significance or an event. Minimization refers to the opposite distortion, that of inappropriately devaluing or reducing the significance of an event. An example of magnification is exaggerating the possible threat or risks associated with meeting new people at a party. An example of minimization would be inappropriately minimizing the danger of leaving your car unlocked in an unfamiliar neighborhood at night.

During the course of PST, some group members may show frequent distortions, misconceptions, or irrational beliefs which require further corrective learning. When this is the case, training can place more emphasis on *cognitive restructuring* (Ellis, 1977) and/or the particular group member(s) can be referred to Ellis and Harper's (1975) *A New Guide to Rational Living* or any of the rational-thinking self-help books focusing on specific problem areas (e.g., sexual problems) which are available from the Institute for Rational-Emotive Therapy in New York City.

Exercise: Gathering Information and Correcting Distortions

Mary and Jane both work in the same sales department in a large corporation. Mary was born in California and Jane was born in Virginia. Jane and Mary were very good friends until Mary received a promotion to sales manager which Jane wanted and expected to get since she had been with the company longer than Mary. According to performance evaluations, however, Mary was rated as having much more leadership potential than Jane. Mary is about 5 ft. 2 in. tall and has black hair. Jane is about 5 ft. 9 in. tall and has red hair. Ever since Mary's promotion, Jane has been hostile towards Mary. In addition, Jane's sales performance has reduced considerably and she has developed a bad attitude toward the company which seems to be having a negative effect on others in the department.

Mary is feeling very upset and threatened. She is concerned about the fact that her teenaged daughter is dating a boy who has been arrested for possession of drugs. She is upset about the loss of the friendship with Jane, the reduction in Jane's sales performance, and the negative effect which Jane's bad attitude is having on the department as a whole. She appraises the problem as a "disaster" for the department and for herself. She believes that Jane's attitude is "horrible" and "intolerable". She is so upset that she is unable to perceive anything good about Jane's behavior or performance; she perceives only the negative characteristics of Jane's behavior at this point. In addition, Mary is beginning to believe that her superiors probably think that she is a very poor sales manager. Mary also thinks that Jane may be trying to turn the other salespeople against her. She is also feeling guilty, thinking that she caused the problem by accepting the promotion. Mary has little hope of finding a solution and is thinking of quitting her job with the company.

1. What are the vague or ambiguous terms in the above problem description? (e.g., "leadership potential," "hostile," "bad attitude," "negative effect on others"). Change them to more specific, concrete, behavioral terms.
2. Identify the information which is *not relevant* to Mary's problem with Jane.
3. Distinguish the *facts* from the unsubstantiated assumptions, beliefs, and inferences in the above problem description.
4. What beliefs of Mary's seem to reflect cognitive distortions?
5. What beliefs of Mary's represent a negative coping style?

Understanding the Problem

A problem can be understood as an imbalance or discrepancy between "what is" (i.e., present conditions) and "what should be" (i.e., conditions that are demanded or desired), together with some obstacle or obstacles preventing the availability of an effective response for reducing this discrepancy. When sufficient relevant, factual information about the problem has been obtained, you should attempt to specify: (a) what present conditions are unacceptable ("what is"); (b) what changes or additions are demanded or desired ("what should be"); and (c) what obstacle(s) are reducing the availability of an effective response. The conditions targeted for change and the obstacles preventing change may both include environmental events, personal events, and interactions between the two. The target conditions may involve environmental events such as physical conditions, task characteristics, the behavior of other people, and structures such as rules, systems, and relations, including relationships between people. These conditions may also include personal events such as your own behavior and behavioral deficits, your physical condition, cognitions such as your values, beliefs and expectations, and emotions such as anxiety or anger. The demands for change may originate in the environment (e.g., job demands) and/or within you, that is, your own personal goals, values, and commitments. In most cases, both sources influence the demands for change. The obstacles are likely to include environmental-personal events such as novelty or unfamiliarity, complexity, conflict, skill deficits, ability deficits, lack of resources, uncertainty, and emotional inhibitions.

Exercise: Understanding the Problem

Identify the following with regard to Mary's problem:

1. "What is"—what present conditions are unacceptable? (to whom?)
2. "What should be"—what conditions are demanded or desired? (by whom?)
3. What obstacle(s) is influencing the availability of an effective response for reducing the discrepancy between "what is" and "what should be?"
4. What is Jane's problem?
5. What is management's problem?

Additional exercises of this type can be performed using the members' real problems or the problem examples presented earlier (Campus crime problem, Nuclear weapons problem, Dating problem, Curfew problem).

Examples: Understanding the Problem

1. *Campus crime problem:*
   "What is": Too much crime on campus.
   "What should be": No crime on campus.
   Obstacles: Uncertainty as to how to reduce discrepancy.
2. *Nuclear weapons problem:*
   "What is": Too many nuclear weapons ready to be used in the world.
   "What should be": Little or no nuclear weapons.
   Obstacles: Conflict or disagreement as to how to reduce discrepancy.

3. *Dating problem:*
"What is": Student is dissatisfied with current dating relationships. He is attracted to a girl whom he has seen frequently on campus but he does not know her. He is afraid of rejection. "What should be": A dating relationship with this girl. Less fear of rejection.
Obstacles: Uncertainty about how to approach girl without getting rejected, not knowing the girl, fear of rejection.
4. *Curfew problem:*
"What is": Daughter keeps violating curfew.
"What should be": Daughter coming home at the expected times.
Obstacles: Unavailability of an effective response.

Setting Goals

The two most important rules in goal-setting are: (a) state the goals in specific, concrete terms and (b) avoid stating goals that are unrealistic or unlikely to be attained. Stating goals in specific, concrete terms helps you to identify relevant, appropriate solutions and facilitates decision-making effectiveness later on in the problem-solving process. Unrealistic goals would change the problem from one which is soluble to an insoluble one, where it would be impossible to find a satisfactory solution. This would result in frustration and more stress.

The general problem-solving goal is to reduce the discrepancy between "what is" and "what should be." For a particular problem, the specific goal(s) may focus on: (a) meeting the demands or expectations for change in the present conditions, (b) overcoming a specific obstacle to meeting these demands, (c) reducing or changing the demands, or (d) some combination of the above. The goals are stated in the form of a "How" or "What" question—e.g., "How can I meet more men?"; "What can I do to reduce the frequency of interruptions when I am trying to study in my dorm room?"; What can I do to reduce my boss' unreasonable demands?

Exercise: Setting Goals

Using the problems previously described, as well as real problems from the members' homework assignments, the members can now practice stating goals. During this process, they should be asked to practice generating *alternative* problem-solving goals, since different problem statements are likely to result in different preferences for solutions, which could affect problem-solving effectiveness.

Examples: Setting Goals

1. *Mary's problem:*
   "How can I . . .(a) get Jane to accept my promotion?"
   (b) get Jane to stop disrupting the work in the department?"
   (c) get Jane to be my friend again?"
   (d) get Jane to improve her performance?"
   (e) calm down so that I can work effectively while I am trying to correct the situation with Jane?"

2. *Nuclear weapons problem:*
   "What plan for eliminating nuclear weapons will the major nations agree on?"

3. *Dating problem:*
   "How can I . . .(a) get the girl to accept a date with me?"
   (b) reduce my fear of getting rejected?"
   (c) get to know the girl?"

Getting at the "Real" Problem

The specific problem you are focusing on may not always be the basic, primary, or most important problem. In some cases, the specific problem may be only part of a more important, broader problem which you are not recognizing. By focusing only on the specific problem, you are limiting your alternatives for dealing with the broader, more important problem. In other cases, the problem you are focusing on might be a consequence or effect of a more important antecedent problem in a cause-effect problem chain. Your attempts to solve the secondary problem might not be successful without solving the primary (antecedent) problem first. Or, if you do succeed in solving the secondary problem, the primary problem might soon cause another problem to occur. A useful technique for getting at the basic or primary problem is to state the problem-solving goal for the problem you are focusing on and then ask "Why?" The answer to this question might help to suggest a broader, more basic problem or a more important primary problem.

Exercise: Getting at the "Real" Problem

1. Arriving at a meeting about 15 minutes early, a speaker noticed that no lectern (lecturer's stand for notes) had been provided for her presentation. Since she anticipated feeling uncomfortable without a place to rest her notes during her talk, she realized she had a problem and stated it in the following way: "Where can I get a lectern in a hurry?" What is the speaker's "real" or basic problem? ("What can I use to rest my notes on while I talk?")*

2. A busy business executive concerned about his poor physical condition is focusing on the problem: "How can I find time to jog three miles each day?" What is a broader, more important statement of this executive's problem that would result in more alternative solutions? ("What can I do to improve my physical condition?")

3. A small church congregation of limited finances wanted to get its church repainted in time for its centennial celebration in two weeks. To keep costs down, they hired a painter who offered to do the job at a very low cost. After several days, it became clear that the painter was very slow and the quality of the work was very poor. The church's repair committee stated its problem as follows: "How can we get the painter to improve the quality and efficiency of his work so that the church will get painted adequately in time for the celebration?" How can this problem be stated more generally to make available a greater range of alternative solutions? ("How can we get the church painted adequately in time for the celebration at the lowest possible cost?")*

4. A professional engineer with a major corporation has reached the mandatory retirement age and must retire from his job, which he enjoys a great deal. He is in good health and he wants to continue being productive and putting his talents and experience to good use. He states his problem as follows: "Where can I find another engineering job where they don't have a mandatory retirement age?" This problem statement did not lead to any success. What is a broader statement of this person's problem that would make available a greater variety of alternatives? ("What can I do to remain productive and put my talents and experience to good use?")

*All asterisks in this chapter indicate that these problems, examples, and/or exercises are taken from Parnes et al. (1977) and Noller et al. (1976).

Dealing with a Complex Problem

When you recognize a broad problem or a cause–effect problem sequence, you may find that it is too complex to deal with as a whole. In that case, the problem might be dealt with more effectively by breaking it down into more manageable sub-problems and solving them one at a time in some predetermined order based on importance or priority. For example, in the case of a cause–effect problem chain, it would be most important to focus on the first problem in the chain, if this is possible. If you have no control over this problem or it is insoluble, then you must deal with the secondary problems which can be solved.

Example: Dealing with a
Complex Problem

1. *The Campus crime problem:* This is a complex problem which might be handled more effectively if it is broken down into more manageable sub-problems, such as "How to reduce burglaries in the dormitories on weekends and vacations?" "How to reduce the frequency of attacks on women in certain areas of the campus?" "How to reduce vandalism and property damage in the academic buildings?"
2. *The Curfew problem:* In order to determine if there is a more basic problem, the parent faced with this problem should ask: "Why do I want my daughter to meet the required curfew?" This might lead to the realization that the curfew problem is really only one part of a broader, more important problem: "How can I get my daughter to respond to family rules and responsibilities" (e.g., coming home when expected, keeping her room clean, helping with chores, attending family activities, etc.) Alternatively, the answer might reveal that the curfew problem is really a *result* of several antecedent problems, such as the daughter's failure to complete homework assignments, her lack of interest in spending time with the family, and the parent's concern about her safety when she is out at night. In either case, identifying the sub-problems which make up the complex problem allows the parent to begin dealing with the more complex problem, either as a single problem or by focusing on the various sub-problems one at a time, depending on the availability of solution alternatives and their potential effectiveness.

Re-appraising the Problem

Once the problem has been clearly defined, it may no longer be as threatening at it appeared to be when it was still vague and undefined. Therefore, you should re-appraise the problem at this point. This is done by considering the benefits and costs to you of solving the problem, as opposed to not solving the problem. You should consider not only the possible immediate benefits and costs, but also the possible long-term benefits and costs. Consider benefits and costs to yourself and to significant others. It might help to ask questions such as "What's at stake?", "What have I got to gain?", "What have I got to lose?" A problem is "benign" (low risk) if you expect little or no costs whether or not the problem is solved successfully. A problem is "significant" or important if you expect significantly *more* benefits and/or *less* costs from solving the problem than from not solving the problem. If you emphasize the possible *costs* of solving and/or not solving the problem, you will probably perceive the problem as a "threat." If you do, the following questions may help you to appraise the threat realistically and avoid magnifying it: "Where's the threat?", "What is the worst thing that can happen?" On the other hand, if you emphasize the *benefits* or opportunities that may result from solving the problem, you will probably perceive the problem as a "challenge", which would help to reduce threat and anxiety, and give you hope and motivation for problem solving."

Exercise: Reappraising the Problem

1. How can Mary reappraise the threat she perceives in her problematic situation?
2. How can Mary view her problem as a challenge?
3. What are the challenging aspects of the following problems: the Campus Crime Problem, the Nuclear Weapons Problem, the Dating Problem, the Curfew Problem.

Unit 5. Generation of Alternative Solutions

Objective: To make available as many alternative solutions (coping options) as possible, in such a way as to maximize the likelihood that the "best" solution will be among them. The first ideas that come to mind when trying to find a solution to a problem are not always the best ideas. Therefore, in order to maximize problem-solving effectiveness, it is necessary to generate as many different options as possible.

Major Blocks to the Creative Generation of Solutions

The major blocks to the creative generation of problem solutions are *habit* and *convention*. We are slaves of our habits. We all repeatedly apply our previously-learned responses to present situations. It feels "right" when we do things in the habitual or conventional way, and it feels "wrong" when we try to change our habits or routine and do something in a different way. Our habits can be helpful and adaptive in many situations. We would be in trouble if we did not develop habits for many everyday situations, such as dressing in the morning and driving a car. Habits can sometimes be helpful in problem-solving as well, when solutions learned in past problematic situations can be applied successfully to new, but similar problems. However, habits can also hinder problem solving when we respond "automatically" to new problems with previously-learned habits without questioning their appropriateness or applicability in the new problematic situation. In order to maximize your *coping effectiveness,* you cannot depend entirely on old habits; you must try out *different* approaches. In order to maximize your *coping creativity,* you cannot limit your thinking to conventional ideas; you must invent new or *original* ideas. [Parnes et al., 1977]

Exercise: Breaking Old Habits
and Creating New Ideas

What are all the uses you can think of for an ordinary (a) brick, (b) wire coat hanger, (c) broom.* Think of as many ideas as possible. Don't give up the search too soon.

Generating Relevant Solution Alternatives

While the generation of alternatives is a creative process which emphasizes imagination and originality, it is not "free association." Rather, the emphasis is on the generation of relevant, goal-oriented solutions. A goal-oriented solution is a coping response(s) aimed at achieving the problem-solving goal(s). The relevant solutions for a particular problem may vary depending on how the goals are stated. Therefore, you should consider alternative goal statements when generating alternative solutions (e.g., meeting task demands vs. reducing task demands, changing an objective situation vs. changing your personal reactions to it). More relevant, potentially effective solutions may be available for one goal statement than for another.

Generating Specific Solutions

Solutions may be generated at different levels of specificity. At the most general level is a solution *strategy,* which is the statement of an objective with the means to the objective being left unspecified or stated only in vague, general terms. At the most specific level is a concrete *course of action,* which describes in behavioral terms the means required to reach an objective. A strategy-level solution would be difficult to evaluate later in the decision-making stage because it is too far removed from the actual behavior. Instead of a specific course of action, it is actually a *class* of coping responses, which may vary considerably in effectiveness. Therefore, if you break down solution strategies into more specific courses of action, you will not only facilitate the decision-making process, but you will also make available more solution alternatives.

Example: Generating Specific Solutions

The parent with the teenaged daughter who has been ignoring the parent's curfew might generate the *strategy:* "Punish her for coming in late." This strategy can include more specific solutions which are likely to vary in effectiveness, such as "Spank her,""Make her do extra work around the house,"or "Take away a privilege.""Take away a privilege" is a somewhat more specific strategy which can still be broken down further into more specific courses of action such as "Ground her on a Saturday night" or "Deny her the use of the family car for one day." In general, the more specifically the solution is stated the better. However, the parent should not waste time generating too many specific alternatives which differ only in minor, trivial details which are not likely to have a significant effect on the effectiveness or feasibility of the alternatives. These minor details are relevant only for solution implementation and can be worked out at the end of the decision-making task or the beginning of the solution-implementation-and-verification task.

Basic Principles for Generating Alternative Solutions

In order to maximize solution production and creativity when generating alternative solutions, you should apply three basic principles: (a) the *quantity principle,* (b) the *deferment-of-judgment principle,* and (c) the *variety principle.*

Quantity Principle

According to the quantity principle, the more alternative solutions that are produced, the more good-quality solution ideas will be made available. To apply this principle, think of as many alternative solutions as possible without limiting your search to conventional solutions, ordinary solutions, or solutions which have worked well in the past. Do not give up the search too soon. If you "block" and can't think of any more ideas, take a break (if the problem does not require an immediate solution) and return to the task later (Osborn, 1963; Parnes et al., 1977).

Deferment-of-Judgment Principle

The deferment-of-judgment principle states that more good quality solution ideas will be generated when you suspend judgment or critical evaluation of solution ideas until later on in the problem-solving process, during the decision-making task. Imagination and judgment are both important for effective problem solving but they tend to clash when you try to use them both at the same time. Imagination and judgment are to the problem solver what a hammer and saw are to the carpenter. They are two kinds of tools, each to be used at a different time for a different purpose. Imagination is used to create or discover new ideas, while judgment is used later to sort out and evaluate these ideas (Parnes et al., 1977). To use this principle effectively, let your imagination "run loose" and try to produce an abundance of original ideas without filtering them through any evaluative screens, such as appropriateness, conventionality, practicality, feasibility, or utility. The wilder the idea the better. Don't worry about wasting time thinking of "silly" or "ridiculous" ideas. A "ridiculous" idea can often be "toned down" or modified to produce a very good, realistic solution which may not have been discovered otherwise (Osborn, 1963; Parnes et al. 1977). For example, "Hire a housekeeper" may not be a feasible solution for some people experiencing a conflict between domestic and career responsibilities, but this idea may suggest the more practical idea "Hire someone to come in a few hours a week to do the ironing."

Variety Principle

According to the variety principle, the greater the range or variety of solution alternatives generated, the more good quality ideas will be made available. When generating specific solution alternatives, you may develop a "set" to produce ideas which reflect only one strategy or general approach to the problem. This narrow set may occur even when the quantity and deferment-of-judgment principles are being applied effectively. To break out of this set, look over your list of solution alternatives after using the quantity and deferment-of-judgment principles and identify all the different strategies which are represented. Basically, this is a classification task, grouping solution alternatives according to some common theme. If any of the strategies have very few specific solutions, try to think of more specific solution alternatives for that particular strategy. Then try to think of *new* strategies which are not yet represented by any of the available solutions and generate additional specific solution ideas for those strategies. For example, consider the problem-solving goal of how to minimize emotional distress in response to a continuing, relatively unchangeable stressful situation. After generating a number of specific solution alternatives, you may realize that all of your coping responses can be grouped into the strategy class; "Take steps to reduce physical tension and fatigue" (e.g., muscle relaxation exercises, breathing exercises, physical exercises, going to sleep earlier). This should then be a cue to generate other strategies for reducing emotional distress, such as "Take steps to reduce unproductive worrying" (e.g., attention diversion or distraction, setting aside a specific time for worrying); "Try to identify and correct irrational thoughts" (e.g., re-appraising threatening expectations, challenging the validity of threatening assumptions); and "Try to view the situation as a challenge or opportunity for personal growth" (e.g., learning to tolerate adversity, learning how to prevent similar problems from occurring in the future, helping others with similar problems).

Exercises: Generating Alternative Solutions

Use the above principles to generate as many alternative solutions as possible to the following problems (a useful procedure for demonstrating the effects of each principle is to conduct one of these exercises following the presentation of each principle, using the same or different problems).

1. What are all the ways you can think of for improving a bathtub? A mailbox? Toothpaste? A bed? A library?
2. Your girlfriend (boyfriend, husband, wife) has asked you to be more affectionate. What are all the possible ways that you can show your affection?
3. A 40-year-old divorced woman working as a bookkeeper in a small office would like to meet a man who is interested in a serious relationship. So far, she has primarily been meeting men in singles bars who are either married or are interested only in a "one-night-stand". She states her problem: "What can I do to meet more men who are interested in developing a serious relationship with a woman?"
4. A foreman in a factory is in charge of a group of workers whose job it is to pack the company's products in boxes for shipping. The workers' productivity has been unsatisfactory because they waste too much time reading the newspapers that are used for packing. Keeping in mind the company's need to keep costs down, the foreman states the problem: "How can I increase the worker's productivity at the lowest possible cost to the company?"
5. A teacher in an elementary school is faced with the problem of having a class in which a number of children keep getting out of their seats, talking out of turn, socializing when they should be working, and not paying attention when the teacher is talking. The teacher states the problem: "How can I get the children to sit in their seats, pay attention, and concentrate on their work?"

Aids for Increasing the Quantity and Quality of Solution Ideas

After generating a list of solution alternatives using the principles described above, you may be able to increase the quantity and quality of solution ideas by using the following procedures:

1. *Combinations.* Look over your list of solution alternatives and consider how individual solutions can be combined to produce new solution ideas.
2. *Modifications and elaborations.* Look over your list of solution alternatives and consider how different solutions can be modified or elaborated on to improve the idea or produce a new one.
3. *Forced relationships.* You can often generate new solution ideas by "forcing" a relationship between two concepts which are different, but yet similar in some ways. For example, in creative problem solving a person might be considering how to improve a bathtub. To use forced relationships to generate ideas, he would think of something that is similar to a bathtub in some ways but different in other ways; for example, a swimming pool. He would then consider how one might improve a bathtub by making it more like a swimming pool (e.g., make it deeper, make it wider, put it where the sun can shine on it, put in a water circulator). In real-life problem solving, you might be able to generate more solution ideas for a particular problematic situation by considering how you can act more like a "model" (another person) who is similar to you in some ways, but different in that he handles that type of situation well. For example, "How can I be more effective in meeting women by acting more like John?"
4. *Visualization.* You may be able to facilitate the identification of potentially effective solution ideas by employing the visualization principle. To use this procedure, construct the problematic situation in imagination, and then imagine yourself attempting to cope with the situation and achieve the problem-solving goal. Your imagination may help you discover a new approach. A variation of this procedure, using the forced-relationships method, is to imagine an effective model coping with the same situation.

Seeking Information about Solution Alternatives

For some difficult, serious, or uncommon problems, it may be necessary to seek information or advice about possible solutions from books, experts, professionals, or other sources of relevent, authoritative information in the community. Some cues that this procedure might be necessary or important are: (a) you cannot think of any possible solutions after trying for some time; (b) your list of alternative solutions is extremely limited; and/or (c) you discover later during decision making or solution implementation and verification that none of your solution alternatives is satisfactory. Information or advice about possible solutions is not sought in a dependent way by acting "automatically" on the advice received, but in an independent, problem-solving manner by making available more good-quality solution alternatives to choose from. Therefore, it is important to not only get information about possible solutions, but about the "pros" and "cons" of each solution as well.

Unit 6. Decision Making

Objective: To evaluate (judge and compare) the available solution alternatives and select the "best" solution for implementation in the problematic situation. In the present model, the "best" solution is the one which is expected to be most effective in achieving the problem-solving goal while maximizing significant benefits and minimizing significant costs.

Rough Screening of Solution Alternatives

You can simplify the decision-making task a great deal by initially going over your list of available solution alternatives and eliminating any that are clearly inferior because of (a) obvious unacceptable risks associated with their implementation, and/or (b) low feasibility. The *unacceptable risks* refer to likely serious negative consequences which significantly reduce the utility of the solution. *Low feasibility* refers to the low likelihood that the solution could be implemented because of lack of ability, lack of resources, or other obstacles.

Anticipating Solution Outcomes

A solution *outcome* refers to the total expected (likely) positive consequences (benefits, gains) and negative consequences (costs, losses) of the particular solution alternative, including long-term as well as immediate consequences, and social as well as personal consequences. The following is a checklist of some of the important *personal consequences* which you should consider.

1. Problem resolution (i.e., expected effectiveness of the solution in achieving the problem-solving goal)
2. Effects on emotional well-being (pleasure vs. pain)
3. Time and effort expended
4. Effects on physical well-being
5. Effects on psychological well-being (e.g., self-esteem)
6. Effects on economic well-being (e.g., job security)
7. Self-enhancement (e.g., achievements, knowledge)
8. Effects on other personal goals, values, and commitments

The following is a check-list of some of the most important *social consequences* which you should consider.

1. Effects on the personal and/or social well-being of significant others
2. Effects on the rights of others
3. Effects on significant interpersonal relationships
4. Effects on personal and/or social performance evaluations (e.g., reputation, status, prestige).

It is clear from the above checklist that solutions in real-life problematic situations may have many different consequences. Considering the limited capacity of the conscious mind to handle large amounts of information, it is important to write down the major significant expected consequences (for example, I am likely to feel very guilty, my parents will be very hurt, in the long run I could lose my job). This will help to facilitate the task of evaluating your solution alternatives.

Evaluating Solution Outcomes

Since the conscious mind does not have the capacity to weigh every expected consequence of each solution alternative when judging and comparing alternatives, the evaluation task is simplified by focusing on the following four major outcome criteria:

1. Problem resolution
2. Emotional well-being
3. Time/effort
4. Overall personal-social well-being

When considering *problem resolution,* you ask: "How likely is it that the solution will achieve the problem solving goal?" For *emotional well-being,* the question is: "If this solution is implemented, how good or bad am I likely to feel?" To consider *time/effort,* you ask: "How much time and effort is this solution likely to require?" *Overall personal-social well-being* refers to the total benefit/cost ratio, considering long-term consequences as well as short-term consequences. You should ask the question: "How favorable (benefits outweigh costs) or unfavorable (costs outweigh benefits) is the total benefit/cost ratio likely to be?"

For a simple, informal evaluation of solution alternatives, consider each solution alternative in relation to the four outcome criteria and judge each solution as either "satisfactory" or "unsatisfactory," or use a simple rating scale, such as "poor," "fair," "good," and "very good." This simple procedure will be sufficient for effective problem solving in most cases. However, if you are interested in making finer discriminations regarding the favorableness or unfavorableness of solution alternatives, then rate each alternative on the following rating scale:

+5 Extremely Satisfactory

+4

+3 Moderately Satisfactory

+2

+1 Slightly Satisfactory

−1 Slightly Unsatisfactory

−2

−3 Moderately Unsatisfactory

−4

−5 Extremely Unsatisfactory

These finer discriminations might be important for "high risk" problem solving, where the consequences of a relatively ineffective solution might be serious.

Some problem-solvers may be interested in a more specific and formal evaluation of solution alternatives where the quality of specific solutions is judged separately for specific outcomes or outcome criteria. For example, the above rating scale can be used to rate each solution separately for *problem resolution, emotional well-being, time/effort,* and *overall personal-social well-being* (total benefit/cost ratio). The quality or utility of each solution alternative can then be based on these four ratings (for example, the sum of the ratings, the average rating). If you prefer to place more weight on one particular outcome criterion, you can do this by multiplying the rating for that criterion by a number which reflects the amount of weight you would like to give it. For example, if you believe that problem resolution is twice as important as the other three criteria, you would multiply the rating for problem resolution by two. Another way to emphasize the importance of a particular criterion is to establish a minimum rating for that criterion. For example, if you felt that emotional well-being was particularly important for a given problem, you might decide to eliminate any solution alternative with a rating less than +3. You can also add new outcome criteria or eliminate criteria, depending on your appraisal of the significance of different outcomes for different problematic situations. For example, in some situations financial cost might be a particularly significant criterion to consider when judging solution alternatives (e.g., what to do when your washing machine breaks down). Instead of considering this criterion as part of the total benefit/cost criterion, you can give it special emphasis by considering it separately.

Keeping in mind the externalization rule, the various solution alternatives and ratings should be written down. To simplify the task of comparing alternatives, they can be summarized in a chart, such as the one in Table 8.5. This chart shows a list of rated solution alternatives for the problem: "How can I get my teenaged daughter to cooperate with our curfew rule more consistently?" On the basis of these ratings, the best alternative appears to be "Reward her by giving her extra gas money." However, the ratings are also consistently favorable for "Reward her by letting her stay out one hour later on Saturday night." Therefore, the problem-solver might choose to include both strategies in his solution plan.

Exercises: Anticipating and
Evaluating Solution Alternatives

It is not always easy to anticipate and evaluate specific consequences of solutions before they are experienced, especially subjective consequences such as feelings and emotions. Two visualization procedures which might be helpful in some cases are *behavior rehearsal* and *imaginal rehearsal* (or covert rehearsal). Behavior rehearsal is useful for interpersonal problems such as dealing with the offensive behavior of another person. To use this technique, a

Table 8.5 Evaluation of solution alternatives for teenage curfew problem

Alternatives	Problem resolution	Emotional well-being	Time/ effort	Benefit/ cost ratio	Total
1. Punish her by denying her the family car.	+5	–3	+5	–1	6
2. Punish her by "grounding" her.	+5	–3	+5	–1	6
3. Reward her by giving her extra gas money.	+5	+4	+5	+5	19
4. Reward her by letting her stay out one hour later on Saturday night.	+3	+2	+2	+4	11
5. Explain how the curfew is for her own good.	–5	–2	+3	–3	– 7
6. Go out and find her and bring her home.	+5	–5	–5	–5	–10

Alternatives rated by four outcome criteria; +5 = extremely satisfactory, –5 = extremely unsatisfactory.

group member introduces an interpersonal problem and alternative ways of coping with it are generated. The member then engages in role-playing with another group member and "tries out" the different approaches. The member playing the other person in the problematic situation can either respond naturally, or he can respond the way the real person is expected to respond in the actual situation. When behavior rehearsal is not possible, group members can be encouraged to use the imaginal-rehearsal technique, which involves experimenting with different coping options in imagination. This procedure is particularly useful in a group setting, where all group members can perform the exercise at the same time, using their own individual problematic situation. Both of these rehearsal procedures may help a person identify and evaluate the various social and emotional consequences of different solution possibilities. In addition, these techniques may also be useful during the next unit of training, namely, solution implementation and verification, for practicing the instrumental skills involved in carrying out different solutions.

*Examples: Evaluating Solution
Outcomes*

1. Bill and Len both had the same problem. They were both divorced, middle-aged men whose problem statement was: "How can I meet more women?" The alternatives both men generated included the following:

   a. Go to singles bars.
   b. Join Parents Without Partners (PWOP)
   c. Go to religion-affiliation social and discussion-group activities
   d. Join a dating service
   e. Put an ad in the personal, singles section in the newspaper.
   f. Go on singles trips and vacations.

After evaluating these solution alternatives using the outcome criteria described above, Bill's first choice was "Put an ad in the newspaper" and his last choice was "Join PWOP." Len's evaluation of the solutions was the opposite. His first choice was "Join PWOP" and his last choice was "Put an ad in the newspaper." The differences in solution preference appeared to be based primarily on different anticipated effects for the outcome criterion "emotional well-being." Bill did not feel "right" about joining PWOP. He perceived this as a threat to his self-esteem. On the other hand, Len did not feel "right" about putting an ad in the newspaper for a date. He viewed this alternative as a threat to his self-esteem. This example illustrates the effects of anticipated emotional outcomes on the preference for solution alternative.

2. Henry is a teacher in an elementary school who has the problem: "How can I get the children to sit in their seats, pay attention, and concentrate on their work?" One of the alternative solutions he generated was "Plan and implement a formal classroom behavior-modification program, using a point system". Henry rated this alternative very high on the problem-resolution criterion. However, he rated it very low on the time/effort criterion. He was not willing to expend all the time and effort which would be required to plan and implement a formal behavior-modification program in the classroom. As a com-

romise, he selected a solution which involved the following procedure: If a child is being very disruptive or has not been paying attention for a specific period of time, the child will be required to place his name on the board under a heading labeled "punishment." On the other hand, if a child has been demonstrating appropriate classroom behavior for a specific period of time, that child will be asked to place his name on the board under the heading "reward." These children will then be given appropriate rewards and punishments later as the opportunity arises (e.g., being allowed to be the teacher's helper for a day, points off on a classroom assignment).

Making a Solution Plan

On the basis of your evaluation of the available solution alternatives, you should then ask three questions: 1. "Is the problem solvable?" (i.e., "Is there a satisfactory solution?"); 2. "Do I need more information before I can select a solution or solution combination for implementation?"; and 3. "What solution or solution combination should I choose to implement?" If you appraise the problem as unsolvable and/or your answer to the second question is positive, then you must return to the problem-definition-and-formulation task to seek more information and/or re-formulate the problem in a way that might make it solvable (for example, goals which emphasize acceptance, emotional control, or personal growth). However, if you appraise the problem as solvable and your answer to the second question is negative, then go to the third question and make a solution plan.

The solution plan should be consistent with the general goal of attempting to resolve the problem satisfactorily while maximizing emotional well-being, minimizing time and effort, and maximizing overall personal-social well-being. The solution plan may be *simple* or *complex*. For a simple plan, you choose a single solution or course of action. When there is one solution which is expected to produce a highly satisfactory outcome, a simple plan may suffice. There are two types of complex plans: a *solution combination* and a *contingency plan*. For a solution combination, you choose a combination of solution alternatives to be implemented concurrently. This is done when it appears that the combination is likely to have greater utility than any solution alone. In choosing a contingency plan, you choose a combination of solutions to be implemented contingently—

you implement solution A, if that does not work, you implement solution B, if that does not work, etc. Another kind of contingency plan occurs when you first carry out one particular course of action (A) and, then, depending on the outcome of A, you will do either B or C. For example, you are very unhappy with your job because you are not getting paid a fair salary and you do not have enough autonomy. Since your major concern is the salary, your contingency plan is to go to the boss and ask for a specific raise which you feel you deserve (A). If he offers an increase which is inadequate, then you will also ask for more autonomy (B). However, if he rejects your request for a raise, then you will tell him you are going to quit the job (C). A contingency plan is chosen when there is enough uncertainty about any one solution or solution combination that it seems wise to have a contingency plan to save time in case the initial solution choice(s) does not work out satisfactorily. Once the solution plan has been prepared, the final step before solution implementation is to fill in the details as to exactly how, when, and where the solution plan will be implemented.

Exercise: Solution Plan

Table 8.5 lists six solution alternatives for the problem: "How can I get my teenaged daughter to cooperate with our curfew rule more consistently?" Based on the ratings for the four outcome criteria in Table 8.5, what is a possible *simple solution* for this problem? What is a possible *solution combination?* What is a possible *contingency plan?*

Unit 7. Solution Implementation and Verification

Objective: To assess the solution outcome and verify the effectiveness or utility of the chosen solution in the actual problematic situation.

At this point in the problem-solving process, the problem has been solved symbolically, but the effectiveness of the solution in coping with the problematic situation in real-life has not yet been verified. The only way to accomplish this verification is to implement the solution plan and evaluate the solution outcome objectively. There are four components to this process: 1. solution implementation, 2. self-monitoring, 3. self-evaluation, and 4. self-reinforcement.

Solution Implementation

Solution implementation involves performance of the behaviors which make up the solution plan. You must recognize that solution performance is likely to be influenced by a number of factors other than problem-solving ability. You may experience unexpected environmental obstacles or personal obstacles, such as emotional inhibitions. You may discover that you lack other required abilities or performance skills. You may discover that you overestimated the environmental rewards for the particular solution and, as a result, you might lose motivation to complete the solution plan. If effective solution implementation is not possible because of these obstacles, you can (a) return to previous stages in the problem-solving process in order to identify an alternative solution which may be implemented more effectively or (b) focus on overcoming the obstacles, such as through the use of the facilitative coping techniques discussed earlier.

At this point, training in specific coping performance skills and/or arousal-oriented coping techniques might be appropriate for some group members who are experiencing obstacles to solution implementation and have serious deficits in performance skills and/or anxiety-management skills. This would also be an appropriate point to utilize once again the behavioral-rehearsal and imaginal-rehearsal techniques used during decision-making training. However, at this time, instead of focusing on the evaluation of solution outcomes, the procedures would focus on the repeated rehearsal of coping responses for the purpose of skill enhancement and/or anxiety reduction.

Self-Monitoring

Self-monitoring involves self-observation of solution performance and/or its products (outcome), and the recording (measurement) of this performance and/or its outcome. There are several ways to record or measure your performance so that your assessment of solution outcome will be accurate and valid. The type of measure which is most appropriate for a particular problem depends on the type of coping behavior or performance you are assessing. The following are some common measures.

1. *Response frequency:* You simply count the number of responses. For example, number of cigarettes smoked, number of times a

child gets out of his seat or talks out of turn in class, number of times your teenaged daughter violates curfew, number of requests for dates.

2. *Response duration:* You record the amount of time it takes to perform a response. For example, the time it takes to complete a report, time spent studying, time spent exercising each day, time spent commuting to work, time spent sleeping.

3. *Response latency:* You record the time between the occurrence of a particular antecedent event or cue and the *onset* of a particular response. For example, the number of minutes late to class, the amount of time beyond curfew, the amount of time late for dinner, the amount of time a child takes to get a job done following a request.

4. *Response intensity:* You rate the degree of intensity of something, such as the degree of anxiety, the intensity or severity of a headache, the degree of depression, the intensity of sexual arousal, the degree of pleasure or satisfaction associated with a particular activity.

5. *Response product:* Your measure here is not of the behavior itself but of the by-products or effects of the behavior. For example, the number of dates accepted, the number of boxes packed per hour, the number of sales made, the number of chapters studied, number of arrests made, the number of problems solved.

At this point the group leader can provide further training in self-recording techniques if he so desires, such as the use of time-sampling procedures and the use of tally sheets and charts or graphs to present a visual summary or illustration of the results of self-monitoring (see Barlow, Hayes, & Nelson, 1984). The latter is often very useful for helping group members assess their rate of progress in solving a problem, especially when the solution plan involves the implementation of an intervention procedure over time.

Self-evaluation

When the solution performance is completed or has been recorded for a sufficient period of time to assess progress, you should judge the solution outcome using the same outcome criteria and rating procedures employed in the decision-making task to judge each solution alternative: (a) problem resolution, (b) emotional well-being, (c) amount of time and effort expended, and (d) total benefit/

cost ratio or overall personal-social well-being. If the "match" between the actual outcome and the anticipated outcome at the time of decision making is "satisfactory," then you can go to the final step in solution implementation and verification, namely, *self-reinforcement*. That is, you reward yourself for a job well done. This can simply be a positive self-statement, such as "Congratulations, you handled that problem very well!" It is also possible to provide yourself with some more tangible reward, such as an enjoyable leisure activity or the purchase of some desirable gift. In addition to self-reinforcement, a powerful reward is likely to be the reinforcement resulting from the positive solution outcome itself, which should also increase your sense of mastery and competence.

If the discrepancy between the actual solution outcome and the anticipated outcome is "unsatisfactory," you must "trouble-shoot" and "recycle"—i.e., return to the problem-solving process and determine where corrections must be made in order to find a more effective solution. If you cannot succeed after several attempts it is best to recognize the futility of further independent problem-solving efforts, and either reformulate the problem as one which must be accepted, or seek help with the problem from someone who might be more knowledgeable about that particular type of problem.

Unit 8. Maintenance and Generalization

Objective: To consolidate training effects and facilitate the maintenance and generalization of effective problem-solving performance.

At this point in the program, training in each of the five components of the problem-solving model has been completed. During these last few sessions, much of the time is spent "putting it all together" and solving real-life problems with a minimum of direction and guidance from the group leader. In addition, the group leader attempts to facilitate the maintenance and generalization of effective problem-solving performance by (a) continuing to provide positive reinforcement and corrective feedback, (b) reviewing positive problem-orientation cognitions and strengthening them by recognizing the group members' progress in learning to cope more effectively with everyday problems, (c) directing the group's attention to the wide range of real-life problems for which the problem-solving approach is applicable, including individual personal problems, interpersonal problems, marriage and family problems, and community problems, and (d) anticipating obstacles to implementing the problem-solving approach or specific solutions in real-life and preparing strategies for dealing with them, using the problem-solving approach.

In connection with the question of obstacles to the application of the problem-solving approach in real-life, unexpected problematic situations often occur in life which require a quick decision and immediate action, thus, precluding the careful, deliberate problem solving described in this program thus far. However, even if an individual has as little as one minute to solve a problem and act, several basic problem-solving principles can still help to maximize problem-solving effectiveness, even under these time-limited conditions (Parnes et al., 1977). In the final session, the following model for rapid problem solving is presented and group members are given the opportunity to practice using this model in the time remaining.

A Rapid Problem-Solving Model

Step #1. Make the following self-statements:
  (a) "Take a deep breath and calm down."
  (b) "There is no immediate catastrophe."
  (c) "Think of this problem as a challenge."
  (d) "I can handle it."
  (e) "Stop-and-think."
Step #2. Ask yourself the following questions:
  (a) "What's the problem?" (State the discrepancy between "what is" and "what should be.")
  (b) "What do I want to accomplish?" (State a goal.)
  (c) "Why do I want to achieve this goal?" (Broaden the goal, if appropriate.)
Step #3. (a) Think of a solution.
  (b) Now think of several other alternative solutions (at least two or three).
Step #4. (a) Think of the most important criteria for evaluating your solution ideas (at least two or three) (e.g., "Will it achieve my goal?" "What effect will it have on others?" "How much time and effort will it take?" Some other important criterion?)
  (b) Decide quickly on the solution alternative that seems best.

        (c) Think of one or two quick ways to improve the so-
lution.

Step #5. (a) Implement the solution.

        (b) Are you satisfied with the outcome?

        (c) If not, try out your second choice if you still have
time to cope with the problem.

If an individual finds it difficult to apply the above model in three
minutes or less, he can reduce the time further by eliminating Step
#2(c) and Step #4(c). Without these steps, the model may still
increase the effectiveness of problem solving under severe time
pressure.

Exercise: Rapid Problem Solving

Solve the following problems (through Step #4) within *five* minutes:

1. You just spilled coffee all over the last page of an important
   business letter which must be mailed out as soon as possible.
   You check the time and see that the last mail pickup at the
   mailbox down the block is due in about five minutes. What
   should you do?*
2. You are a college student returning to your dormitory room
   after a late class. You have a very important exam the next
   morning at 9 A.M. and are getting ready to begin studying for
   the entire evening because you are behind in your readings.
   Someone comes in and gives you the message that your girlfriend called to say that she is very depressed over something
   terrible that happened to her at work and that she *must* see you
   as soon as possible. You would like to help your girlfriend but
   you also want very badly to get a good grade on the exam. She
   is waiting for you to call. What should you do?

Solve the following problems within *three* minutes.

1. You are at a very expensive restaurant about one hour's drive
   from your home on a first date with a lady whom you would like
   very much to impress. You have just finished dinner and the
   waiter has brought you the check. As you reach for your wallet,
   you realize that you left it at home. What should you do?
2. You are driving home alone from your job at about 2 A.M. and
   you think that a car has been following you since you left the
   parking lot at your job. You have two weeks' pay in your wallet.
   What should you do?

Solve the following problems within *two* minutes.

1. Three times each week you wake up about 5:30 A.M. and jog about six miles before going to work, three miles away from your home and three miles back. One day you are on the return trip about two miles from your home when you see this huge dog about 50 yards up the road looking toward you and barking fiercely. You must get home as soon as possible in order to get to work on time. What should you do?

2. You live in an apartment building and are very friendly with the couple who lives in the next apartment. One night at 2 A.M. you are awakened by loud banging and screaming in their apartment. What should you do?

Solve the following problems within *one* minute.

1. You are working at your desk at about 10 A.M. one day when someone tells you that the boss wants to see you in his office. At that moment you remember that the boss told you the day before that he wanted an important report done by 10 A.M. today. You planned to complete it last night at home but you forgot all about it. What should you do?

2. You are alone in a subway in New York City late at night when three tough looking young men come into the subway, approach you and ask you to "lend" them $50. You only have $50 with you and you need money to pay for your car at the parking garage and for tolls to get home. What should you do?

Summary

A PST program is described which may serve as a model for PST as a treatment method, a maintenance strategy, or a prevention program with goals of increasing social competence and reducing stress. As described here, the program is designed as a time-limited competence enhancement/stress-management training "package," which can be carried out in approximately 15 two-hour weekly sessions. The program may be adapted to an individual (one-to-one) setting, a small group setting, or a large group setting, such as a classroom situation. The program provides training in problem orientation, problem definition and formulation, the generation of alternative solutions, decision making, and solution implementation and verification. Training is also provided in facilitative coping skills, which includes training to control and prevent interfering cognitions and disruptive emotional arousal. A rapid problem-solving method is also included in the training to help individuals deal with problematic situations which require quick effective action. The next chapter will describe how these methods can be implemented in a clinical situation as part of a broader therapy program conducted within a general PST framework.

Coming from a different field and perspective (industry), Alex F. Osborn (1952, 1963) was a strong voice calling for the development of training methods and techniques to nurture and enhance creative performance. He was instrumental in the development of one of the earliest and most influential PST programs, the Creative Problem-Solving Program, now located at the State University College at Buffalo. Originated over 30 years ago at the University of Buffalo, this program focused initially on the stimulation of productive thinking and creative performance using Osborn's "brainstorming" techniques, which tap several of the creative abilities identified by Guilford. Later, under the directorship of Sidney J. Parnes, who was influenced by both Osborn and Guilford, the goals and procedures of the program were broadened considerably and now focus on the facilitation of *general competence* (i.e., productive thinking, creative performance, and personal-social effectiveness) (Parnes, 1962; Parnes, Noller, & Biondi, 1977). In addition to the training program, which is conducted in academic courses and a week-long Annual Creative Problem-Solving Institute, a comprensive longitudinal research investigation was initiated in 1969 to study the effectiveness of the program. PST programs based on the Osborn-Parnes program have multiplied at a rapid rate in recent years.

9

Case Illustrations

It was explained in the previous chapter that PST can be conducted as a group-oriented, time-limited, competence-enhancement/stress-management "package," or it may be applied within a broader, individualized, open-ended therapy program. In the latter application, it was recommended that therapy be conducted within an overall PST framework, where other treatment procedures are applied at appropriate points during the training program, as needed. Conducted within the latter program, the goals of therapy include not only the reduction in maladaptive behavior, but also the facilitation of independent problem-solving performance in a positive direction in order to produce more generalized and durable behavior changes and prevent future psychological problems.

Four clinical cases are presented below that illustrate the application of PST within a broader, individualized therapy program for clinical disorders involving generalized anxiety, depression, obsessive-compulsive behavior, and a neurological deficit (developmental learning disability). All four cases are characterized by the possession of a negative coping style, including the client's perception of "uncontrollability" (inability to control negative events) and ineffective problem-solving performance. In three cases, the negative coping style is associated with a high degree of stress and its negative by-products, including anxiety, depression, and low self-esteem. In the fourth case (Mr. D.), the client appears to be insulated from these negative stress effects by a supportive, overprotective social environment. The goal of problem-solving-oriented therapy in each case was to reduce negative stress effects and maladaptive behavior by developing a more adaptive, problem-solving coping style and facilitating effective, independent problem-solving performance.

Case #1: Generalized Anxiety

Mrs. S. was a 36-year-old housewife and part-time art teacher. At the time she came into therapy she had been married for eight years, to a bank vice-president. The couple had one child—a six-year-old boy. It was Mrs. S.'s second marriage. The first had ended in divorce. Mrs. S. contacted me [T. J. D.] for therapy after she had been arrested for shoplifting at a local drug store. She had stolen only a lipstick, but the store manager had suspected her of shoplifting at the drug store for some time, because she frequently bought items and then returned them for refunds. He believed that she had been buying an item, stealing another one of the same type, and then later returning one of them and getting a refund using the receipt from the item she had bought. Mrs. S. denied this accusation, claiming that the theft was her first one, and that she frequently browsed in stores and bought things because she was bored and had nothing else to do. She would later realize that she did not really need many of the things that she had bought, or that she had spent too much money, so she often returned them.

Mrs. S. did not believe that the shoplifting was a problem, except for the fact that she did not understand why she did it. Her major presenting complaints were a high level of general anxiety, depression, and poor self-esteem. She described herself as extremely tense, uptight, impatient, indecisive, and fearful. She reported worrying about "everything" (for example, chemicals in the food, people who might try to take advantage of her, her health). She even worried about worrying too much—that worrying might eventually make her physically ill.

In addition to anxiety, Mrs. S. reported feeling very unhappy, bored, and dissatisfied with her life. Her self-confidence and self-esteem were very poor. She perceived herself as inadequate, incompetent, and lacking in control over her life and her emotions. She reported that her self-esteem had been deteriorating steadily since she left her full-time job about six years before as an art teacher in an elementary school. Mrs. S. had stopped working soon after she became pregnant with her son. She had started working again after he started school, but she could only find a job working 45 minutes each day as an art teacher in a junior high school. In addition to the short working time each week, Mrs. S. was not satisfied with the job because she had much more difficulty managing the behavior of the junior high school students in her class than she had had managing the elementary school students in her previous job.

In addition to gathering information about the dimensions of the above emotional and self-esteem problems and their development over time, the pretreatment assessment phase of therapy focused also on the identification of current life problems and stresses, consequences of problem behaviors and emotional responses, assessment of problem solving and other coping skills, and initial structuring for therapy. The latter included an explanation and discussion of the rationale and course of problem-solving therapy, with the major goals being to develop a problem-solving cognitive set and strengthen expectations of benefit. Problem solving and other coping skills were assessed using the Problem-Solving Inventory (PSI) and the Problem-Solving Self-Monitoring (PSSM) method (see Chapter 6). In addition to these assessment methods, self-ratings were used to assess anxiety state, mood, and self-esteem throughout the course of therapy. These variables were rated on a scale from 0 to 10, with 10 being the negative end of the scale in each case. During the first three weeks, the ratings were made daily at a randomly selected time in the morning, afternoon, and evening. Thereafter, the ratings were made during three randomly selected days each week.

Mrs. S. was seen in therapy for 28 sessions. The major specific problems and stresses identified and focused on during therapy fell into five problem areas: (a) her mother's health, (b) son's well-being (health and school problems), (c) work and other personal achievements, (d) social relationships, and (e) marriage. In addition to the problems in the above areas, a major problem that occurred during therapy was related to her husband's expected transfer to a new job in another state within the next three months.

About four months before entering therapy, Mrs. S. was informed that her mother had cancer. At the time Mrs. S. started therapy, the prognosis of her mother was still uncertain. About two months after learning about her mother's cancer, Mrs. S.'s son caught a bad cold, which developed into pneumonia. Both of these illnesses created considerable stress for Mrs. S., which reduced her ability to deal effectively with these problems. Shortly after beginning therapy, more anxiety was produced when Mrs. S. was informed by her son's school teacher that he had a reading problem which was interfering seriously with his school performance. This problem was also handled poorly by Mrs. S.

With regard to work and personal achievements, Mrs. S. was not involved in any meaningful work or constructive activity which could give her a sense of mastery or competence. During her brief work period each day as an art teacher, she did not believe that she was managing the class effectively. Mrs. S. was also unhappy because she had no close friends. Since she engaged in few activities outside of the home, she rarely had opportunities to meet people. On a few occasions when she did meet someone new, the person failed to show an interest in her as a friend later.

At first, Mrs. S. described her husband as a wonderful person for being so patient and understanding about the shoplifting and about her anxiety problems. Later, however, she complained that he was against her going for therapy before the shoplifting incident because he believed you should not discuss your personal problems with a stranger. Moreover, she complained that her husband never praised her or gave her recognition for anything. Instead, he frequently criticized her and put her down. They spent very little time together because he commuted a long distance to work each day and, as a result, would arrive home sometime between 7:30 P.M. and 11 P.M., eat dinner, and go right to bed. On weekends, he frequently spent hours doing paperwork related to his job. When she complained about their lack of time together, he told her that there was nothing he could do about it and that she was wrong to complain. With regard to the husband's expected job transfer, Mrs. S. was fearful because she did not know anything about the area and she was concerned that they would not be able to find a satisfactory residence in so short a period of time.

The problem-solving and coping-skills assessment revealed significant deficits in problem-solving-oriented coping. The major deficits were in problem orientation and problem definition and formulation, which precluded any further effective problem solving (generation of alternative solutions, decision making, etc.). Mrs. S. tended to appraise a problem as a "threat to be avoided" instead of a challenge or "problem to be solved," which caused fear and anxiety. She also tended to appraise the threat to her well-being (or a loved one's well-being) as being more serious or significant than it actually was on the basis of minimal information, which exacerbated the anxiety. She blamed herself for the problem, ignoring the important role of other factors, and tended to conclude, inappropriately, that there was nothing she could do to change the problem or reduce its stressfulness. This contributed to a feeling of helplessness and a sense of losing control. For example, when the teacher told Mrs. S. about her son's reading problem, her immediate response was: "I failed him. If I didn't have so many problems, he wouldn't have problems." She then cried and apologized profusely to the teacher for her son's reading problem instead of beginning to gather information about the problem and consider alternatives for dealing rationally and effectively with it. When a woman from the neighborhood whom Mrs. S. met and had lunch with one day seemed to ignore her the next day, Mrs. S. blamed herself, thinking that she had said or done something wrong. She felt rejected and upset and did nothing further to clarify the problem or try to spend more time with the person.

The anxiety generated by the negative problem-orientation cognitions, together with the failure to gather sufficient information to clarify, understand, and reappraise a problem accurately, tended to result in misconceptions and distortions which created pseudoproblems. These pseudoproblems, reflecting Mrs. S.'s fears and anxieties, were more threatening than the real problems. For example, Mrs. S. believed, incorrectly, that the woman whom she had met in the neighborhood was rejecting her. When her son showed signs of developing a cold, she thought that he had developed pneumonia again. When her husband informed her that he was going to be transferred to a new job within three months, she believed, without clarifying the problem, that it would be impossible to find a satisfactory home in so short a period of time.

In addition to the above deficits in problem orientation and specific problem-solving skills, it was determined during training that Mrs. S. also had deficits in *facilitative coping skills,* which are important for overcoming cognitive and emotional obstacles to effective problem solving (see Chapter 7). Moreover, when it was necessary to implement her problem solutions, it was learned that she had deficits in some of the instrumental skills that were required to implement certain problem solutions effectively—assertiveness skills and communication skills. Toward the latter part of therapy, it also became increasingly clear that it was going to be necessary for the husband to become involved in conjoint communication/problem-solving training, because he sometimes responded very negatively to her assertive problem solutions and other attempts to communicate and resolve the conflicts between them. However, he was very resistant to the idea of therapy.

A major goal of therapy was to help Mrs. S. develop a more effective problem-solving coping style. Instead of viewing a stressful problem primarily as a threat and worrying about it, she gradually learned to approach the problem as a challenge or problem to be solved. This prompted her to gather relevant information and to state the problem in problem-solving terms. Some of the problem statements that were developed and focused on in her therapy were the following:

1. What can I do to minimize my distress about my mother's cancer?
2. What can I do to help my mother adjust to having cancer? (an alternative statement of the problem involving her mother's cancer)
3. My son is showing symptoms of a cold. What can I do to prevent a more serious illness from developing?
4. What can I do to ensure a safe, healthy diet for my family?
5. What can I do to find a satisfying, productive full-time job?
6. What can I do to give myself a greater sense of personal achievement and accomplishment? (a broader statement of problem #5)
7. How can I reduce disruptive behavior in my classroom?
8. What can I do to overcome feelings of boredom when I am home alone?
9. How can I meet more people?
10. How can I communicate with people in a way that will ensure that they will enjoy my company and want to be my friend?
11. How can I get my husband to praise me more often and recognize the good things that I do to please him?
12. What can I do to get my husband to stop criticizing me and putting me down so often?
13. What can my husband and I do to make available more time to spend together?
14. How can my husband and I improve the quality of the time we spend together?
15. How can I persuade my husband to participate with me in marital counseling?

Instead of simply providing solutions to the above problems and helping Mrs. S. implement them effectively, the therapist attempted to teach her how to generate alternative solutions on her own, evaluate the solutions, select the "best" solution or solution combination, implement it, and evaluate the outcome. When Mrs. S. was not able to generate any more solution alternatives using the principles she was taught, the therapist sometimes suggested additional alternatives in order to maximize her effectiveness and build her response repertoire for future, similar problems. When certain solutions required instrumental skills that Mrs. S. did not have (e.g., assertiveness skills), training was provided in these skills using skill-training methods such as coaching, modeling, behavior rehearsal, performance feedback, and positive reinforcement.

In addition to the above training in goal-oriented coping skills (discovering and implementing problem solutions), training was provided in facilitative coping skills, when cognitive and emotional obstacles to effective problem solving occurred (e.g., exaggerated appraisals of threat, irrational assumptions, intense emotional arousal). Mrs. S. required training in both cognition-oriented facilitative coping (e.g., cognitive restructuring) and emotion-oriented facilitative coping (e.g., relaxation). For example, Mrs. S. was taught to test the validity of threatening beliefs and assumptions instead of accepting them automatically. A problem-solving approach was used for this purpose. When the woman in the neighborhood ignored Mrs. S., Mrs. S. assumed that she had said or done something wrong and that, as a result, the woman disliked her and did not want to be her friend. Instead of accepting this threatening assumption, Mrs. S. was taught to generate as many alternative explanations for the woman's behavior as possible (e.g., she was in a bad mood, she was preoccupied and did not see Mrs. S., she has poor eyesight and did not recognize Mrs. S.). She was then asked to generate or seek as many facts as possible for and against each explanation and to decide which one was most likely to be valid.

To deal with excessive emotional arousal, Mrs. S. was trained in progressive muscle relaxation and meditation. In addition, a desensitization procedure was used, which involved verbal problem solving in the session while at the same time attempting to apply relaxation skills (e.g., muscle relaxation, slow and deep breathing).

During the first four weeks of therapy, which focused primarily on assessment, Mrs. S.'s average weekly anxiety ratings were consistently "high" (8–10) and her average weekly mood and self-esteem ratings were consistently "poor" (8–10). As she developed more effective problem-solving-oriented coping skills during the next 12 weeks of therapy, her anxiety ratings dropped to the "moderate" (4–7) range, while her mood and self-esteem ratings changed to "fair" (4–7) and then to "good" (0–3). At about the 16th week of therapy, Mrs. S.'s anxiety ratings increased to the "high" range again and her mood and self-esteem ratings deteriorated from "good" to "fair" for a few weeks. These changes occurred when Mrs. S.'s husband informed her about the expected job transfer within the next three months. Her immediate response was: "We don't know anything about that area. How are we going to find a place to live in three months? What if we don't like it there?" Mrs. S. experienced considerable anxiety because she appraised the problem as a significant threat to the well-being of the entire family and was inclined to believe that it could not be satisfactorily solved before gathering sufficient information to clarify and understand the nature of the problem. When she was encouraged to view the situation as a "problem to be solved" and to use her problem-solving skills, she was able to clarify that she was concerned mainly about the health and safety of the neighborhood in which they would live and about the quality of the schools. This clarification led to relevant information-gathering strategies during the next few weeks, which resulted eventually in the purchase of a satisfactory home within the three-month period.

As Mrs. S. made progress in coping with the job-transfer problem, her average weekly anxiety ratings were reduced to "low-moderate" again and her mood and self-esteem ratings returned to "good." The ratings remained at this level for the next several weeks of therapy, after which treatment was terminated because the family moved. At that point, Mrs. S. felt that she could handle all of her current problems on her own except for some of the marital problems (e.g., the lack of positive feedback, the lack of time together). It was recommended that the couple seek marital counseling in their new location. However, in a follow-up telephone conversation three months later, Mrs. S. indicated that her husband was still refusing to become involved in marital therapy. As a result, her dissatisfaction with the marriage remained, but she was coping well with her other problems.

Case #2: Depression

Mr. C. was a 48-year-old high school guidance counselor who had been separated from his wife for approximately one year. He had been married for 26 years and had three children, aged 24, 22, and 20. There were no previous marriages. Mr. C.'s wife had insisted on the separation after a long history of serious marital problems and several previous separations. She was in the process of filing for a divorce at the time that Mr. C. entered therapy.

Mr. C. was a large, handsome man, although slightly balding. He stood about 6'4" and weighed about 220 lbs. His presenting problems included moderate to severe depression, with occasional suicidal feelings, fear and anxiety about the future, poor anger control, and poor self-esteem. Mr. C.'s depression was related primarily to his wife's rejection and its effect on his self-esteem. He reported that he loved his wife and could not accept that his marriage was over. For the past year, he had been trying desperately to win his wife back by attempting to see her and talk to her as often as possible, but he was rejected consistently. His wife told him flatly that she no longer loved him and that there was no chance for a reconciliation. Even his children were urging him to accept the fact that the marriage was over and to start a new life of his own. However, he could not bear the thought of his wife being with another man and he did not believe that he could ever love another woman. He was afraid that he would be alone and unhappy the rest of his life. Although he occasionally thought of suicide, he reported that these were fleeting thoughts and that he never seriously considered acting on them.

Mr. C. accepted most of the responsibility for his past marital problems. He attributed most of the problems to his poor anger control. Instead of approaching conflicts and disagreements with his wife in a calm and rational manner, he angrily insisted that he was right, refused to compromise in any way, and attempted to coerce her into giving in to his demands by using threats and verbal abuse. Physical violence was frequent, but was limited to throwing objects and hitting walls. No one was ever hurt. When Mr. C.'s aggression did not get him his way, he punished his wife by refusing to communicate with her for days and even weeks at a time. Mr. C. tended to use a similar, although less intense aggressive approach to interpersonal conflicts and disagreements with peers in the work setting and in other social situations. As a result, he alienated many people and had no close friends.

Because of the constant rejection from his wife, his inability to control his anger, the lack of satisfying social relationships, and his inability to do anything about these problems, Mr. C.'s self-esteem was at a very low point when he entered therapy. He felt very inadequate and helpless, perceiving that he had no control over himself, his present life, or his future. However, one personal asset that prevented a complete breakdown in his self-confidence was the fact that he was considered a good guidance counselor and was well liked by the students, if not by his peers.

Mr. C. was seen in therapy for 33 sessions. Assessment methods included the PSI, the PSSM method and self-ratings of mood, anxiety state, and self-esteem. Specific current problems and stresses that were focused on in therapy can be grouped into six categories: (1) his wife's relationship with another man, (2) interpersonal conflicts and disagreements in the work setting, (3) his relationships with women, (4) friendships, (5) feelings of loneliness, and (6) feelings of inadequacy. Following the initial assessment and structuring phase, therapy focused on training in problem-solving-oriented coping skills.

The assessment revealed that Mr. C had deficits in all components of the problem-solving process. He showed several negative problem-orientation cognitions. For example, he tended to perceive problems primarily as threats to his well-being, and did not approach them as "problems to be solved." Instead of taking the time to gather information, clarify the problem, and generate alternative solutions, he responded impulsively and automatically to the perceived threat, often in an angry and aggressive manner. Whenever he did stop to think before acting, he often failed to anticipate important consequences, especially the long-term effects of his actions on his social relationships. After responding ineffectively, he often failed to recognize all the negative consequences, or he disregarded them and failed to correct his behavior.

Mr. C. could not tolerate seeing his wife with her new boyfriend, Dave. Since Mr. C. still had hope of winning his wife back, he perceived Dave as a threat to his relationship with her. Since Dave was not well-educated and worked only as a laborer, Mr. C. also perceived the relationship between Dave and his wife as a threat to his self-esteem. Mr. C. responded impulsively to this threat with extreme anger and aggression. On one occasion when he met Dave outside of his home after Mr. C. visited his son, he threatened him with physical violence if Dave ever saw his wife again. A few weeks later, when he saw Dave dancing with his wife at a Parents Without Partners (PWOP) social function, Mr. C. invited him to go outside and fight. When PWOP officials saw what was happening, they forced Mr. C. to leave the dance.

While learning to clarify and define this problem in therapy, Mr. C. initially stated the problem as follows: "How can I make Dave get out of my wife's life?" However, while exploring the possibility that this problem was not the "real" (primary) problem, he realized that it was secondary to the more important problem: "How can I win my wife back?" A review of past attempts to solve this problem and the failure to come up with any new alternatives that might work helped Mr. C. to realize that he had to accept this problem as insoluble and begin to seek a new relationship. Although it was a difficult step for Mr. C., he reformulated his problem with Dave in the following manner: "How can I control my anger and aggressive behavior toward Dave?" One of his solutions was to keep telling himself that the relationship with his wife was over for good and that Dave and his wife had every right to see each other if they wanted to. Mr. C. was taught to use cognition-oriented facilitative coping (rational restructuring) to deal with the threatening assumption that the relationship between Dave and his wife somehow meant that he (Mr. C.) was "inadequate." A second solution to this problem was to avoid as many situations as possible where he might see Dave with his wife. A contingency plan related to this solution was that if he did happen to be in the same situation with Dave and his wife, he would act "friendly" (you can't be friendly and too aggressive at the same time) and then leave the situation as soon as possible.

The above solution proved to be almost life-saving on one occasion. Mr. C. met Dave and his wife one day at another PWOP dance. Because of the previous incident when Mr. C. invited Dave to go outside to fight, Dave brought three tough friends along to wait outside for Mr. C. and beat him up after he left the dance in order to convince him to leave Dave alone. These men waited in a nearby bar for the dance to end at about 12 midnight. However, Mr. C. implemented his solution and left the dance at about 10:30 P.M.. The men who were there to beat him up were drinking beer at the bar and never saw him leave. Thus, Mr. C.'s solution enabled him to avoid a beating.

With regard to interpersonal conflicts and disagreements in the work setting, Mr. C. also tended to perceive these problems as threats to his self-esteem, and he responded in a similar impulsive, angry, aggressive manner. His problem appraisal in these situations was based on several distorted or irrational beliefs and assumptions. He believed that there were only two sides to every issue or conflict: a "right" side and a "wrong" side. Since he always believed that his point of view was the "right" one, he assumed that the other person's point of view had to be "wrong." Furthermore, he believed that if a person held to a "wrong" viewpoint, and could not recognize the "right" viewpoint, then that person had to be "stupid" or "incompetent" and, therefore, did not deserve to be treated with respect. Thus, it became clear that Mr. C. felt very threatened when someone challenged his views or disagreed with his demands because he did not want to be perceived as "wrong" and "incompetent."

In order to reduce anger, avoid impulsive and aggressive responding, and make time available for rational problem-solving thinking, Mr. C. was taught to use rational restructuring to correct the above irrational assumptions. For example, he was taught that two people could hold different viewpoints without either one being "wrong" (i.e., different evaluative criteria). He was also taught to understand that a person could make a mistake and be wrong in a particular instance without being "stupid" or "incompetent."

Once he was able to inhibit his impulsive, aggressive responses and devote time to problem definition and formulation and the generation of alternative solutions, Mr. C. began to generate more appropriate *assertive* strategies for dealing with interpersonal disputes and disagreements. In addition, once he realized that he did not have to "win" every argument or dispute, he was able to consider alternative strategies for resolving conflicts, such as compromising, negotiating a *quid pro quo* agreement (one person agrees to something in exchange for something else), and sacrificing (one person "gives in" or defers to the other person's demands). Since some conflict situations required quick thinking and quick action (e.g., an unexpected confrontation), Mr. C. was also taught to use the rapid problem-solving method (see Chapter 8). In connection with this method, he was taught how to respond initially to an unexpected confrontation so as to give himself at least a few minutes to think before acting (for example, "I can't talk to you about this right now. Where are you going to be? I'll get back to you in a few minutes." "I don't have an answer for you right now. Let me think about it a few minutes and I'll get back to you." "I'm not sure how I feel about this right now. Let me think about it awhile and I'll get back to you.")

In the area of relationships with women, Mr. C. initially had little hope of finding another woman whom he could love and who would love him. As noted above, he also maintained the hope that he would win his wife back. As a result, he was devoting very little time and effort to exploring ways of meeting women at the time he entered therapy. After Mr. C. accepted the need and desirability of developing new relationships, problem-solving training focused on such problems as: "Where can I go to meet women?" "How can I let women know that I am available?" "How should I approach a woman whom I don't know and start a conversation?" "How can I make myself as attractive as possible to women?" "How and when should I make sexual advances?" "What kind of woman would satisfy me the most?" Mr. C. soon became adept at generating a variety of solutions to these problems and implementing them. For example, he decided that he preferred to meet women at PWOP functions, church-related activities, and work-related activities (e.g., seminars, conferences, workshops). He preferred to avoid singles bars and personal ads in the newspaper. He bought new clothes to make himself look attractive and he asked all friends and relatives to let people know that he was single and available. During generation-of-alternatives training, the therapist suggested additional alternatives when Mr. C.'s response repertoire was depleted and only a few good alternatives were generated. However, this aid was not often necessary. In order to maximize solution implementation effectiveness, some training in instrumental skills was required (communication and conversational skills). However, in most cases, once Mr. C. considered all the alternatives carefully and decided on the "best" solution, he was usually able to implement it effectively. He was soon meeting women and dating frequently.

Mr. C. was unhappy about the fact that he had no close friends, although he had several acquaintances with whom he was on friendly terms. In addition to solving his anger-control problems, problem-solving training also focused on other positive strategies for developing closer relationships with particular individuals. Some of the solution strategies generated by Mr. C. included friendly greetings, being a good listener, expressing empathy, giving reassurance and support, expressing positive feelings, giving positive feedback, offering help, and inviting the person to participate in activities together more often. Very little training was required in the specific instrumental skills needed to implement these strategies. Most of these skills were already present in Mr. C.'s response repertoire and were already being applied in his counseling activities. Problem solving helped him to generalize these skills to his everyday social relationships.

Early in therapy, Mr. C. often felt lonely because he spent much of his time in his apartment alone. He also felt inadequate because he was not experiencing much positive reinforcement in his life. These feelings were problematic because they aggravated his depression, which in turn, threatened to interfere with effective problem solving. Therefore, although it was recognized that these negative feelings would probably be reduced once the current antecedent problems causing them were solved, it was also believed that by focusing on these feelings directly as "problems to be solved," Mr. C. might be able to get some immediate relief from depression, which might facilitate further problem-solving therapy related to the antecedent problems. These "emotional problems" were stated as follows: "What can I do to feel better when I feel lonely?" "What can I do to feel better about myself?" With regard to the first problem, Mr. C. found that several of his relatives and acquaintances were quite willing to talk to him and offer support and understanding when he felt lonely and depressed. However, since he did not want to make too many demands on relatives and friends, he considered a variety of other strategies as well, and found that a particularly effective one was to take a long drive in the country.

For the problem of feeling inadequate, Mr. C. generated alternatives, which included reminding himself of the students he helped as a guidance counselor, putting in extra time counseling, taking a continuing education course and attending workshops to improve his counseling skills, helping a friend, developing some new hobbies, and taking steps to pursue a life goal of getting into school administration. The above strategies, once implemented, proved to be helpful in reducing feelings of loneliness and inadequacy early in therapy.

As therapy progressed and improvement was observed in problem-solving-oriented coping, this improvement was reflected in Mr. C.'s self-ratings of mood, self-esteem, and anxiety. During the first seven weeks of therapy, average weekly self-ratings showed "high" anxiety and "poor" mood and self-esteem. In the eighth week, anxiety ratings reduced to "moderate." Two weeks later, mood and self-esteem ratings improved to "fair." By the 25th session, anxiety was "low-moderate" and mood and self-esteem were "good." When these ratings stabilized over a period of several weeks and Mr. C. felt that he could cope with his current problems on his own, therapy was faded and then terminated. A few weeks before therapy ended, Mr. C. was divorced from his wife. He handled this event well. A follow-up telephone conversation six months after termination revealed that Mr. C. was continuing to do well. He was no longer depressed. Anxiety was moderate to low. Self-esteem was very good and was being reinforced by frequent positive feedback from women. Although he was dating frequently, he was not yet "in love." However, he felt confident that he would fall in love and be married again some day.

Case #3: Obsessive-Compulsive Disorder

Mr. K. was a 38-year-old elementary school teacher who had been divorced for four years and had no children. He was short, slight, bearded, and balding, but he was neat and personable. His presenting complaints included obsessive-compulsive behavior, generalized anxiety, physical pain, depression, and low self-esteem.

Mr. K. was leaving a five-year psychotherapeutic relationship with a psychiatrist who had given him the diagnosis "obsessive-compulsive neurosis." During the five years of therapy, there had been little lasting improvement in Mr. K.'s condition. For the first three years, treatment was psychoanalytically oriented. During the last two years, the psychiatrist's conceptualization of Mr. K.'s disorder changed from a psychoanalytic formulation to a biological one. He was told that he would have to live with his condition the rest of his life and that the only way to minimize the symptoms was through psychiatric medication. The last two years of treatment primarily involved supportive therapy and experimentation with various kinds of psychiatric drugs. Mr. K. came to the author for therapy on the advice of a friend who recommended that he try a cognitive-behavioral approach.

When asked about the history of his problems, Mr. K. reported that he had difficulty handling stress for most of his life. He typically reacted to stressful situations with extreme anxiety and tension, which he could not control very well. In recent years, this tension tended to aggravate an undiagnosed physical condition involving almost constant pain in many of the joints in his body, especially in his hands, arms, and legs. Doctors told Mr. K. that the condition could be the result of the beating his body took in a serious motorcycle accident about five years earlier. However, no doctor had been able to make a specific diagnosis.

In addition to aggravating his pain, the stress and anxiety in Mr. K.'s life also tended to increase the frequency of several disturbing obsessions and compulsions. Since adolescence, Mr. K. had an obsessive concern about his "masculinity" and a compulsive need to engage in various physical activities to "prove" his masculinity, including motorcycle riding, weight lifting, mountain climbing, marathon running, and long-distance swimming. Mr. K. engaged in these activities as often as possible and with much intensity. All of his friends were people who participated in these activities. He was compulsively driven to not only excel at these activities, but to show that he was the best of all those who participated. All of these physical activities suddenly came to an end when Mr. K. had his serious motorcycle accident, which resulted in a long hospital stay with head, back, and leg injuries. He recovered eventually from most of the injuries, but was left with permanent damage in one knee and the pain he developed in his joints. The pain was aggravated a great deal whenever he tried to engage in any strenuous physical activity. A vicious circle soon developed where Mr. K. would avoid all strenuous physical activities because of the pain, become bored and depressed, attempt to engage in the physical activities again in order to relieve these negative feelings, experience the pain and be forced to avoid the activities once again, and so on. Mr. K. could not break out of this vicious circle.

Mr. K. also had obsessions about "flaws" in women whom he dated. Since his divorce four years earlier, Mr. K. had been having difficulty meeting women and developing new relationships. When he met a woman and dated her, the relationship did not last. Some women rejected him and he rejected some others. When he rejected a woman it was usually because he became obsessed about certain "flaws" that he noticed, such as facial hair, a skin imperfection, or small breasts. Once he noticed such a flaw, his attention was constantly drawn to it and considerable anxiety was created. Consequently, he would begin to avoid the woman and, if the problem continued, as it usually did, he would eventually terminate the relationship. This problem was increasing in frequency in recent years.

Two compulsive rituals disturbed Mr. K. One was a compulsion to go to the bathroom and try to urinate at least eight times each night before going to bed. He could not relax enough to go to sleep if he did not perform this ritual. The second was the compulsion to masturbate every evening. Like the urination compulsion, masturbation seemed to relieve tension and allow Mr. K. to sleep. However, masturbation also created guilt. Therefore, before he could relax, he also felt compelled to punish himself by eating his "seed" (semen). Mr. K. reported that he had tremendous guilt over masturbation since, as a child, he saw his father run out of the bathroom, naked and with an erection, being chased by his mother who was screaming, "Masturbator! Masturbator!"

When Mr. K. first came in for therapy, his self-esteem was very low and he was feeling discouraged, helpless, and depressed. He could not control the stress and anxiety in his life. He could no longer participate and excel in the physical activities which had been providing most of the positive reinforcement in his life and contributing most to his self-esteem, which was dominated by his view of "masculinity" as the ability to excel in physical activities. Furthermore, he could not develop a lasting relationship with a woman, he was sexually frustrated, and he had compulsions that he disliked and could not control. He felt completely dominated and controlled by his "neurosis" and was told by his doctor that his only hope was psychiatric drugs. Thus, it was not surprising that he felt inadequate and depressed.

Mr. K. was seen in therapy for 54 sessions. Assessment methods included the PSI, the PSSM method, and self-ratings of anxiety, mood, and self-esteem. In addition, Mr. K. was asked to keep a record of the frequency of obsessive thoughts (women's flaws) and compulsive behaviors (trips to the bathroom before bed, masturbation, eating his semen, strenuous physical activities which should be avoided). The stress in Mr. K.'s current life was conceptualized in terms of specific life problems in four major categories: (1) problems in the work setting, (2) problems in relationships with women, (3) the massive loss and failure to regain positive reinforcement in his life, including important social reinforcement, and (4) inability to cope with physical pain.

The assessment revealed that several cognitive variables contributed to Mr. K.'s stress. These included negative problem-orientation variables, such as exaggerated appraisals of threat to well-being and problem attributions involving judgments of personal inadequacy. In addition, stressful pseudoproblems were created because of perfectionistic behavioral standards and expectations and negative judgments about others who did not share his values and ideals. In addition to the effects of these cognitive variables, Mr. K. also showed an emotional oversensitivity to stressful stimuli such as conflict, frustration, and loss of reinforcement. Partly due to the high level of stress and anxiety, Mr. K. usually failed to respond to problematic situations with careful, thoughtful problem-solving behavior. Instead, he tended to respond impulsively to the demands of the situation with ineffective goal responses, or he focused on his anxiety and responded with self-defeating, maladaptive attempts to reduce anxiety.

After the initial assessment and structuring period, therapy focused on the problem-solving approach to stress management, which emphasizes training in problem-solving-oriented coping (see Chapter 7). The coping skills focused on in training included goal-oriented coping (discovering and implementing solutions to specific stress-producing life problems) and facilitative coping (overcoming cognitive and emotional obstacles to effective problem solving). Facilitative coping included cognition-oriented coping, such as reappraisal of threat and correcting irrational assumptions, and emotion-oriented coping, such as relaxation and desensitization procedures. Mr. K. required intensive training in these facilitative-coping skills. He responded particularly well to progressive muscle-relaxation training and found this method to be very useful for relieving general tension and preparing himself for rational problem solving. In addition to the above skills, training was also required in some specific instrumental skills, which were needed in order to implement certain goal-oriented solution responses (e.g., assertiveness). Finally, although it was hypothesized that the obsessions and compulsions would be reduced when Mr. K. became capable of managing stress and anxiety more effectively, these problems were also treated directly using self-monitoring, attention diversion, and response prevention (thought stopping, use of incompatible responses).

In the work setting, stress resulted from problems involving disruptive behavior in the classroom and interpersonal conflicts with peers, students, and parents. In general, Mr. K. enjoyed the reputation of being a very conscientious, dedicated, effective teacher who was very interested in the well-being of his students. He was quite concerned about behavior that might disrupt the learning process in the classroom, such as talking out of turn, getting out of one's seat, and failing to pay attention when the teacher is talking. Mr. K. was having much difficulty controlling his students' disruptive behavior, causing him considerable anxiety. Therefore, one problem statement focused on in problem-solving training was: "How can I control disruptive classroom behavior?" Alternatives generated ranged from a formal classroom behavior modification program to an informal behavioral procedure of praising appropriate behavior and ignoring inappropriate behavior. He eventually implemented a very effective reward and punishment procedure that represented a compromise between the two extremes. Since Mr. K. was familiar with behavior-modification principles from a psychology course that he had taken recently, he was able to formulate his solution with little direct help from the therapist.

Mr. K. was more liberal in his values, ideals, and politics than most of his peers and most of the students and parents in the area, who tended to have conservative values. Mr. K. was quite concerned about issues such as discrimination, racism, the environment, nuclear energy, cigarette smoking, and unhealthy diets. It was stressful for him to hear opinions and observe behavior that conflicted with his strongly held beliefs. However, his response was usually to either say nothing, which increased the stress, or to assert himself inappropriately in a way that antagonized and alienated others. For example, one day during the early phase of therapy, Mr. K. was invited by several male teachers to join a group that watched Monday night football games together. During the game, several men made racial slurs against some of the black football players. Mr. K. said nothing at the time. However, the next day he put a note in the mailboxes of all the men in the group, castigating them for their racism, and indicating that he did not want to belong to a racist group. This approach created much hostility and tension.

In therapy, Mr. K. was asked to generate alternative, more effective ways for handling such a problem (e.g., direct, appropriate verbal assertion). Training in cognition-oriented facilitative coping was needed for interpersonal conflicts such as these, to help Mr. K. deal with his tendency to expect people to be perfectly moral and just at all times and to judge them harshly when they were not.

A conflict in values also occurred with the students in Mr. K.'s class. In the classroom, Mr. K. often expressed his opinions in favor of a low fat, low cholesterol, low salt, low sugar diet, and against some of President Reagan's policies (e.g., Reaganomics and "Star Wars" technology). One day, he received a note signed by about one-half of the students in the class which said: "Stop trying to make us be vegetarians and against President Reagan." (In fact, he did not advocate vegetarianism, but merely the reduction of fat in the diet.) When clarifying and defining this problem, Mr. K. realized that he did not prepare the students very well for a discussion of these issues and he was probably too "intense" in his manner of presenting his viewpoint to sixth-grade children who tended to come from relatively conservative families. His approach tended to make them feel threatened and pressured. In therapy, he worked on the problem: "How can I present and discuss controversial issues in class without threatening the students and making them feel pressured?"

An example of a conflict with parents occurred toward the end of the school year when 13 parents called the principal and said that they did not want their children to be assigned to Mr. K. for the next school year because of the complaints from some of his present students and their parents about his teaching (see above). Another problem occurred when several parents called to complain that special written material that Mr. K. occasionally sent home with the children often contained misspelled words. Mr. K. admitted that he had a problem with spelling. Problem definition and formulation led to the following problem statements: "How can I convince the 13 parents that I would be a good teacher for their children?" "How can I improve my spelling?" "How can I ensure that material containing misspelled words will not be sent home with the children?" Problem solving for the latter problem resulted in the principal's agreeing to proofread Mr. K.'s written material before it was given to the children to take home, provided that he also took steps to improve his spelling.

In the area of relationships with women, stress was resulting primarily from Mr. K.'s frustration over not being able to meet more women and the threat of rejection once he did. In the first two years after his divorce, Mr. K. approached and dated a number of women, but he was frequently rejected when he approached them, or after one or two dates. He later developed his obsession about "flaws," which appeared to be a maladaptive response to the perceived threat of rejection, enabling Mr. K. to avoid rejection by avoiding the woman, which was, however, obviously self-defeating. When clarifying and defining a problem of frequent rejection from women at singles bars when he first approached them, Mr. K. realized that he had primarily been approaching tall, slim, model-type, beautiful women. Since Mr. K. is only about 5 ft. 5 in. tall and is not as handsome as Robert Redford, he realized that his perfectionistic standards regarding women might have been responsible to a great degree for the high frequency of early rejections. When he was able to reduce these standards and make them more realistic, his frequency of rejections decreased.

In addition to his perfectionistic standards, there were other reasons why Mr. K. had been getting rejected so often, which were related to his communication patterns and his "intensity" during the early phase of a relationship. Assessment of his communication patterns revealed that he frequently monopolized the conversation, focused the conversation on himself, boasted about his past athletic accomplishments, and showed very little interest in the woman and *her* life. Mr. K.'s "intensity" during the early phase of the relationship was partly due to the deprivation and frustration of his affectionate and sexual needs and his resulting impatience. It was also partly due to his failure to consider carefully the effects of his behavior on the woman's feelings. He tended to express his strong affectionate and sexual feelings too early, and to make too many demands on the woman's time, which tended to threaten many women who were not ready to become so closely involved so soon. For example, on one first date he invited the woman to go away with him the next weekend. She made an excuse and he never saw her again.

After clarifying and defining the problems in this area, some of the resulting problem statements were: "How can I meet more women?" "What should I talk about when meeting a woman for the first time?" "How can I communicate with a woman in a way which would make her enjoy my company?" "How and when should I make sexual advances?" "How often should I see a woman early in a relationship?" "What activities should I suggest early in a relationship that a woman would feel comfortable with and enjoy?" In addition to generating and implementing problem solutions in this area, much therapy time was also spent on cognition-oriented coping (reappraisal of threat, rational thinking), emotion-oriented coping (applied relaxation), and training in communication skills.

When Mr. K. was forced to eliminate or severely curtail the physical activities he had engaged in so frequently, he suffered a massive loss of positive reinforcement and a significant loss of self-esteem. This included a loss of social reinforcement and social support, since the only interest that he had in common with many of his friends was the particular sport or physical activity that they participated in together. Instead of engaging in problem solving toward the goal of replacing this loss, he developed the self-defeating vicious circle described earlier. In therapy, this problem was clarified and the following problem statements were formulated: "What can I do to increase my social contacts and make new friends?" "What activities can I engage in that will increase my satisfaction with my life and myself?" These statements led to the generation of a wide range of new alternative activities, including outdoor activities, music, poetry, art, teacher's union activities, and other community activities. For example, Mr. K. decided to experiment with a variety of nonstrenuous outdoor activities, such as camping, fishing, and nature walks. He also began to take flute lessons, learned that he had the ability to write poetry, and found that he enjoyed attending concerts. He soon met a number of new friends while experimenting with these new activities.

The final problem area was Mr. K.'s inability to cope satisfactorily with his physical pain. This problem was partially resolved when he finally broke the vicious circle and stopped trying over and over again to continue his earlier strenuous physical activities. In addition, he focused on generating alternative solutions for the problem: "What can I do to reduce the pain in my joints?" The alternatives generated included such strategies as physical relaxation, meditation, heat, listening to music, alcohol, pain medication, attention diversion, and acupuncture. Among other strategies, he implemented the last and was surprised to find that it did, in fact, result in some relief. However, more effective strategies were muscle relaxation, meditation, heat, and attention diversion. He preferred to avoid using alcohol and pain medication too often.

Significant progress began to occur in Mr. K.'s case after about two months of therapy. Self-ratings of anxiety reduced to the "moderate" level, ratings of mood and self-esteem improved to "fair," and the obsessions and compulsions occurred less frequently. Mr. K. also reported an increase in assertive behavior at this time. During the next eight months of therapy, anxiety fluctuated within the "moderate" range, mood and self-esteem fluctuated between "fair" and "good," and the obsessions and compulsions continued to decrease in frequency. At this point, Mr. K. reported that he had much more confidence in his ability to control the obsessions and compulsions.

As Mr. K. continued to make progress in solving his problems and managing anxiety during the last two months of therapy, the self-ratings showed less fluctuation. Anxiety tended to stabilize at a "low-moderate" level and mood and self-esteem were most often "good." Mr. K. reported that the obsessions and compulsions were very low in frequency and were no longer a problem. He believed that he was managing stress more effectively and he was satisfied with his new activities and his new friends. He was dating more regularly and having sex. Although he had not yet developed a serious relationship with any one woman, his relationships were lasting longer and were more satisfying. Regular therapy was terminated at that point, but Mr. K. continued to come in for one session each month for several months in order to review his progress and reinforce the use of his problem-solving-oriented coping skills.

Case #4: Neurological Disorder

Mr. D. was a 27-year-old unmarried man with a developmental learning disability. He lived with his parents, who were both about 50 years old, and worked as an assembler in an electronics factory where his father was an engineer. No one else lived at home. A

23-year-old married brother lived in another town. Mr. D. came in for therapy at the request of his parents because of their concern about his ability to function independently in the community. They realized that they were getting older and that the day would come when Mr. D. might have to live alone and take care of himself. However, they believed that they might have been overprotective with Mr. D. over the years because of his disability and, as a result, limited the opportunities for him to learn to be more independent.

Mr. D. was seen in therapy for 38 sessions. He was always well-groomed and dressed neatly. He was friendly, sociable, cheerful, and highly motivated to learn how to solve problems more effectively and become more independent. Speech, communication, and comprehension were quite good. Mr. D.'s social behavior was always appropriate. Emotionality was also appropriate and within normal limits. However, attention and concentration were only fair. Mr. D. would occasionally become distracted during problem solving in session. For example, he might stop in the middle of a problem-solving task and talk about something more interesting to him (e.g., sports). It was never difficult to direct his attention back to the relevant task. However, the fact that he became distracted in this way was problematic for his real-life independent functioning.

In addition to interviews with Mr. D. and his parents, assessment methods included the Wechsler Adult Intelligence Scale (WAIS), adaptive behavior ratings provided by the parents, verbal problem-solving tests using hypothetical problems, and the PSSM method. Information on cognitive abilities was also available from a recent neuropsychological assessment. Information on progress in independent functioning in the real-life setting during the course of therapy was based on the PSSM and reports from the parents.

On the WAIS, Mr. D. earned a Full Scale IQ score of 80. Verbal Scale IQ was 83 and Performance Scale IQ was 77. Mr. D.'s functioning approached the average level for men of his age in vocabulary, factual information, and abstract thinking. However, he showed significant deficits in several abilities that are important for social problem solving, including judgment, mental concentration, attention span, visual concentration (alertness to environmental events), and anticipation (ability to anticipate cause-effect relationships). Data from the WAIS and previous neuropsychological testing also showed significant deficits in short-term memory and visual-motor integration.

Adaptive behavior ratings were provided by Mr. D.'s parents for the following behavior categories: self-care, self-direction (initiation of constructive activity, persistence without prompting and supervision), stress tolerance (emotional control), independent problem solving, communication skills, motor skills, social skills, work habits, and money management. Little or no deficiencies were reported in self-care, stress tolerance, communication skills, social skills, work habits, and money management. Moderate deficits were reported in self-direction and motor skills. Independent problem solving was rated as severely deficient. Mr. D. tended to respond to problems by doing nothing and waiting for someone else to take care of the problem, leaving the situation, or asking someone else for help. In addition, the parents tended to protect him from problematic situations at home and at work. Therefore, he was rarely forced to experience any serious negative environmental or emotional consequences of unsolved problems.

Further assessment of social problem-solving skills revealed that Mr. D. was significantly deficient in the ability to recognize real-life problems, the ability to gather relevant information and define problems, the ability to generate a large number and variety of alternative solutions, and the ability to evaluate alternative solutions. He regularly generated too few alternatives within a limited range and he tended to choose a solution too quickly, without carefully evaluating all the important consequences.

Except for the above deficiencies in cognitive abilities and adaptive functioning, the assessment did not reveal any other serious cognitive, behavioral, or emotional disorder. Mr. D. seemed to be fairly well-adjusted both socially and emotionally. However, the parents reported that he tended to be "shy" and rarely initiated social contacts. Although he interacted well with women and was well-informed about sexuality, he did not seem to be in touch with his own sexual feelings and he never approached women for dates. Most of his socializing was done with an organized social group connected with an organization for people with developmental disabilities. This group met for a social activity once each week.

Therapy for Mr. D. closely followed the PST format described in Chapter 8, except that training involved one-hour weekly sessions instead of two-hour sessions. Mr. D. required very little training in facilitative coping skills. He showed few cognitive distortions or irrational beliefs and he showed no emotional oversensitivity to stress, although as noted above, Mr. D.'s parents tended to protect him from stress both at home and at work. Mr. D. did require some training in instrumental performance skills that were required for some of his problem solutions (e.g., assertiveness, verbal expression of feelings). PST focused on both hypothetical problems and real problems. The latter were reported by both Mr. D. and his parents, who came in for several sessions during the course of therapy. In addition, there were several telephone conversations with one of the parents.

Since Mr. D. showed a lack of sensitivity to problems, training focused initially on problem recognition. Mr. D. was provided with a problem checklist and homework assignments were given to identify and record problems that occurred during everyday living. One obstacle to problem recognition was the fact that Mr. D. often failed to identify accurately his own feelings and the feelings of others in particular situations. The problem-solving approach was used to help him learn to identify feelings accurately, to express and cope with his own feelings, and to respond effectively to the feelings of others. Problem solving focused on problem statements such as the following:

1. You forgot your mother's birthday. What might be her feelings (e.g., hurt, angry)? What could you do to make her feel better?
2. Jane is in your social group. She is pretty. You like to talk to her. You have fun together. She says nice things about you. What might you be feeling when you are with her (e.g., affection, sexual feelings)? How can you show her how you feel?
3. Your friend promised to come to your house Saturday morning to help you fix your car. He did not show up. What might be your feelings (e.g., anger, disappointment)? What can you do or say to show him how you feel?

Following the training in problem recognition, subsequent sessions focused on other problem-orientation cognitions, problem definition and formulation, generation of alternative solutions, decision making, and solution implementation and verification. There was a particular emphasis on the generation of alternatives and decision making. The following problem statements illustrate the kinds of problems that were focused on in training.

1. Your car breaks down on your way to work about five miles from the factory. What can you do to get to work on time and get the car fixed as soon as possible?
2. A fellow worker is always making fun of you and playing practical jokes on you. What can you do to get him to stop?
3. You have just gotten into a minor automobile accident. The other person hit you in the rear when you were stopped at a stop sign. What can you do now to make sure that neither you nor your insurance company will have to pay for the damages?

4. What new activities would you like to participate in by your-self or with friends that would be fun and interesting?
5. You are out eating dinner at a restaurant with your parents. You see a nice-looking young woman at another table with two people who look like they might be her parents. What can you do to meet this woman?
6. Your parents keep telling you what to do all the time. How can you tell them to stop and let you make your own decisions without hurting their feelings?
7. You are at home alone on a Sunday afternoon and you feel bored and lonely. What can you do to feel better?
8. There are a few people in your social group with whom you would like to develop a closer friendship. What can you do to become better friends with these people?
9. Your parents have gone away for a few days and you are home alone. You go to the laundry room to wash some clothes that you will need and you find that the washing machine won't work. How can you get your clothes washed?
10. What can you do to make sure that you will have light in case the power in your neighborhood goes out?

After about 30 sessions of therapy, Mr. D. had made very good progress in solving problems *in the sessions*. However, the generalization of these skills to the real-life setting was only mod-erate. In addition, there was only slight improvement in other independent activities (e.g., social activities with friends). In an attempt to facilitate generalization, a greater emphasis was placed on homework assignments during the last eight weeks of therapy. These assignments involved instructions to solve specific problems, carry out specific solutions, and engage in specific independent activities, such as asking a friend to go out with him to a movie. In addition, a session was held with the parents to discuss obstacles to the generalization of independent problem-solving behavior and the performance of more independent activities. Despite these efforts, overall improvement remained at a moderate level.

There are several possible reasons for Mr. D.'s failure to obtain greater improvement in real-life problem-solving performance and independent behavior. One possibility is that Mr. D.'s intellectual deficits (judgment, concentration, short-term memory, etc.) set limits on his level of social problem-solving ability (see Chapter 2). Without much prompting and guidance, Mr. D. might not be capable of applying problem-solving principles effectively on his own. A second possibility is that Mr. D.'s social environment failed to set the occasion for and reinforce more independent behavior. Mr. D.'s parents reported that they still held back from providing opportunities for independent functioning because they still had fears about his safety and security. For example, although Mr. D. did very well when the parents went away for a weekend, they would not try going away for a longer period of time. Although they let Mr. D. drive to work alone each day, they would not let him drive alone on a weekend when they went away, nor would they let him drive alone to his therapy sessions at night. Although they reported that they wanted Mr. D. to develop closer friendships, they rarely encouraged him to go out with friends in the evening or on weekends, except for the organized social-group activities, which were supervised.

Mr. D.'s parents were advised that counseling for themselves might help them to understand their fears about Mr. D. better and to learn how to deal more effectively with them. For example, they were told that it would be important for them to be able to discriminate accurately between realistic and unrealistic fears, and to overcome the unrealistic fears so that they could gradually provide more opportunities for Mr. D. to perform independently. After a period of six months, Mr. D.'s parents had not yet followed this advice. Moreover, Mr. D. had an accident; he fell off a swing and injured his spine seriously. It was not yet determined whether there would be any permanent disability that would tend to limit his independent activities further and reinforce his parents' fears.

Summary and Discussion

Four clinical cases are presented to illustrate the application of PST as part of a broader, individualized therapy program for clinical disorders involving generalized anxiety (Mrs. S.); depression (Mr. C.); obsessive-compulsive behavior (Mr. K.); and a neurological deficit or developmental learning disability (Mr. D.). All four cases were characterized by a negative coping style, which includes the perception of uncontrollability and ineffective problem-solving performance. In three of the cases, this negative coping style is associated with negative stress effects such as anxiety, depression, and low self-esteem. In the fourth case (Mr. D.), the client appears to be protected by a supportive environment from experiencing these negative stress effects. Problem-solving-oriented therapy seemed to be successful in developing a more adaptive problem-solving coping style, increasing effective problem-solving performance, and reducing negative stress effects, although the amount of improvement was limited in two cases (Mrs. S. and Mr. D.). In the case of Mr. D., deficits in intellectual abilities may have set limits on his social problem-solving ability (see Chapter 2).

In addition to the common emphasis in these cases on goal-oriented coping (discovering and implementing problem solutions), the four clients required different amounts of training in facilitative coping (removing cognitive and emotional obstacles to effective problem solving). All clients required some training in cognitive restructuring to correct negative problem-orientation cognitions (e.g., exaggerated, threatening problem appraisals) and distortions in problem definition and formulation (e.g., perfectionistic behavioral standards). Mrs. S. and Mr. K. also required training in relaxation and desensitization skills because of their emotional oversensitivity to stressful problematic situations, which could not be reduced sufficiently through cognitive restructuring and problem solving alone. Although Mr. C. showed strong emotional reactivity as well, relaxation training was not conducted because cognitive restructuring and problem solving were successful in reducing emotional arousal. Mr. D. did not require relaxation training because he did not show a problem with stress or emotional arousal.

Two of the case studies (Mrs. S. and Mr. D.) illustrate how the generalization of problem-solving training effects may be limited when the client's social environment fails to set the occasion for and reinforce independent problem-solving behavior. In these cases, it is necessary to involve significant others from the client's social environment in the therapy in an attempt to create a more supportive environment, which encourages and reinforces problem-solving behavior. In the case of Mrs. S., the husband "punished" assertive problem solutions and refused to participate in conjoint problem solving to resolve interpersonal conflicts. In the case of Mr. D., his parents failed to encourage and reinforce independent behavior because of their anxiety about Mr. D.'s safety and security.

In the next two chapters, more applications of PST will be described, in which PST is used as a treatment procedure or a treatment maintenance strategy with other clinical problems. In addition, several programs will be described in which PST is used with a "normal" but "vulnerable" population in an attempt to enhance personal-social effectiveness and prevent clinical problems.

10

Variations in PST Programs

PST programs reported in the literature have varied in terms of (a) target population, (b) program goals, (c) training setting, (d) amount of training in other coping skills within the overall PST framework, (e) instructional methods used, and (f) overall program structure (see D'Zurilla & Nezu, 1982; Spivack et al., 1976). The target populations have included hospitalized psychiatric patients; substance abusers; cigarette smokers; hypertensives; people with stress and anxiety problems; people with weight-control problems; depressed individuals; people with marital and family problems; academic underachievers; elderly persons with social-skill deficits and problems related to aging; students with problem-solving skills deficits; low-income people receiving public assistance; and community problem-solving groups (e.g., a community policymaking committee). PST has been conducted in both individual and group settings (mostly group), and in both clinical and nonclinical community settings (e.g., the home, the classroom). Program goals have included treatment goals (reduction in psychopathology or maladaptive behavior); maintenance goals (prevention of "relapse" and new problems following therapy); prevention goals (prevention of psychopathology in vulnerable or at-risk groups); and positive competence-enhancement and stress-management goals.

Training in other coping skills within an overall PST framework has included training in specific self-control skills (e.g., stimulus control, behavioral contracting), cognitive-restructuring skills, anxiety-management skills, and instrumental performance skills. Instructional methods have included: verbal instruction, group discussion, self-instruction, problem-solving demonstrations and examples (modeling), problem-solving exercises and homework assignments (rehearsals), using workbooks and other written materials (e.g., the PSSM method) as well as videotapes and audiocassettes; role-playing; covert rehearsal; performance feedback; positive reinforcement; and shaping. The overall program structure has differed on such variables as number of sessions, duration of sessions, time devoted to different problem-solving skills, time devoted to training in other coping skills, and emphasis on different instructional methods. At the present time, there is a lack of data relevant to the question of what variations result in the most efficient and effective problem-solving training. The following program descriptions are presented only to illustrate some of the variations.

Coché's Group Therapy Program

Coché and his associates have developed a group problem-solving therapy program for psychiatric patients at Friends Hospital in Philadelphia (Coché & Flick, 1975; Coché & Douglas, 1977; Coché, 1985). There are three main criteria for acceptance into the program: (a) the patient must have a reasonable degree of intellectual capability; (b) the patient must not have any serious memory disturbances; and (c) the patient must not show any significant disruptive or antisocial behaviors that would undermine the group's progress.

Training is conducted in groups of four to ten patients over a two-week period. Four sessions are held each week, for a total of eight sessions. The length of a session is 60–90 minutes. The duration of training is determined to a great extent by the expected length of stay at Friends Hospital, which is a median of 25 days.

In the first session, the purpose of the group and the course of training are described. Patients are told that the purpose of the group is to get experience in interpersonal problem solving. They are told that members of the group will bring up problems for discussion, and that the group will then try to come up with as many possible solutions as can be found. The group leader's main responsibility is to guide the group through the necessary steps in problem solving and to remind the patients from time to time of the primary goal of learning to solve problems. In some groups, there is also a co-leader to assist the leader.

Training focuses on the following six steps for each problem presented: (1) bringing up a problem; (2) clarifying the problem and information-gathering; (3) presenting solutions; (4) discussion of feasibility; (5) role-playing; and (6) reporting back to the group. In "bringing up a problem," group members are encouraged to present problems for discussion. These may be practical problems, personal problems, or interpersonal problems. If no problems are introduced by the patients at first, the leader presents hypothetical problems to start the discussion. In "clarifying the problem and information-gathering," the leader encourages members to restate the problem in specific, concrete terms, and to seek more information, asking questions to help the group learn how to seek relevant information. In "presenting solutions," the deferment-of-judgment principle is emphasized and members are reinforced by the leader for generating quantity. A written log of solutions generated is kept by the leader or co-leader. In "discussion of feasibility," the group is asked to give opinions on which solution is best. The group focuses on two questions: Which idea is most likely to be successful? and What is the cost likely to be if one solution is chosen over another? The question of how to implement the chosen solution is presented to the group as a new problem to be solved. "Role-playing" of the solution, when possible, is designed to facilitate transfer of solution performance to the real-life setting. The technique of role-reversal is used to teach perspective-taking. In the final step, "reporting back to the group," the member who implemented the solution reports back to the group about how the solution worked out. If the solution did not work out satisfactorily, this is accepted as a challenge for the group to deal with the problem again and come up with a new solution.

In a recent publication, Coché (1985) describes his group therapy program in detail as well as some recent research findings. Included is a discussion of the qualities of a good group leader and how a leader can deal with special problems in the group such as deviations from the group's goals, disputes among group members, monopolizers, boredom, "psychotic" or bizarre solutions, and problems involving institutional staff. On the basis of his research, Coché concludes that this short-term problem-solving group program can be a valuable adjunct to the treatment regimen in a psychiatric hospital setting, that it can increase the self-confidence of the participants, reduce depressions, and contribute to the better functioning of the institution.

Mahoney's Personal Science Paradigm

Mahoney (1977, 1980) describes a self-management approach to therapy, which focuses on teaching the client to be his own cognitive-behavior therapist. This approach adopts a broad coping-skills perspective in combination with an emphasis on self-control and personal problem solving. The therapist is viewed as a consultant or coach whose primary responsibility is to teach the client how to assess his own problems, plan an appropriate self-management intervention program, and implement it effectively. Therapy is viewed as an apprenticeship in cognitive-behavioral assessment and self-management-oriented intervention. The role of the client, therefore, is one of active collaboration and participation.

Consistent with the general behavioral approach, the therapy program is cast within a "scientific" or experimental framework, which Mahoney calls "personal science." Mahoney showed considerable creative problem-solving ability in being able to organize the social-problem-solving model into seven steps mnemonically represented by the letters of the word "science." These seven steps are: (1) specify general problem area; (2) collect data; (3) identify patterns or sources; (4) examine options; (5) narrow and experiment; (6) compare data; and (7) extend, revise, or replace.

In stage one ("specify general problem area"), the client is trained to define the area or areas that are of current concern in his day-to-day transactions with the environment. In the second stage ("collect data"), the client is taught to gather more specific information regarding the parameters and correlates of the presenting problems. This stage includes specific training in assessment methods (e.g., self-observation, analog-assessment techniques). The third stage of therapy ("identify patterns or sources") focuses on training in the identification of possible antecedent determinants of the problem—factors responsible for the development and/or maintenance of the problem behavior. Three general categories of determinants are considered: (1) aspects of the physical environment, (2) aspects of the social environment, and (3) cognitive or skill factors.

In the fourth stage of therapy ("examine options"), training is provided in the generation of alternative solutions, with an emphasis on deferment of judgment. These solutions are divided into goals (desired changes) and means (specific procedures for implementing the goals). Since the client is not likely to be aware of or skilled in many behavioral intervention procedures, instruction is provided during this stage in such techniques as stimulus control, modeling, behavior and covert rehearsal, and shaping. In the fifth stage "narrow and experiment", the client is taught to narrow the possible options to those that are most feasible and promising. When the most feasible option has been selected, it is implemented in the form of a personal "experiment." In the sixth stage "compare data", the effects of the personal experiment are assessed by comparing the current status of the problem behavior (frequency, intensity, duration) to its status prior to intervention. If the outcome of that comparison is not satisfactory, the experimental solution is either extended, revised, or replaced in stage seven "extend, revise, or replace. "

Mahoney (1977) describes several ways in which the therapist can facilitate training, including the use of modeling, stimulus control, motivational incentives, task gradation, and active rehearsal. The personal-science paradigm appears to be a useful and promising framework in which to conduct cognitive-behavioral therapy. Instead of focusing on the therapist's skills in assessing and modifying the client's problem behavior, the approach focuses on *training the client to assess and control his own problem behavior,* which should lead to more generalized and durable behavior changes. In addition, since "faith" in the treatment and expectations of benefit are widely recognized as important factors influencing therapeutic efficacy, an approach emphasizing *personal science* might have strong appeal to a population of clients who place a high value on "science," "control," and "competence."

Black's Weight-Control Program

In an attempt to improve the efficacy of weight-control treatment, particularly with regard to maintenance of weight loss, Black and his associates have developed a problem-solving program to be used along with other behaviorally oriented weight-control methods (Black, in press; Black & Scherba, 1983; Black & Threlfall, 1986). The goal of the problem-solving program is to train clients to cope more effectively with problematic situations involving either overeating or underexercising. In one particular study (Black, in press), subjects attended 20 two-hour sessions over a period of 10 consecutive weeks. In another study, PST was implemented as a home-study bibliotherapy program (Black, & Threlfall, 1986) in which subjects are assisted in learning the problem-solving procedures by their spouses. The program involves training in seven problem-solving steps: (1) identifying the problem, (2) listing alternatives, (3) evaluating the alternatives, (4) choosing one or more alternatives for implementation, (5) putting the plan into action, (6) evaluating progress, and (7) beginning again, if unsuccessful. In addition, one study added a general problem identification step, which involves "tests of reality" (i.e., identification and assessment of a general weight problem). Training emphasizes repeated practice applying these seven steps to specific real problems.

In the first step, a problem that prompts overeating or prevents exercising is identified and described. The second step involves the generation of all possible solutions, using the deferment-of-judgment principle. In the third step, the effectiveness of each solution is rated. The solutions with the highest ratings are chosen in the fourth step. The fifth step involves the preparation of a solution plan specifying how, when, where, and how often the chosen solutions will be used. In the sixth step, a measure of the effectiveness of the solution plan is recorded, such as a reduction in caloric intake, an increase in caloric expenditure, or weight loss. If the plan was not successful, each problem-solving procedure is reviewed in the seventh step, necessary revisions are made, a new plan of action is prepared, and the subject tries again, repeating this process as often as necessary.

Black's approach has produced some of the best results reported in the behavioral weight loss literature to date (Black, in press; Black & Scherba, 1983; Black & Threlfall, 1986). These results will be discussed further later.

Heppner's Prevention Program

Heppner and his associates developed a PST program for college students with problem-solving deficits; it was conducted within a one-credit-hour academic course on Applied Problem Solving at the University of Missouri-Columbia (Heppner, Baumgardner, Larson, & Petty, 1983). Since problem-solving deficits tend to be associated with maladjustment (see Chapter 5), this program can be viewed as a prevention-oriented PST program with a vulnerable or at-risk population. The goals of the program were to increase the students' awareness of their problem-solving style and to examine how they might enhance their problem-solving effectiveness. In addition to training in problem-solving skills, instruction was also provided in a number of self-management principles (e.g., self-reinforcement, cognitive restructuring, coping self-statements) within the overall PST framework.

The program was conducted over a period of eight weeks, meeting once a week for 1½ hours. The course was conducted by a psychologist and two graduate students. Each session included an introductory lecture by one of the instructors on the content of training for that particular session. These lectures were typically followed by small-group discussions and exercises, and subsequently dyadic discussions and exercises. The content of the sessions emphasized (a) the concept of problem-solving style and its influence on problem-solving performance, (b) the use of self-management principles to cope with obstacles (cognitive, affective, behavioral) often encountered in problem solving, and (c) the specific problem-solving steps or skills (problem definition, generation of alternatives, etc.).

Another example of a university-based PST program for college students is Sidney Parnes's popular Creative Problem Solving Program at the State University of New York College at Buffalo (Parnes et al., 1977). Although this comprehensive PST program is not specifically prevention-oriented (i.e., it is not targeted specifically for a vulnerable or at-risk population), its goals and methods appear to be quite appropriate and potentially useful for a prevention program. Parnes's program is described in detail in two publications: *Guide to Creative Action: Revised Edition of Creative Behavior Guidebook* (Parnes et al., 1977) and *Creative Actionbook* (Noller et al., 1976).

Although the Heppner and Parnes programs are both designed for college students and conducted within an academic course structure, the language, examples, and instructional methods can easily be modified so that the program would be suitable for individuals at lower intellectual and/or educational levels. These programs could be targeted for other populations with deficiencies in problem-solving ability or performance who are experiencing an increase in the frequency and/or complexity of problems and stresses with which they must cope (e.g., the elderly, single parents, recently divorced individuals, adolescents). The effectiveness of the Heppner and Parnes programs will be discussed in a later chapter.

Jacobson's Marital Therapy Program

Jacobson developed a behavioral marital therapy (BMT) program, which involves two major components: (a) behavior exchange and (b) training in communication/problem-solving skills (Jacobson, 1977a; Jacobson & Margolin, 1979). Unlike most forms of marital therapy, Jacobson's behavioral approach attempts to teach couples a specific set of skills designed to aid the couple in the resolution of their current marital conflicts, and even more importantly, to help the couple deal more effectively with new problems that arise subsequent to the termination of therapy.

Behavior-exchange procedures are focused on during the early stages of BMT because they are both nondemanding and likely to generate early positive changes, which can serve as a foundation upon which other improvements can be built. In the generic sense of the term, *behavior exchange* refers to any procedure that increases the frequency of desired behaviors in a relationship. Although there are many variations of behavior-exchange procedures, two basic steps are common to all of them. First, behaviors described as desirable by one or both spouses are specified. Second, some attempt is made to increase the frequency of these behaviors. In behavioral terms, behavior exchange is a structured way for spouses to increase the positive reinforcement they provide for one another.

Training in communication/problem-solving skills is conducted through the use of three methods: (a) feedback, where couples are provided with information about their current maladaptive communication patterns; (b) instructions, where the therapist teaches alternative, more desirable communication patterns; and (c) behavior rehearsal, where couples practice the new communication patterns. Training focuses initially on general communication skills, such as empathy, listening skills, and assertiveness. Later, the focus of training shifts to the problem-solving process, with an emphasis on problem definition, generation of alternative solutions, and evaluation of solutions. Each problem-solving session has two distinct phases: a definition phase and a solution phase. During the definition phase, the goal is to develop a clear, specific statement of the problem. Suggested solutions are not allowed during this phase. Then, once the problem has been clearly defined, the discussion enters the solution phase, during which an attempt is made to find a mutually satisfactory resolution of the problem.

According to Jacobson, PST is a very powerful treatment strategy for a wide variety of distressed couples. Its power appears to stem from two sources. First, it focuses simultaneously on content and process. Couples solve current distressing problems and, at the same time, they acquire general skills that lead to more reinforcing interactions and allow them to solve their own future problems more effectively. Second, PST reinforces a collaborative set. In the process of resolving relationship problems, couples learn that they will be much happier working collaboratively to improve their relationship than dealing with their conflicts as adversaries.

Robin's Parent-Adolescent Program

Robin (1979, 1980) developed a Problem-solving Communication Training Program which is designed for the treatment of parent-adolescent conflicts. The program involves three components: (1) general communication training, (2) PST, and (3) generalization programming.

General communication training is designed to teach parents and adolescents appropriate, facilitative communication skills. An attempt is made to decrease negative communication habits, such as accusations, interruptions, lectures, put-downs, overgeneralizations, commands, sarcastic expressions, and inattentive postures, and replace them with more positive communication habits, such as verification of meaning, passive listening, active listening, I-messages, appropriate eye contact, and appropriate nonverbal posture. Instructional methods include modeling, instructions, and intensive behavior rehearsal. Several communication patterns are targeted per session.

PST follows a four-step model: (1) defining the problem, (2) generating alternative solutions, (3) decision making, and (4) planning implementation. In the first step, family members identify a conflict and each person states the nature of the problem explicitly from his or her point of view. In the second step, family members take turns suggesting ideas for solving the problem, following the three rules of "brainstorming": (a) defer judgment, (b) quantity, not quality, of ideas counts, and (c) be creative and "freewheeling." The third step begins with an independent evaluation of each solution by each family member, using a benefit/cost analysis. Then, the evaluations are discussed and an attempt is made to reach a consensus regarding the best solution. If a consensus cannot be reached, the family members negotiate a compromise agreement. The final step in the process involves a discussion of the details specifying who will do what, when, where, and how to fulfill the agreement. The family members also establish behavioral criteria and monitoring systems for evaluating compliance with the solution.

Generalization programming, the third component of Robin's Problem-solving Communication Training Program, involves a set of procedures designed to facilitate the use of effective communication/problem-solving skills in the natural home environment. These procedures include discussions of factors affecting the use of problem-solving at home. Also included are homework assignments that require family members to: (1) implement specific solutions agreed upon during problem-solving discussions in sessions; (2) conduct additional problem-solving discussions at home; and (3) apply component problem-solving communication skills in daily interactions with each other.

Training in Robin's Problem-solving Communication Training Program involves 7 to 12 one-hour sessions, preceded by and followed by a two-hour assessment session. At the beginning of the first training session, the rationale for problem solving is presented, written outlines of the four-step problem-solving model are distributed, and a topic is selected for an initial problem-solving discussion. The therapist models each step of problem solving and then asks the family members to practice the procedure, using the written outline of the model as a guide. Instructions, prompts, behavior rehearsal, and feedback are used to facilitate training. At each successive session, an additional conflict is discussed and resolved. In the later sessions, the therapist attempts to fade out direct instruction and corrective feedback, encourages family members to progress naturally from step to step, and helps them to recognize when they are getting bogged down.

Summary

PST programs vary in terms of (a) target population, (b) program goals, (c) training setting, (d) amount of training in other coping skills within the overall PST framework, (e) instructional methods used, and (f) overall program structure. The following PST programs are presented to illustrate some of these variations: (a) Coché's Group Therapy Program, (b) Mahoney's Personal-Science Paradigm, (c) Black's Weight-Control Program, (d) Heppner's Prevention Program, (e) Jacobson's Marital Therapy Program, and (f) Robin's Parent-Adolescent Program. In the next chapter, outcome studies are presented that evaluate the efficacy of programs such as these.

11

Outcome Studies

PST outcome studies have focused on a variety of different target populations and program goals. Target populations have ranged from hospitalized psychiatric patients to normal individuals and groups who want to maximize their general personal-social competence. In different studies, PST has been used as a treatment method, a maintenance strategy, and/or as a prevention or community program. The studies reviewed below are grouped according to type of subject or target behavior focused on.

Psychiatric Patients

Siegel and Spivack (1976a, 1976b) developed a problem-solving therapy program for chronic psychiatric patients. The program attempts to improve their general social competence. It focuses on four problem-solving skills: (a) the ability to recognize interpersonal problems; (b) the ability to define problems; (c) the ability to think of alternative solutions; and (d) the ability to decide which solution is best. Training consists of a series of 14 gamelike exercises involving the use of didactic presentations, slides, and cassette tapes. For example, one of the exercises for problem definition is called "Thirty Questions." Designed to train patients to seek relevant information, this exercise requires the patient to ask a maximum of 30 questions in order to obtain information about a problem from the therapist. Siegel and Spivack (1976a, 1976b) conducted two pilot studies using this program. They suggested that the program is feasible and that patients respond favorably to it; however, no objective outcome data were reported.

Three studies by Coché and his associates have provided more objective data on the efficacy of PST with psychiatric patients.

Coché and Flick (1975) compared group PST; an attention-placebo group (play-reading); and a no-treatment control group. In the attention-placebo group, subjects met to read and discuss various plays; different subjects were assigned different roles from the play. Both the PST and play-reading groups met for eight one-hour sessions over a period of two weeks. The major dependent measures were three scores derived from the MEPS (Means-Ends Problem Solving procedures, Platt & Spivack, 1975): number of relevant means, number of irrelevant means, and the relevancy ratio. The results showed that the patients who received group PST improved significantly more on all three measures than the attention-placebo and no-treatment control groups. No differences were found between the attention-placebo and no-treatment control groups on any measure.

In an attempt to evaluate the effects of PST on outcome measures other than the MEPS, Coché and Douglass (1977) conducted a similar study, which included two self-report measures of personal adjustment in addition to the MEPS. Three groups similar to those in the Coché and Flick (1975) study were compared: group PST; an attention-placebo group in which subjects read and discussed comedies; and a no-treatment control group. Contrary to the findings of the previous study, no significant differences were found by Coché and Douglass between PST and the control groups on any of the MEPS measures. They explain the failure to replicate the MEPS results of the 1975 study by pointing out that subject attrition resulted in a higher level of pretreatment problem-solving ability in the problem-solving group, leaving this group with less "room to grow" than the other two groups. Although the MEPS failed to provide support for PST in the Coché and Douglass study, the PST group did show significantly greater improvement than both control groups on several measures of personal adjustment, including impulse control, self-image, feelings of mastery and competence, and depression.

In another study, Coché, Cooper, and Petermann (1984) compared group PST with "interactive group therapy," which focuses on interpersonal relationships. Both types of groups met for eight sessions over a two-week period, each session lasting 90 minutes. Outcome measures included self-report measures of self-esteem, self-confidence, and psychopathology, and ratings of improvement for the three most salient target complaints for each patient by the nurse on the hall. The results showed no significant differences between treatments. However, there was a significant interaction effect between sex and treatment. Men improved more with PST and women improved more with interactive therapy. The results of this study are difficult to interpret for two reasons. First, the duration of therapy is very short. It seems unlikely that effects strong enough to demonstrate the superiority of one therapy over another can be produced in just eight sessions with psychiatric patients. Second, the PST groups were led by females only. This difference in therapists may have contributed to the significant interaction effect between sex and treatment.

Viewing PST as part of a deinstitutionalization program involving the teaching of practical skills to chronic psychiatric patients, Edelstein, Couture, Cray, Dickens, and Lusebrink (1980) evaluated a problem-solving therapy program with 12 of these patients. Training involved a series of four modules, which focused on five problem-solving skills: problem identification and definition, generation of alternative solutions, selection of the best alternative, implementation of the solution response, and evaluation of resulting outcomes. Each training module was structured to begin with a didactic presentation of the underlying principle or principles, and then gradually increase patient participation while decreasing therapist involvement.

The Edelstein et al. (1980) study had a multiple-baseline design, with each subject serving as his own control. A verbal problem-solving test using an interview format was administered at pretreatment and after each of the four training modules. In this procedure, subjects were required to respond to hypothetical problems similar to those that might be encountered in the community after leaving the hospital (for example, problems preparing meals independently, conflicts with a landlord, or problems budgeting money). Four problems were presented at each testing. Problem-solving performance was evaluated in four skill areas: correct identification of the "main problem," number of alternative solutions generated, adequacy and realism of stated consequences and solution choice, and adequacy of statements of solution implementation: how one would actually go about carrying out the solution. A combination behavioral-verbal problem-solving test was also administered at pre- and posttreatment in order to assess for generalization from verbal problem-solving to overt problem-solving performance. The test involved a simulated problematic situation in which a customer (the subject) was overcharged by the cashier in a grocery store. In addition to role-playing a response to the situation, the subject also responded verbally to questions regarding the same skills as were assessed on the verbal test.

The results for the verbal problem-solving measure showed significant increases in the four skill areas as a function of each respective training module. In addition, the data also suggested that training in one problem-solving operation can affect the ability to perform other operations: training in problem identification and definition seemed to facilitate the subjects' generation-of-alternatives performance, and training in the generation of alternatives appeared to improve the subjects' ability to evaluate alternative solutions. The effect of training in problem identification on generation of alternatives is consistent with results reported by Nezu and D'Zurilla (1981b). Significant improvement in all four skill areas was also found in pre- to posttest comparisons. Analysis of the behavioral-verbal problem-solving data showed significant pre-post increases in adequacy of solution choice and adequacy of solution implementation.

A similar PST program was evaluated by Bedell, Archer, and Marlowe (1980). In addition to didactic lectures and exercises aimed at providing patients with an understanding of important problem-solving concepts, the training program included a "skill enhancement/generalization" component designed to facilitate problem-solving performance. This component included the use of structured role-playing, journal writing, practice sessions, and "homework assignments." Twenty hospitalized psychiatric patients participated in the study. In addition to their participation in the PST program, these patients were also involved in a traditional residential treatment program, which included both medical and psychiatric care. The patients were divided into two groups: a PST group and a control group that engaged in a recreational program for an equal period of time.

Three self-report measures of problem solving were developed for the study and administered before and after treatment: (a) the Problem Solving Knowledge and Information Test (PKIT); (b) the Problem Solving Self-Evaluation Test (PSET); and (c) the Problem Solving Performance Evaluation Test (PPET). The PKIT assessed the subjects' knowledge about the problem-solving process. The PSET consisted of self-ratings of the frequency of performing various problem-solving operations. The PPET measured the subjects' verbal problem-solving performance in several areas: problem identification, listing the basic elements of the problem, generating possible solutions, rank-ordering the solution alternatives with regard to feasibility, and providing reasons for selecting the different solutions. The results showed that the PST group improved significantly more than the control group on the PKIT and the PPET, but not on the PSET.

In a study described in detail earlier in Chapter 3, Hansen et al. (1985) trained seven chronic aftercare psychiatric patients in five problem-solving component skills: problem identification, goal definition, solution evaluation, evaluation of alternatives, and selection of a best solution. The effects of training were assessed using measures of problem-solving ability and verbal problem-solving performance, which focused on actual problematic situations the patients were likely to encounter in the community. The results showed that training significantly increased both problem-solving ability and problem-solving effectiveness, with improvement generalizing from problematic situations used in training to unfamiliar, untrained situations. Before training, the patient sample showed a significant deficit in problem-solving effectiveness compared to a criterion sample of 20 "normal," nonpsychiatric individuals living in the community. Following training, the patients' problem-solving effectiveness was equal to that of the criterion sample.

Alcoholism

Intagliatia (1978) conducted a study to assess whether PST would improve on the results of a typical VA alcoholism treatment program, involving six weeks of inpatient medical and psychiatric care. Sixty-three male alcoholic patients were randomly assigned to either an experimental group, which received PST in addition to the VA alcoholism program, or a control group, which received only the VA program. The PST group participated in 10 one-hour training sessions over a four-week period, which were designed to teach the problem-solving steps: problem recognition, problem definition, generation of alternatives, and selection of the best solution. Both groups were administered the MEPS and a social competency scale at pre- and posttreatment assessments. Additionally, shortly prior to discharge from the alcoholism program, all subjects participated in a structured interview to discuss "discharge planning," covering such areas as employment, living arrangements, and the use of leisure time. The subjects' interview responses were scored for: (a) number of discrete instrumental acts described as plans for coping with problems, (b) number of obstacles recognized, (c) number of solution alternatives that were considered but not yet decided upon, and (d) number of discrete acts that the person planned to implement.

The results showed that the PST group improved significantly more than the control group on one MEPS score: the number of relevant means. Trends were observed in favor of PST on the other MEPS scores but none of the differences were significant. With regard to the interview data, however, the problem-solving group performed significantly better than the control group in all four response categories, indicating better planning and preparation for coping with problems in living after returning to the community. No significant findings were reported for the social competency scale. A one-month follow-up evaluation included only the problem-solving group in order to determine how well they remembered the problem-solving principles and whether or not they were applying these principles in real life. Although many subjects who were contacted had forgotten significant portions of the training information, 70% of them reported using problem-solving principles in coping with real-life problems.

A similar study with alcoholics was conducted by Chaney, O'-Leary, and Marlatt (1978). The forty male patients who participated as subjects in this study were also in an inpatient VA alcoholism treatment program. These subjects were randomly assigned to either a PST group, a placebo control group, or no-treatment control group. The placebo control group met to discuss their feelings and reactions to various problematic situations involving alcohol. The PST and placebo groups met for eight 90-minute sessions over a four-week period. The no-treatment control group received only the regular VA alcoholism program.

The major outcome measure in this study was the Situational Competency Test (SCT), which involved the presentation of tape-recorded problematic situations involving alcohol that the patients might encounter in the real-life social setting. The subject's task was to imagine being in the situation and then verbally respond to the question: "What would you do or say?" Verbal responses were scored for latency of response; duration of response (number of words); compliance (whether or not the subject "gave in" to the situation); and specification of new alternative behaviors. A second outcome measure was a "drinking profile," which involved the use of a structured interview to obtain information about the subject's drinking behavior. The SCT was administered at pretreatment, at termination of training, and at a three-month follow-up. The drinking profile was taken at pretreatment and after follow-up periods of one, three, six and twelve months.

The results for the SCT showed that the PST group performed significantly better than both control groups on scores for duration of response and specification of new alternative behaviors; however, these differences diminished at the three-month follow-up assessment. Since no significant differences were found between the two control groups on the measures of drinking behavior from the drinking profile, this data was pooled and then compared to the data from the PST group. For the one-year period following treatment, the PST group was found to be significantly more improved on the following measures: number of days drunk, total number of drinks, and mean length of a drinking period. No significant differences were found in the actual number of relapses between the groups; however, one can conclude from the other drinking measures that the duration and severity of relapses were reduced as a function of PST.

Cigarette Smoking

Karol and Richards (1978) investigated the use of PST as a maintenance strategy for cigarette-smoking reduction. Thirty-eight habitual smokers were randomly assigned to behavioral treatment, behavioral treatment and maintenance strategy, or waiting-list control. The behavioral treatment; consisting of self-monitoring, stimulus control, and alternative behavior planning, involved five sessions over a three-week period. The goal of the program was to gradually reduce smoking and then quit completely by a predetermined target date. The maintenance strategy consisted of PST and the use of a "buddy system" involving scheduled telephone contacts between pairs of subjects following the behavioral treatment program.

The results at treatment termination indicated a significant reduction in smoking frequency in both treatment groups, but not in the waiting-list control group. Follow-up assessments via telephone interviews were conducted after two-, four-, and eight-month periods. The group that received the maintenance strategy showed very little relapse on follow-up, whereas the relapse rate for the other two groups was substantial. For example, at the eight-month follow-up evaluation, the average number of cigarettes smoked above the posttreatment assessment level was 1.1 for the maintenance strategy group, whereas the number for the other two groups was 14.8.

Depression

In an important, well-controlled, well-executed outcome study focusing on unipolar depression, Nezu (1986a) randomly assigned 26 clinically depressed community-residing subjects to one of three conditions: (1) problem-solving therapy (PST); (2) problem-focused therapy (PFT); or (3) waiting-list control (WLC). Both therapy conditions were conducted in a group setting over eight weekly sessions lasting from one and one-half to two hours. PST involved training in the problem-solving skills described by D'Zurilla and Nezu (1982). PFT involved discussions of the subjects' current life problems with a problem-solving goal, but no systematic training in problem-solving skills was provided.

Dependent measures were obtained at pretreatment, posttreatment, and at a six-month follow-up assessment. These measures included the Beck Depression Inventory (BDI), the Depression Scale of the Minnesota Multiphasic Personality Inventory (MMPI-D), the Problem-Solving Inventory (PSI), and the Internal-External Locus of Control Scale (I-E).

Both traditional statistical analyses and an analysis of the clinical significance of the results indicated substantial reductions in depression in the PST group, which were maintained over the six-month follow-up period, as measured by both the BDI and the MMPI-D. Moreover, the improvement in depression in the PST condition was significantly greater than in the PFT and WLC conditions. The superiority of PST over PFT was maintained at the six-month follow-up evaluation. The results for the PSI and the I-E scale showed that the PST subjects increased significantly more than the other two groups in self-appraisal of problem-solving effectiveness, and also changed significantly in locus of control orientation from external to internal. The improvements on the PSI and I-E scale were also maintained at the six-month follow-up. These results provide support for the basic assumption that PST produces its effects by increasing problem-solving ability and strengthening personal-control expectations.

Hussian and Lawrence (1981) compared the use of PST with a

social-reinforcement program for the treatment of depression in a group of geriatric patients living in a nursing home. Thirty-six patients who scored in the severely depressed range on the BDI were randomly divided into three groups: problem-solving training (PST), social reinforcement (SR), and waiting-list control (WLC). Both treatment groups met for five 30-minute training sessions during a one-week period of time. PST was based on the D'Zurilla and Goldfried (1971) model. Training was carried out on an in-dividual basis and involved discussion of each of the five stages of the model as well as practice solving real-life problems generated by the subjects in a previous pilot study. The major objective of the social-reinforcement program was to increase the rate of reinforce-ment the subjects were receiving in their daily lives. Subjects were prompted to engage in various activities such as arts and crafts and given social reinforcement for attendance, participation in a specific activity, perseverance, and interaction with other patients.

After the first week of treatment, each of the three groups was randomly divided in half to produce six subgroups. One PST sub-group received a second week of PST (PST-PST), while the second PST subgroup participated in the social-reinforcement program (PST-SR). One SR subgroup received a second week of social reinforcement (SR-SR), while the second SR subgroup received PST (SR-PST). Finally, one WLC subgroup remained on the waiting list for the second week (WLC-WLC), while the second WLC subgroup was changed to an informational control group (WLC-IC), which met to discuss the various life changes that accompany aging. The major outcome measures were the BDI and self-ratings of depres-sion. Other outcome measures included the Hospital Adjustment Scale (HAS), which measures the general level of daily functioning and adjustment in the institutional environment, and a written problem-solving test using hypothetical problems. The BDI, HAS, and self-ratings were administered at pretreatment, at the end of the first treatment week, at the end of the second treatment week, and after follow-up periods of two weeks and three months. The written problem-solving test was administered at pretreatment and at the end of the first treatment week.

After the first week of treatment, both the PST and SR groups showed significantly less depression on both measures than did the WLC group. As expected, the PST group showed significantly better performance on the problem-solving test than did the SR group. An analysis of differences between pretreatment assessment and the posttreatment assessment at the end of the second week provided for a comparison between the combined treatments. The results showed a significant reduction in depression on the BDI only for groups that received PST. The PST-PST group was significantly less depressed than both the WLC-IC and WLC-WLC groups, and the SR-PST group was significantly less depressed than the WLC-IC group. The differences between the SR-SR group and the control groups were not significant.

Differences on self-ratings of depression and on the HAS emerged in the analysis of differences between the end of the first treatment week and the end of the second treatment week. The groups that received PST during the second week reported less depression than the groups that received social reinforcement during that week. On the HAS, the group that received PST for both weeks showed significantly more improvement than the two-week social reinforcement group and the two-week waiting-list control group. The superiority of PST was maintained at the two-week follow-up. Two PST groups (PST-PST and PST-SR) were found to be significantly less depressed on the BDI than the two-week waiting-list control group. On self-ratings of depression, the two-week PST group was significantly less depressed than the two-week social reinforcement group and the two-week waiting-list control group. Although the differences were no longer significant at the three-month follow-up assessment, the trends in the data were similar to the findings at the two-week follow-up.

Academic Underachievement

Richards and Perri (1978) evaluated the relative effectiveness of PST and faded counselor contact as maintenance strategies used in conjunction with a behavioral-counseling program for poor study habits and academic underachievement in college students. The subjects were 69 introductory psychology students who volunteered for the study. They were randomly assigned to six groups: (1) study–skills advice; (2) self-control training; (3) self-control training with PST; (4) self-control training with faded counselor contact; (5) self-control training with PST and faded counselor contact; and (6) no-treatment control. In addition, a no-contact, nonvolunteer control group of 11 students was included in the study.

The study–skills advice group participated in a training program that offered direct information regarding textbook reading, study scheduling, note-taking, exam-taking and writing. Self-control training provided instruction in the use of behavioral self-control procedures such as self-monitoring, stimulus control, and self-reinforcement in addition to the study–skills advice. PST followed the five stages of the D'Zurilla and Goldfried (1971) model. The five treatment groups met for four sessions over a three-week period. The two groups that included faded counselor contact met with 2-, 5-, and 14-day intervals between sessions. The other three treatment groups met with one-week regular intervals between sessions.

The outcome measures included exam grades from the introductory psychology course and semester grade point averages (GPA). Course grades were available during the week following counseling and at six and twelve weeks after counseling. GPAs from before counseling and 12 weeks and one year following counseling were analyzed. A written test designed to assess knowledge of the problem-solving skills was also administered at posttreatment and at a 12-week follow-up.

Results for the course exams showed that the two groups receiving PST were significantly superior to all other groups at the 6- and 12-week posttreatment evaluations. The faded counselor contact procedure was not effective as a maintenance strategy. Results from the problem-solving test indicated that the two PST groups did, in fact, learn the requisite skills and maintained this knowledge at the 12-week follow-up assessment.

Vocational Indecision

Mendonca and Siess (1976) evaluated the relative effectiveness of anxiety-management training and PST for reducing anxiety resulting from vocational indecision in college students. The subjects were 32 undergraduate college students with this problem, who were divided into five groups: (a) anxiety management; (b) problem solving training; (c) anxiety management and problem solving training combined; (d) discussion placebo; and (e) no-treatment control.

Anxiety-management training involved relaxation training, group systematic desensitization, and the use of self-coping imagery. PST used a group-discussion format and was based on the D'Zurilla and Goldfried (1971) model. The combined condition included the essential features of both treatments with an equal emphasis on the two methods. The subjects in the placebo condition met to discuss their career indecision and attempt to gain insight into the causes of their anxiety.

Outcome measures included measures of the frequency and variety of vocational search behavior (for example, visiting a job site, discussing career plans with a professor), state and trait anxiety, and problem solving. The problem-solving measure was a timed written test involving imaginary role-playing in response to tape-recorded vignettes of common problematic situations in a college setting. Three subtests produced scores for the following problem-solving behavior: concrete information gathering, generation of alternatives, and choice behavior.

Results for vocational search behavior showed that the combined treatment (group c) and the anxiety-management group improved significantly more than the problem-solving training and no-treatment control groups. There was no significant difference between the combined treatment and anxiety management. No significant differences were found in anxiety reduction on either anxiety measure. On the information-gathering subtest of the problem-solving measure, the problem-solving training group performed significantly better than anxiety management and both control groups; the combined-treatment group performed significantly better than both control groups; and anxiety-management was significantly better than the no-treatment control. On the generation-of-alternatives subtest, the combined treatment group was significantly better than both control groups, and the problem-solving group performed significantly better than the placebo control group. No significant results were found on the measure of choice behavior.

The findings for the problem-solving test supported the efficacy of PST in this study, but the results for the measures of anxiety reduction and vocational search behavior did not. Since none of the treatments produced significant anxiety reduction, it is possible that the vocational problems of the students were not sufficiently resolved by the end of the study for them to show a significant relief from the anxiety of their vocational indecision. A follow-up assessment would have been desirable to assess for possible later anxiety-reducing effects resulting from the different treatments. With regard to vocational search behavior, it is possible that the college students in this study were already quite aware of the importance of exploratory behavior in making vocational decisions; thus, PST would not be expected to add any new information or skills in this area. The self-coping imagery and covert rehearsal involved in the anxiety-management condition might have been more useful than PST in actually *facilitating* the students' search behavior.

Marital and Family Problems

Jacobson's behavior marital therapy (BMT) program involves behavior-exchange procedures and training in communication/
problem-solving skills (Jacobson, 1977a; Jacobson & Margolin,
1979). The BMT program was initially evaluated in an outcome
study involving 10 maritally distressed couples, who were randomly
assigned to either a treatment group, involving 10 sessions of therapy, or a waiting-list control group.

The early therapy sessions focused on PST; behavior exchange
began in the fourth session. In the remaining sessions, the couples
applied all of their skills to the discussion of specific problems in
their relationship. Outcome measures included a problem-solving
performance test, in which couples were observed interacting in a
problem-solving discussion situation, and a self-report scale of
marital adjustment. Scores were obtained for problem-solving performance by coding the couples' verbal behavior into positive, negative, and neutral categories. Both measures were administered at
pre- and posttreatment. The marital adjustment scale was also
administered after a one-year follow-up. In addition, throughout
treatment couples were asked to monitor and record behaviors in
the home that had been defined as problematic during pretreatment
assessment. This resulted in a multiple-baseline type of design,
allowing for an assessment of the specific effects of the treatment
intervention on particular problematic behaviors.

The results showed that the couples receiving BMT improved
significantly more than the waiting-list control group on both the
measures of problem-solving behavior and marital adjustment. At
the one-year follow-up, the treatment gains on the marital adjustment scale were maintained. On the measure of frequency of
problematic behaviors in the home, the treated couples showed
significant improvement, which could be attributed to the specific
treatment procedures.

Jacobson (1978) conducted a second study designed to replicate
the above findings with the addition of a nonspecific therapy group
to control for nonspecific factors such as attention and expectation of
benefit. The nonspecific group included discussions of relationship
problems but no specific training in PST and no behavior-exchange
procedures. The credibility of the nonspecific therapy was checked
by having the couples rate the therapists and the two treatment
conditions on factors related to expectations of benefit, and by having an independent sample of subjects rate written descriptions of

both treatment conditions. No significant differences in credibility were found between the two treatment conditions.

The results of the 1978 Jacobson study replicated the findings of the first study regarding the comparisons of BMT with the waiting-list control. In addition, the results also showed that BMT produced significantly more improvement than the nonspecific treatment on the measures of problem-solving behavior and marital adjustment. The gains on the marital adjustment scale were maintained at a six-month follow-up assessment.

Since both of the above studies focused on a university-based population (relatively young, moderately distressed, relatively high intelligence), Jacobson (1977c) conducted a study with a more severely distressed population in an urban psychiatric hospital setting. These subjects were not only experiencing serious relationship problems, but many also had serious individual psychological problems as well. Six couples participated in the study, each of which was studied separately, using a single-subject, multiple-baseline design, focusing on problematic behaviors recorded by the couples in the home.

PST with each couple was compared to a baseline involving three to four weeks of a behavior-exchange procedure in which the couple was instructed to increase positive behavior. After these three or four weeks, individual problem areas were treated with the problem-solving approach. The behavioral data recorded in the home showed significant improvement in five of the six couples from baseline to posttreatment. In the sixth couple, although positive changes were reported on a self-report measure, these changes were not substantiated by the home behavioral data. Of the five improved couples, four maintained their gains at a six-month follow-up, as measured by the marital-adjustment scale. With four of the five improved couples, PST appeared to be effective and sufficient for producing significant therapeutic change. However, the fifth improved couple needed further direct instruction aimed at increasing positive behavior before significant change could be produced.

In another study, Jacobson (1984) compared BMT with its two major components presented alone: behavior exchange (BE) and communication/problem-solving training (CPT). The subjects were 33 married couples who were seeking therapy; they were randomly assigned to one of the three treatment groups (BE alone, CPT alone, or BE and CPT) or a waiting-list control group. The study involved 12–16 sessions of treatment and a six-month follow-up. Dependent measures included global marital satisfaction, problem checklists, and spouse reports of behavior at home. The results at posttest showed that the three treatments were equally effective in improving marital satisfaction and reducing presenting problems. At the six-month follow-up, however, 44% of the BE couples reversed their progress, whereas virtually all couples receiving CPT—either alone or in conjunction with BE—generally maintained their treatment gains or continued to improve.

In a later report, Jacobson and Follette (1985) presented data from an additional 24 couples. In terms of marital satisfaction, differences between groups began to emerge at the six-month follow-up. BE couples deteriorated in marital satisfaction again at very high rates, whereas deterioration was rare among CPT and BMT couples. Moreover, some of the couples in both the CPT and BMT conditions continued to improve from posttest to follow-up, whereas none of the BE couples improved.

Robin's (1979, 1980) problem-solving communication training program for the treatment of parent-adolescent conflict involves communication training, PST, and generalization programming. The latter involves several procedures designed to facilitate the use of effective problem-solving and communication skills in the natural home environment. This program has been evaluated in three clinical outcome studies.

In the first study, Robin, Kent, O'Leary, Foster, and Prinz (1977) randomly assigned 22 mother-adolescent dyads to a problem-solving communication training (PSCT) group or a waiting-list control group. The dyads in the PSCT condition met with a therapist for five sessions, in which they were taught problem solving and communication skills. Three of the five sessions focused on hypothetical conflicts and the other two focused on real conflicts. No generalization programming was included in the training program in this study. Dependent measures included an observational measure of problem-solving behavior based on problem-solving discussions held before and after the treatment sessions, and self-report measures of parent-adolescent conflict and communication behavior in the home environment. The results showed dramatic improvement in problem-solving behavior in the PSCT group relative to the control group at the posttreatment assessment, but no clear-cut evidence of improvement in conflict resolution or communication behavior at home.

In the second study, Foster, Prinz, and O'Leary (1983) randomly assigned 28 families (25 triads, 3 dyads) to a waiting-list control group; a PSCT group with generalization programming (homework assignments and discussions of factors affecting the use of problem-solving skills at home); or a PSCT group without generalization programming. The treatment groups met for seven sessions, in which training focused on currently distressing *real* conflicts. In this study, no significant improvements were found on the observational measure of problem-solving behavior, which may have been due to the great variability among the families in this study on that measure at the pretreatment assessment. However, the results showed that both treatment groups improved significantly more than the control group on several measures of parent-adolescent conflict and communication behavior at home. These results were generally maintained at a six- to eight-week follow-up assessment. Since there were no significant differences between the two treatments on these measures, the generalized treatment effects cannot be attributed to the generalization-programming procedures. Instead, they are more likely to be a result of other improvements in the PSCT program in this study, such as the addition of two more training sessions, the inclusion of fathers in the training program instead of mothers only, and the emphasis during training on the families' *real* problems instead of on hypothetical problems.

In the third study (Robin, 1981), PSCT was compared to a less structured "best alternative treatment" in an attempt to control for nonspecific factors such as demand characteristics and expectations of benefit. The alternative treatment was short-term family therapy characterized by the family therapists who conducted it as "eclectic," "family systems," or "psychodynamic." There were 33 families, who were randomly assigned to the two treatment groups or a waiting-list control group. Treatment involved seven sessions in both groups. The results showed that both treatments produced significant improvement in conflict resolution and communication behavior at home; however, only PSCT resulted in significant improvement on the observational measure of problem-solving communication. Most treatment effects were maintained at a 10-week follow-up. In addition, parents consistently rated PSCT more favorably than the alternative family therapy with regard to improvement in their relationship with their adolescents, improvement in their adolescents' behavior at home, improvement in problem-solving discussions at home, and the extent to which the program fulfilled their expectations.

There are some inconsistencies in results within and between the above three studies, which make it difficult to draw definite conclusions. However, taken together, the general findings strongly suggest that PSCT is a promising approach to the treatment of parent-adolescent conflict which can (a) facilitate the acquisition of effective problem-solving and communication skills and (b) produce generalized improvements in conflict resolution and communication behavior at home. It also appears that the improvements in problem-solving communication skills that follow PSCT are due to the specific training procedures and not to nonspecific factors such as demand characteristics and expectancy effects.

Weight-Control Problems

Several studies have focused on the use of PST to enhance the efficacy of weight-control programs. Black and Scherba (1983) investigated the effects of two types of behavioral contracting assignments on weight loss following a behaviorally oriented weight-control program. Fourteen subjects who were at least 25% overweight attended seven weekly sessions, which focused on the weight-control program of Mahoney and Mahoney (1976). Following the completion of the program, all subjects attended follow-up sessions three, six, and twelve months after treatment. In addition to the regular requirements of the weight-control program, half of the subjects were asked to complete contracts that required them to practice behavioral weight-control skills (e.g., stimulus control, self-reinforcement, physical exercise) during treatment and the follow-up periods. The other half had contracts requiring the completion of problem-solving forms describing the application of a seven-step problem-solving procedure to specific weight-related problems during treatment and the follow-up periods (see Chapter 10). The results showed that the subjects who contracted to practice problem solving lost significantly more weight from posttreatment to the six-month follow-up than did the subjects who contracted to practice behavioral weight-control skills.

In another study, Black (in press) evaluated the efficacy of a weight-control program that consisted of a "minimal intervention" followed by his PST program for weight control. The subjects for this study were seven moderately obese women (27% to 54% overweight). The minimal intervention consisted of verbal instructions regarding nutrition, physical activity, gradual weight loss, and self-monitoring of weight and calories consumed and expended. The duration of this intervention varied for different subjects, ranging from six weeks to twelve weeks. The PST program involved 20 two-hour sessions over a 10-week period, which focused on the seven-step problem-solving procedure described earlier (see Chapter 10). If subjects had difficulty progressing through the problem-solving steps for any particular problems, specific facilitative coping techniques were suggested, including covert modeling, self-reinforcement, attention diversion, relaxation, and behavioral contracting. In addition to weight-loss measures, the dependent measures included a measure of the frequency of weight- and exercise-related life problems, and a problem-solving ability measure using hypothetical problematic situations and a "think aloud" procedure, which permitted the assessment of specific problem-solving cognitions. After the formal treatment period, three- and six-month follow-up meetings were held.

The major findings were: (a) weight loss increased dramatically during the PST program, compared to the minimal-intervention program; (b) weight loss was variable during minimal intervention but very homogeneous during PST; (c) weight loss continued after treatment, with six subjects losing weight by the three-month follow-up and three subjects continuing to lose weight by the 12-month follow-up; (d) clinically significant weight losses occurred for five subjects; and (e) a strong relationship was found between weight loss and problem-solving ability and between weight loss and the number of weight-related problems during the PST period. Greater weight losses were associated with higher problem-solving ability and less frequent problems. The average weight loss of 25 pounds in this study is one of the best reported in the behavioral weight loss literature to date.

In another recent study, Black and Threlfall (1986) evaluated the efficacy of a "stepped approach" to weight control. In this approach, treatment begins with a minimal intervention; more intensive procedures are added for particular subjects as needed. In the present study, the procedure that was added for subjects who needed a more intensive program was a home-study bibliotherapy program based on the same seven-step problem-solving procedure used in the two previous studies. The study focused on 26 moderately obese subjects and their partners, who helped with the home-study PST program. The minimal-intervention program was introduced first; if subjects were not losing weight, the PST program was added. It was necessary to add the PST program for 22 of the 26 subjects. The duration of the program was one year, after which there was a three-month follow-up evaluation. During this time, subjects completed a variety of forms and written assignments related to problem solving and self-monitoring and mailed them in to the treatment staff. In addition, subjects were required to read, and were quizzed on, information related to behavioral weight-control skills (Mahoney & Mahoney, 1976) and nutrition and health.

The results showed that the subjects substantially decreased in weight and percentage overweight by the end of the one-year program and maintained the improvement at follow-up. Six subjects reached ideal weight by the three-month follow-up and nine subjects were in the acceptable range for body-mass index. Overall, subjects lost an average of 22.1 pounds by the three-month follow-up. An important additional finding was that subjects who complied well with the requirements of the PST program lost significantly more weight than those who complied poorly. This finding suggests that the specific problem-solving procedures were a significant determinant of weight loss in this study.

Straw and Terre (1983) reported results similar to those of Black and Scherba (1983). Straw and Terre evaluated three behavioral weight-control treatments: (a) group-administered standardized treatment; (b) individually administered standardized treatment; and (c) individualized treatment. These treatments were crossed with two maintenance strategies: (a) individual problem-solving training (PST) and (b) optional weigh-ins. Forty-two obese women completed the 10-week treatment program. The results at a 9½-month follow-up showed that subjects who received the standardized group treatment and subjects who received the individualized treatment continued to lose weight, while the subjects who received the individually administered standardized treatment regained much of the weight they lost during treatment. Of most interest here, the PST maintenance strategy was significantly more effective than optional weigh-ins for facilitating and maintaining weight loss during the follow-up period.

Agoraphobia

Jannoun, Munby, Catalan, and Gelder (1980) compared programmed practice with problem solving for the treatment of agoraphobia. These investigators set out to replicate under more controlled conditions the findings of a previous study in which 12 agoraphobic patients were successfully treated with a home-based programmed-practice approach involving graded in vivo exposure to feared situations, with assistance and social reinforcement provided by the patient's spouse or some other significant person. As a comparison treatment, the investigators decided to use an approach that would enable them to establish whether exposure to the feared situations is an essential component of the treatment of agoraphobia. The treatment they employed for this purpose was a problem-solving approach involving the identification of relevant life problems and stresses and the discovery of ways of solving or reducing them.

The subjects were 28 agoraphobic patients, who were randomly assigned to the two treatment conditions and to one of two therapists. Each therapist treated seven patients in each treatment condition. Treatment was carried out in the home for a three-week period. In both treatments, the patient's partner was actively involved in planning treatment targets and reinforcing progress. In the programmed-practice condition, patients were instructed in the use of the graded-exposure method and asked to practice going out for at least an hour each day. In the problem-solving condition, patients were instructed to keep a daily record of life problems and stresses and taught how to set problem-solving targets and deal with them. The patients and their partners were instructed to discuss relevant problems and stresses for at least an hour each day. The partners were instructed in how to assist the patients in solving these problems and reinforcing their attempts at doing so.

Dependent measures included ratings of phobic severity and anxiety by an independent assessor and by the patients themselves, and daily measures of time away from home and number of journeys made. Assessments were made before and after treatment and at three- and six-month follow-ups. On the measure of phobic severity, both the assessor's ratings and the patient's ratings showed significant decreases after treatment for both treatment conditions, with improvement continuing in both conditions during the follow-up period. Although improvement was significantly greater for the programmed-practice treatment at the three-month follow-up, there was no longer a significant difference at the six-month follow-up, indicating that the problem-solving group continued to improve at a faster rate. On both the assessor's and the patient's ratings of anxiety, both treatment conditions showed a significant decrease at the end of treatment, which continued during the follow-up period so that at the six-month assessment both groups showed only mild anxiety. There were no significant differences between treatment conditions.

On the measure of average time away from home each week, the programmed-practice group reported a greater number of hours per week at the end of treatment than the problem-solving group, but the difference was not significant. (It should be noted that the programmed-practice subjects were asked to go out daily as part of their treatment, whereas the problem-solving subjects were not.) However, an unexpected finding was that the scores of the programmed-practice group *decreased* slightly between the three- and six-month follow-ups, while the problem-solving group reported an *increase* in time away from home during this period. The same pattern of results was found on the measure of average number of journeys per week.

The above results show that by the six-month follow-up, problem solving and programmed practice were equally effective in reducing anxiety and phobic severity. Moreover, there appeared to be a greater tendency for the problem-solving group to continue to improve during the follow-up period. These findings indicate that a treatment aimed at coping more effectively with life's problems and stresses can be effective for agoraphobia and might even result in better long-term maintenance effects.

Stress and Ineffective Coping

Several PST studies have focused on programs that had goals of reducing stress and anxiety, enhancing general coping effectiveness, and preventing maladaptive behavior. Although several of the studies that focus on positive competence enhancement do not include any measures of adjustment or psychopathology, they are included here because of the relevance and potential utility of these programs for prevention.

Ewart, Taylor, Kraemer, and Agras (1984) studied the effects of a communication/problem-solving training procedure on the blood pressure reactivity of hypertensive patients during marital problem-solving discussions in a laboratory setting. Twenty hypertensive patients seeking stress-management treatment were randomly assigned to a communication/problem-solving group or a no-treatment control group. The results showed that subjects who mastered reflective problem-solving techniques engaged in fewer hostile exchanges compared to no-treatment controls, and also showed a significantly greater reduction in blood pressure. Similar results were found in a previous study by Ewart, Burnett, and Taylor (1983), which used an A-B-A-B design to study two hypertensive males during problem-solving discussions with their spouses.

Moon and Eisler (1983) compared the effectiveness of three behaviorally oriented treatments for anger control. They randomly
assigned 40 male undergraduates who scored above the mean on an
anger inventory to the following groups: (a) stress inoculation (SI),
(b) problem-solving training (PST), (c) social-skills training (SST),
and (d) a minimal-attention control (MA). In this study, SI focused
on the use of neutral or rational coping self-statements, PST was
based on the D'Zurilla and Goldfried (1971) social problem-solving
model, and SST focused on assertive training. All treatment groups
received training on a weekly basis over a five-week period. The
primary assessment method was a role-playing procedure focusing
on anger-provoking situations. The measures obtained using this
procedure included self-reported anger, assertion, and aggression.
In addition, subjects were asked to monitor their responses to real-
life anger-provoking situations. The results showed that SI significantly decreased anger-provoking cognitions when compared to the
MA group, but did not increase appropriate assertiveness, whereas
PST and SST both significantly reduced anger-provoking cognitions
and increased assertive or socially skilled behaviors. According to
the investigators, the data suggests that PST and SST facilitate
effective interactions with the environment, whereas SI tends to
foster withdrawal from anger-provoking situations.

Tableman, Marciniak, Johnson, and Rodgers (1982) assessed the
effectiveness of a Stress Management Training Project (SMTP) for
low-income women supported by public assistance. The objectives of
the program were to help the women (a) feel better about themselves, (b) accept responsibility, (c) take control of their lives, and (d)
handle stress more effectively. Training was conducted in groups of
six to twelve women for 10 weekly sessions lasting 1½ to 3 hours.
The program was characterized as providing training in four component coping skills: (a) belief in one's power and potential (problem-orientation cognitions); (b) life planning (setting and working
toward life goals); (c) problem-solving aimed at changing the negative aspects of one's life; and (d) specific techniques for reducing
stress generated by unplanned or uncontrollable events. Over a
two-year period, complete data were obtained from 39 women who
attended 7 to 10 training sessions (experimental subjects) and 35
subjects who attended no sessions (control subjects). Pretest data
were collected within 30 days before the first session and posttest
data were collected 3½ months after the last session. The results
showed that the experimental subjects improved significantly more
than the control group subjects on psychological tests measuring
general psychological distress, depression, anxiety, inadequacy,

self-confidence, and ego strength. Although no follow-up was reported and there were no measures of coping performance or competence, the SMTP represents an important step toward primary prevention with one particular "vulnerable" population.

Petty, Moeller, and Campbell (1976) developed a community-based support group program for elderly persons experiencing moderate stress and anxiety as a result of the aging process. Participants were 30 people (26 women and 4 men) in four support groups, with 6 to 9 persons in each group. The members ranged in age from 62 to 85 years. Structured as informal workshops, the group program involved 10 two-hour sessions, consisting of two 45-minute group problem-solving discussions separated by a refreshment break. The sessions focused on specific problems related to aging, which were generated by the group members themselves, including problems related to memory, vision and hearing, interpersonal relationships (e.g., asking family members to meet their needs), health management (e.g., asking for clarification of health problems from physicians), death and loss, and housing and relocation. These problem-solving discussions emphasized "brainstorming" principles (generating as many solution ideas as possible, suspending judgment, generating a variety of different solution ideas). A pre- and posttest questionnaire was administered which assessed attitudes about aging and current life activities. In general, the questionnaire results suggested that group members had become more adept at both analyzing specific antecedents of physical and psychological discomfort and at adopting new coping behaviors to deal more effectively with these concerns. Although the Petty, Moeller, and Campbell study is an uncontrolled case study, it is another important step toward a potentially useful prevention program for a vulnerable population in our society.

Another workshop designed to improve the problem-solving effectiveness of senior citizens was developed by Toseland (1977). The workshop provided training in the following problem-solving skills: (a) problem definition; (b) evaluation of thoughts and feelings concerning the particular problematic situation; (c) explication of the desired emotion, behavior, and consequences for the problematic situation; (d) generation of alternative solutions; (e) decision making; and (f) practice in solution implementation. Although the workshop emphasized training in general problem-solving skills, the content of the group meetings focused on stressful problematic situations requiring assertive behavior, such as confrontation, turning down unreasonable requests, and giving negative feedback. Six volunteers from a senior citizen center participated in the six-session workshop. Dependent measures included a self-report assertiveness scale and a problem-solving performance test involving the role playing of responses to assertion situations. These measures were administered one week before and after training. The results showed significant pretest-posttest improvement on both measures.

In addition to the above stress-reduction programs, PST is also considered to be an important component in the stress-inoculation programs of Meichenbaum and Cameron (1983) and Novaco (1979). Stress inoculation is a multicomponent stress-management approach, which involves training in a variety of coping skills, including cognitive skills, emotion-focused skills, and instrumental skills. The PST component emphasizes the adoption of a positive problem-solving "set" and training in problem definition, the generation of alternative solutions, anticipation of consequences, and the evaluation of alternatives. Support for the stress inoculation approach has been provided in a number of studies (Meichenbaum & Jaremko, 1983; Novaco, 1979). However, the specific contribution of the PST component is not known at the present time.

Christoff, Scott, Kelley, Schlundt, Baer, and Kelly (1985) evaluated the effectiveness of a group training program for shy young adolescents. The program had two components: (a) training in problem-solving skills and (b) training in social performance skills (conversational skills). The subjects were four adolescents ranging in age from 12 to 14 years who were referred to the training program because they were socially withdrawn and lacking in social skills. Using a multiple baseline design, problem-solving training (PST) was conducted in four sessions, followed by four sessions of social-skills training (SST). The major dependent measures were a MEPS-type problem-solving test, focusing on the number of relevant means and a global effectiveness rating, and an observational conversation skills measure. These measures were administered during four baseline sessions and at the end of each training session. Additional measures used to assess generalization effects included a self-observational measure of the frequency of social interactions, a self-report measure of social interaction skills, and a self-esteem scale.

The results showed that PST resulted in a significant increase in both problem-solving skills and specific conversational skills. The introduction of SST produced further improvement in conversational skills. Moreover, the training program resulted in significant increases on the two measures of social interaction, and an increase on the self-esteem scale that approached significance. All improvements were maintained at a five-month follow-up assessment.

Sarason and Sarason (1981) evaluated a problem-solving training program for high school students, which used modeling and role-playing to demonstrate both problem-solving cognitions and effective coping behavior for specific problematic situations relevant to teenagers. The subjects were 127 students from a high school with high dropout and delinquency rates. The study was conducted within the context of the regular high school health course. Subjects were divided into two groups: an experimental group, which received the training program in 13 class sessions, and a control group, which received no special training. The problem-solving cognitions focused on during training included perceiving a problem from another person's viewpoint, considering probable consequences of one's actions, and thinking of several alternatives before acting. The dependent measures included a MEPS-type problem-solving test, a generation-of-alternatives test, and ratings of behavioral effectiveness during a job interview situation conducted several months after the training program.

The results showed that the experimental group performed significantly better than the control group on both problem-solving tests and was rated more effective in the job interview situation. During a one-year follow-up period, the experimental group also had lower rates of tardiness and fewer absences and problem behavior referrals.

Schinke, Blythe, and Gilchrist (1981) evaluated a small group training program with high school students aimed at the prevention of adolescent pregnancy. The subjects were 36 high school sophomores, who were assigned to a no-training condition or a group training condition in which subjects received contraceptive information, instruction in problem-solving skills, and practice in communicating decisions to others about sexual behavior. Compared to the control subjects, the subjects who received the training showed more positive posttest scores on measures of sexual knowledge and interpersonal problem solving. At a six-month follow-up, the trained subjects had better attitudes toward family planning and were practicing more effective contraception.

Dixon, Heppner, Petersen, and Ronning (1979) assessed the effects of an intensive problem-solving workshop with college student volunteers. The subjects, 50 undergraduates, were randomly assigned to three groups: a PST group, a pretest-posttest control group, and a posttest-only control group. PST was conducted in five, 1½-hour group sessions consisting of didactic presentations, group discussions and directed practice. Homework assignments were also given, which were designed to facilitate generalization and transfer of skills beyond the workshop setting.

The major dependent measure was a problem-solving test consisting of a generation-of-alternatives subtest and a choice-behavior subtest. Another measure was a self-report problem-solving inventory which assessed the subjects' appraisal of their problem-solving skills. The results for the generation-of-alternatives subtest showed that the problem-solving group and the pretest-posttest control group increased equally in the *quantity* of solution alternatives produced, but that the problem-solving group improved significantly more on scores related to the *quality* of alternatives. The brief opportunity to practice generating alternatives on the pretest seemed to be sufficient to produce a significant increase in the number of alternatives generated in the pretest-posttest group; however, more intensive PST was required to produce a significant improvement in the quality of solution ideas. No significant results were found for the choice-behavior subtest. The results for the self-report problem-solving inventory showed that the problem-solving group performed significantly better than the combined control groups, with the difference resulting primarily from the subjects' report of less impulsivity in problem-solving situations.

In an outcome study referred to earlier, Heppner et al. (1983) evaluated a prevention-oriented PST program for college students with problem-solving deficits. Subjects were obtained from a group of students enrolled in a large introductory psychology class on the basis of their scores on the Problem-Solving Inventory (PSI) (Heppner & Petersen, 1982). These subjects were randomly assigned to the PST group or a delayed treatment control group. Training was conducted in eight weekly 1½-hour sessions. A follow-up evaluation was held after one year. Dependent measures included the PSI, a comprehensive problem checklist, a self-assessment measure of problem-solving skills, and a measure of coping. Following training, the subjects in the PST group, compared to the control subjects, reported fewer problems on the problem checklist, more problem-solving confidence, a greater tendency to approach rather than avoid problems, and a more favorable self-assessment of their problem-solving skills. These gains held up at the one-year follow-up evaluation.

Sidney Parnes's (Parnes et al., 1977) creative problem-solving program at the State University College at Buffalo has been referred to a number of times in this book. This program has been emphasized because of its potential value for prevention. Parnes and Noller (1973) have conducted an extensive two-year evaluation of the program, which was given as a four-semester curriculum of creative problem-solving courses. Entering college freshmen were invited to take the curriculum as an elective and about 350 accepted. From this group of applicants, 150 were randomly assigned to an experimental group, which took the creative problem-solving courses, and another 150 were assigned to a control group, which did not take any of these courses.

A variety of outcome measures were obtained at the beginning of the program and at intervals during the two years. Among these measures were: (a) tests of cognitive abilities based on Guilford's Structure-of-Intellect (SI) model; (b) a test of problem-solving (coping) performance based on Goldfried and D'Zurilla's (1969) competence-assessment model; (c) self-ratings of problem-solving performance and confidence; (d) several personality scales; and (e) a measure of nonacademic achievement (e.g., leadership, social service, business, art). Results over the two-year period showed significantly greater gains for the experimental group than for the control group on a number of SI tests of ability, including tests related to the operations of *divergent production, convergent production,* and *cognition.* With regard to *content,* the significant gains were mostly on tests involving semantic and behavioral information, which are the content categories most closely related to social problem solving. Experimental subjects also rated themselves significantly higher on self-confidence and ability to solve real-life problems, and showed significantly greater improvement on the problem-solving performance test. Although there were no significant group differences on the personality scales, differences were found in the expected direction on 10 out of 10 scales that were predicted before the data analysis to most likely reflect differences in growth as a result of the program. On the measure of nonacademic achievement, the experimental subjects showed a tendency to surpass the control subjects, but the differences were not significant. However, it was noted that the accomplishments assessed by this measure take considerable time and effort. Since the subjects were only college juniors after the two-year program, the potential effects in this area may not have had sufficient time or opportunity to develop.

The above results indicate that Parnes's PST program significantly enhances basic problem-solving abilities as well as an individual's confidence in his ability to deal more effectively with life's problems. The results also suggest that these gains in ability and confidence tend to translate into improvements in problem-solving performance and competence. These results support the view that Parnes's program should be examined for its potential efficacy as a prevention program for populations who show deficiencies in problem-solving performance and competence.

Community Problems

All of the studies reviewed above focused on the problems of individuals, couples, or small groups. PST may also have a useful application in community psychology to increase the effectiveness of special groups or committees in solving problems confronting entire communities (for example, crime, air pollution, inadequate services, unemployment, and racial conflict). The members of such problem-solving groups might include volunteers from the community, elected officials, supervisors, employees, and management or administrative personnel. Community problem-solving groups might also include committees from various professional and special interest organizations (for example, lawyers, doctors, psychologists, trade unions) who are charged with the responsibility of attempting to find solutions to problems facing the organization.

One study evaluating PST for a community-based problem-solving group was conducted by Briscoe, Hoffman, and Bailey (1975). The study focused on a policy-making board from a university-sponsored rural community project. The nine board members were elected representatives from the community. The responsibilities of the board included the identification and resolution of community problems and the administration of a $20,000 budget for community projects. Earlier assessment of the board's activities found that its problem-solving attempts were unsystematic and relatively unsuccessful. In order to remedy this, three problem-solving steps were identified for training: (1) problem identification and isolation; (2) generation and evaluation of alternative solutions; and (3) selection of a solution with concomitant plans for its implementation. A multiple-baseline design across subjects and skills was used. Seven of the nine board members received individual training in the problem-solving skills; the remaining two served as control subjects and received no training. Training methods included prompting, modeling, fading, role playing, and social reinforcement. The major outcome measure was verbal problem-solving behavior based on an analysis of videotapes of board meetings. The verbal statements of board members were judged by two university professors who taught problem-solving courses and by two active community leaders.

The results for both group and individual data generally showed increases in the use of key problem-solving statements following training in the relevant skill. Follow-up assessments of one week to two months following training in each skill indicated that although the positive changes were not always maintained at a high level, they consistently remained higher than baseline. The two control subjects did not show any changes in the quality of their problem-solving statements.

Summary and Conclusions

PST outcome studies have focused on a wide variety of target populations, ranging from hospitalized psychiatric patients to normal individuals and groups interested in maximizing their general problem-solving effectiveness. Taken together, the results of these studies have produced very promising results, which contribute support for the use of PST as a clinical intervention approach for a variety of clinical problems. In addition, there are results which show that PST can be useful for prevention and for enhancing the effectiveness of community problem-solving groups. However, although the overall results are very encouraging, some of the studies have methodological problems, which preclude definition conclusions about the efficacy of PST in these particular studies.

A problem in some of the studies is that PST is conducted as part of a treatment package that includes other treatment techniques. It is not possible to isolate the specific effects of PST in these studies. A second problem is that a few studies do not include the necessary controls to account for the effects of extraneous variables (e.g., time, intercurrent life experiences) on behavior change. A third problem is the failure in most studies to include procedures to account for the effects of nonspecific factors associated with treatment. In other studies, such procedures have included attention-placebo control groups and ratings to assess client expectations of benefit. However,

O'Leary and Borkovec (1978) have questioned the use of attention-placebo groups in therapy outcome research on conceptual, methodological, and ethical grounds. These authors have suggested alternative procedures for controlling for attention-placebo effects. It has also been argued that placebo factors are an inherent part of psychological treatment and need not be controlled for in outcome research (Wilkins, 1984). However, despite the appeal of this argument, a minimum requirement when two or more treatments are being compared should be to obtain ratings of expectations of benefit during the early phase of treatment in order to rule out the possibility that the superiority of one treatment over another was due primarily to the fact that the treatment generated more favorable client outcome expectations.

A fourth methodological problem is that some studies failed to include any measures of social problem solving among the outcome measures used. Without these measures, it is not possible to determine whether the training program achieved its major immediate objective of improving problem-solving ability or performance, a result that would have helped to support the conclusion that PST, rather than attention-placebo factors, was primarily responsible for the positive changes in adjustment. A fifth problem is that some studies used a problem-solving outcome measure only, without including any measures of adjustment, psychopathology, or maladaptive behavior. The failure to include these measures reduces the clinical significance of the findings. Finally, some studies failed to include any follow-up evaluations. Without a follow-up, the question of the durability of treatment effects cannot be answered.

In addition to the limitations resulting from the above methodological problems, definite conclusions are not possible for a few target populations because only one outcome study has been reported thus far (e.g., for agoraphobia). These studies must be replicated before conclusions about the efficacy of PST for these particular target populations can be made with confidence.

Although the evidence from some studies is limited and inconclusive at the present time, the consistency with which positive treatment effects have been found with programs involving PST argues strongly for the efficacy of this approach as a clinical intervention strategy for a variety of different clinical problems. The evidence indicates that PST contributes not only to immediate treatment effects, but to the maintenance of treatment effects as well. The maintenance effects have been particularly impressive with weight-control problems. In addition, the results of studies focusing on prevention-oriented programs in nonclinical community settings suggest that PST is also effective in reducing stress effects and enhancing personal-social effectiveness among various vulnerable or at-risk groups in the community. Finally, the results of one study strongly suggest that PST can also be useful in enhancing the problem-solving effectiveness of community policy-making groups, which has important implications for community psychology.

Concluding Commentary

In this book a problem-solving approach to clinical intervention was presented which has important implications not only for treatment, but also for the generalization and maintenance of treatment gains and for prevention. The theoretical basis for this approach is a prescriptive model of social problem solving, which has five components: (a) problem orientation (problem-solving cognitive set); (b) problem definition and formulation; (c) generation of alternative solutions; (d) decision making; and (e) solution implementation and verification. Empirical studies were reported that provide support for the model's five components. Studies were also reported that provide support for the hypothesis that a relationship exists between social problem solving and adjustment. The important role of emotions in social problem solving was discussed and various approaches to the assessment of social problem-solving skills were described. An important issue in assessment is the distinction between problem-solving ability and problem-solving performance. The former refers to the knowledge or possession of requisite problem-solving skills (i.e., the problem-solving *process*), whereas the latter refers to the application of these skills to a particular problem (i.e., the problem-solving *product*).

A transactional/problem-solving model of stress was presented which argues for the potential efficacy of problem-solving training (PST) as a stress-management approach. A specific PST program was described that may serve as a model for PST as a treatment method, a treatment maintenance strategy, or a prevention program with goals of increasing social competence and reducing stress. Outcome studies on PST have focused on a variety of different target populations and program goals. Although there are methodological problems in some of these studies that limit the conclusions that can be drawn, the consistency with which impressive results have been reported in programs employing PST argues strongly for its efficacy.

Future Directions

There are several important areas for future research on PST. In the area of treatment, PST seems to be a particularly appropriate treatment for stress-related disorders and depression because of the possible important role of perceived uncontrollability in the etiology and/or maintenance of these disorders (Abramson et al., 1978; Hamberger & Lohr, 1984). More outcome studies are needed which focus on these disorders. In the area of maintenance, the impressive results reported in studies on weight control and cigarette smoking suggest that PST might be useful as a maintenance strategy in the treatment of other disorders as well. This possibility should be explored in future studies. A promising direction in the mental health field today is primary and secondary prevention, focusing on competence enhancement (Felner, Jason, Moritsugu, & Farber, 1983; Wine & Smye, 1981). The potential utility of PST as a model for competence-enhancement-oriented prevention programs should be investigated further (Heppner, Neal, & Larson, 1984; Durlak, 1983). Studies in this area have produced very promising results, but most of them have been uncontrolled case studies. In order to facilitate research in the above areas, more comprehensive, reliable, and valid assessment measures of social problem-solving ability and performance are badly needed. Finally, continued research is needed on the social problem-solving model itself. As more is learned about the specific abilities required for effective social problem solving, the model can be modified and improved which, in turn, will lead to refinements and improvements in PST programs.

Cautions and Conclusions

Before ending the discussion of PST as a clinical intervention approach, a few cautions are in order. One concerns the danger of failing to recognize when other intervention methods are necessary or more appropriate for a particular case. A second caution refers to the dangers of viewing PST primarily as a "rational" or "intellectual" form of therapy, instead of viewing it as an active coping process involving an interaction of cognitive, behavioral, and emotional variables. A third caution, which is somewhat related to the second, concerns the danger of failing to recognize that a positive therapeutic relationship is important for the success of PST as a clinical intervention method.

It was argued in this book that most, if not all, clients are likely to benefit from conducting therapy within an overall PST framework, where a concerted effort is made to teach clients general skills that will enable them to assess and cope more independently and effectively with their own problems. However, within this overall framework, the amount of emphasis on training in problem-solving skills will vary across clients and therapy sessions, depending on the needs of the particular client. The therapist must possess the clinical skills to recognize when it is important to deviate from PST procedures in order to apply some other intervention strategy or technique which may be necessary for the effective management of a particular case. At some point in therapy, it may be necessary for the therapist to deal *directly* with an immediate problem involving particularly difficult or severe environmental conditions, emotional reactions, or maladaptive behaviors which cannot be handled adequately by the client through independent problem solving alone. For example, a highly anxious client may require immediate relaxation training before other methods can be applied effectively, an agoraphobic client may require a series of in vivo exposure sessions in order to facilitate fear reduction, and a depressed client may require intensive cognitive restructuring, social-skills training, or marital communication training in order to achieve a sense of mastery or control.

Social problem solving has been described in this book as an active coping process involving an interaction between cognitive, behavioral, and emotional variables. The danger in viewing PST primarily as a "rational" or "intellectual" therapy is that the important role of behavioral and emotional factors in social problem solving may be neglected. Important behavioral variables include actively seeking information about the problem, actively experimenting with options, and actively self-monitoring to evaluate the solution outcome. In order to facilitate problem-solving effectiveness, emotional factors must be taken into account when setting goals, evaluating solution alternatives, and evaluating solution outcome. In addition, it is often necessary to control intense emotional arousal in order to facilitate problem-solving efficiency. If these behavioral and emotional variables are ignored in PST, then problem solving may become a mere intellectual exercise, which may result in the failure to achieve the real therapeutic effects of improvement in coping actively with real-life problems and stresses.

Subjective and emotional factors also play an important role in the development of a positive therapeutic relationship. A therapeutic relationship characterized by such factors as warmth, empathy, genuineness, and support is important for the success of any psychological treatment, and PST is no exception. Some clients enter therapy with little faith in the particular treatment, or in any psychological treatment. Some clients lack the commitment to change, for various reasons. Some are actually afraid to change or try out new behaviors. Because of these factors, clients may show resistance to PST requirements in a number of different ways (see Goldfried, 1982). A positive therapeutic relationship will help to overcome these resistance problems. If the variables associated with a positive therapeutic relationship are neglected, then therapeutic success will be limited.

In conclusion, PST appears to be a useful and effective intervention strategy for a variety of clinical problems, particularly in cases where the treatment goals include an increase in *independence and general competence* (effectiveness in coping independently with a variety of life problems and stresses). Such cases are likely to include clinical problems ranging from the more severe disorders, such as schizophrenia, to the relatively minor maladjustments, such as academic underachievement. PST is likely to be particularly appropriate and useful in cases where a core problem is a generalized feeling or perception of uncontrollability. This is often the case with anxiety disorders, depressive disorders, and other stress-related disorders. In addition to its use as a treatment strategy, PST is likely to be useful as a maintenance strategy following treatment, and as a prevention strategy in community psychology programs focusing on vulnerable or at-risk populations, such as the elderly or adolescents experiencing adjustment difficulties. I would like to close this discussion by referring the reader once again to the quote by Mahoney (1974) concerning the promise of problem solving for therapy: "In terms of adaptive versatility and the ability to cope with an ever-changing array of life problems, these cognitive skills may offer an invaluable personal paradigm for survival." Since this statement was published in 1974, there has been significant progress toward the fulfillment of this promise.

References

Abramson, L. Y., Seligman, M. E. P., & Teasdale, J. D. (1978). Learned helplessness in humans: Critique and reformulation. *Journal of Abnormal Psychology, 87,* 49–74.

Appel, P. W., & Kaestner, E. (1979). Interpersonal and emotional problem solving among narcotic drug abusers. *Journal of Consulting and Clinical Psychology, 47,* 1125–1127.

Azar, S. T., Robinson, D. R., Hekimian, E., & Twentyman, C. T. (1984). Unrealistic expectations and problem-solving ability in maltreating and comparison mothers. *Journal of Consulting and Clinical Psychology, 52,* 687–691.

Baddeley, A. D. (1972). Selective attention and performance in dangerous environments. *British Journal of Psychology, 63,* 537–546.

Badia, P., Suter, S., & Lewis, P. (1967). Preferences for warned shock: Information and/or preparation. *Psychological Reports, 20,* 271–274.

Bandura, A. (1971). Vicarious and self-reinforcement process. In R. Glasner (Ed.), *The nature of reinforcement.* New York: Academic Press.

Bandura, A. (1977). Self-efficacy: Toward a unifying theory of behavioral change. *Psychological Review, 84,* 191–215.

Bandura, A. (1980). Gauging the relationship between self-efficacy judgment and action. *Cognitive Therapy and Research, 4,* 263–268.

Barlow, D. H. (Ed.). (1981). *Behavioral assessment of adult disorders.* New York: Guilford.

Barlow, D. H., Hayes, S. C., & Nelson, R. O. (1984). *The scientist practitioner: Research and accountability in clinical and educational settings.* New York: Pergamon.

Baumgardner, A. H., Heppner, P. P., & Arkin, R. M. (August 1983). *Perceived problem solving effectiveness: Relationship to causal attribution for interpersonal and intrapersonal problems.* Paper presented at the 91st Annual Convention of the American Psychological Association, Anaheim, California.

Baumgardner, P., Heppner, P. P., & Arkin, R. M. (August 1984). *The role of causal attribution in personal problem solving.* Paper presented at the 92nd Annual Convention of the American Psychological Association, Toronto.

Bayless, O. L. (1967). An alternative pattern for problem-solving discussion. *Journal of Communication, 17,* 188–197.

Beach, L. R., & Mitchell, T. R. (1978). A contingency model for the selection of decision strategies. *Academy of Management Review, 3,* 439–449.

Beck, A. T. (1967). *Depression.* New York: Hoeber.

Beck, A. T. (1970). Cognitive therapy: Nature and relation to behavior therapy. *Behavior Therapy, 1,* 184–200.

Bedell, J. R., Archer, R. P., & Marlowe, H. A., Jr. (1980). A description and evaluation of a problem solving skills training program. In D. Upper & S. M. Ross (Eds.), *Behavioral group therapy: An annual review.* Champaign, IL: Research Press.

Beech, W. R., Burns, L. E., & Sheffield, B. F. (1982). *A behavioural approach to the management of stress: A practical guide to techniques.* New York: Wiley.

Bellack, A. S. (1979). A critical appraisal of strategies for assessing social skills. *Behavioral Assessment, 1,* 157–176.

Bellack, A. S., & Hersen, M. (1977). Self-report inventories in behavioral assessment. In J. D. Cone & R. P. Hawkins (Eds.), *Behavioral assessment: New directions in clinical psychology.* New York: Brunner/Mazel.

Bernstein, D. A., & Borkovec, T. D. (1973). *Progressive relaxation training: A manual for the helping professions.* Champaign, IL: Research Press.

Black, D. R. (in press). A minimal intervention program and a problem-solving program for weight control. *Cognitive Therapy and Research.*

Black, D. R., & Scherba, D. S. (1983). Contracting to problem solve versus contracting to practice behavioral weight loss skills. *Behavior Therapy, 14,* 100–109.

Black, D. R., & Threlfall, W. E. (1986). A stepped approach to weight control: A minimal intervention and a bibliotherapy problem-solving program. *Behavior Therapy, 17,* 144–157.

Bloom, B. S., & Broder, L. J. (1950). *Problem-solving processes of college students.* Chicago: University of Chicago Press.

Brilhart, J. K., & Jochem, L. M. (1964). Effects of different patterns on outcome of problem-solving discussion. *Journal of Applied Psychology, 48,* 175–179.

Briscoe, R. V., Hoffman, D. B., & Bailey, J. S. (1975). Behavioral community psychology: Training a community board to problem solve. *Journal of Applied Behavioral Analysis, 8,* 157–168.

Butler, L., & Meichenbaum, D. (1981). The assessment of interpersonal problem-solving skills. In P. C. Kendall & S. D. Hollon (Eds.), *Assessment strategies for cognitive-behavioral interventions.* New York: Academic Press.

Carver, C. S., & Scheier, M. F. (1982). Control theory: A useful conceptual framework for personality-social, clinical, and health psychology. *Psychological Bulletin, 92,* 111–135.

Chaney, E. F., O'Leary, M. R., & Marlatt, G. A. (1978). Skill training with alcoholics. *Journal of Consulting and Clinical Psychology, 46,* 1092–1104.

Christoff, K. A., Scott, W. O. N., Kelley, M. L., Schlundt, D., Baer, G., & Kelly, J. A. (1985). Social skills and social problem-solving training for shy young adolescents. *Behavior Therapy, 16,* 468–477.

Ciminero, A. R., Calhoun, K. S., & Adams, H. E. (Eds.). (1977). *Handbook of behavioral assessment.* New York: Wiley-Interscience.

Claerhout, S., Elder, J., & Janes, C. (1982). Problem-solving skills of rural battered women. *American Journal of Community Psychology, 10,* 605–612.

Coché, E. (1985). Problem-solving training: A cognitive group therapy modality. In A. Freeman & V. Greenwood (Eds.), *Cognitive therapy: Applications in psychiatric and medical settings.* New York: Human Sciences Press.

Coché, E., Cooper, J. B., Petermann, K. J. (1984). Differential outcomes of cognitive and interactional group therapies. *Small Group Behavior, 15,* 497–509.

Coché, E., & Douglas, A. A. (1977). Therapeutic effects of problem-solving training and play-reading groups. *Journal of Clinical Psychology, 33,* 820–827.

Coché, E., & Flick, A. (1975). Problem solving training groups for hospitalized psychiatric patients. *Journal of Psychology, 91,* 19–29.

Cone, J. D., & Hawkins, R. P. (Eds.). (1977). *Behavioral assessment: New directions in clinical psychology.* New York: Brunner/Mazel.

Corah, N. C., & Boffa, J. (1970). Perceived control, self-observation, and response to aversive stimulation. *Journal of Personality and Social Psychology, 16,* 1–4.

Cormier, W. H., Otani, A., & Cormier, S. (1986). The effects of problem-solving training on two problem-solving tasks. *Cognitive Therapy and Research, 10,* 95–108.

Coyne, J. C., Aldwin, C., & Lazarus, R. S. (1981). Depression and coping in stressful episodes. *Journal of Abnormal Psychology, 90,* 439–447.

Davis, M., Robbins Eshelmann, E., & McKay, M. (1982). *The relaxation and stress reduction workbook* (2nd. ed.). Oakland, CA: New Harbinger.

DeLongis, A., Coyne, J. C., Dakof, G., Folkman, S., & Lazarus, R. S. (1982). Relationship of daily hassles, uplifts, and major life events to health status. *Health Psychology, 1,* 119–136.

Dixon, D. N., Heppner, P. P., Petersen, C. H., & Ronning, R. R. (1979). Problem-solving workshop training. *Journal of Counseling Psychology, 26,* 133–139.

Dobson, D. J., & Dobson, K. S. (1981). Problem-solving strategies in depressed and nondepressed college students. *Cognitive Therapy and Research, 5,* 237–249.

Doerfler, L. A., Mullins, L. L., Griffin, N. J., Siegel, L. J., & Richards, C. S. (1984). Problem-solving deficits in depressed children, adolescents, and adults. *Cognitive Therapy and Research, 8,* 489–499.

Doerfler, L. A., & Richards, C. S. (1981). Self-initiated attempts to cope with depression. *Cognitive Therapy and Research, 5,* 367–371.

Douglass, M. E., & Douglass, D. N. (1980). *Manage your time, manage your work, manage yourself.* New York: AMACOM.

Durlak, J. A. (1983). Social problem-solving as a primary prevention strategy. In R. D. Felner, L. A. Jason, J. N. Moritsugu, & S. S. Farber (Eds.), *Preventive psychology: Theory, research, and practice.* New York: Pergamon.

D'Zurilla, T. J., & Goldfried, M. R. (1971). Problem solving and behavior modification. *Journal of Abnormal Psychology, 78,* 107–126.

D'Zurilla, T. J., & Nezu, A. (1980). A study of the generation-of-alternatives process in social problem solving. *Cognitive Therapy and Research, 4,* 67–72.

D'Zurilla, T. J., & Nezu, A. (1982). Social problem solving in adults. In P. C. Kendall (Ed.), *Advances in cognitive-behavioral research and therapy* (Vol. 1). New York: Academic Press.

Easterbrook, J. A. (1959). The effect of emotion on cue utilization and the organization of behavior. *Psychological Review, 66,* 183–201.

Edelstein, B. A., Couture, E. T., Cray, M., Dickens, P., & Lusebrink, N. (1980). Group training of problem-solving with chronic psychiatric patients. In D. Upper & S. Ross (Eds.), *Behavioral group therapy: An annual review* (Vol. 2). Champaign, IL: Research Press.

Edwards, W. (1954). The theory of decision making. *Psychological Bulletin, 51,* 380–417.

Edwards, W. (1961). Behavioral decision theory. *Annual Review of Psychology, 12,* 473–498.

Ellis, A. (1962). *Reason and emotion in psychotherapy.* New York: Lyle Stuart.

Ellis, A. (1977). The basic clinical theory of rational-emotive therapy. In A. Ellis & R. Grieger (Eds.), *Handbook of rational-emotive therapy.* New York: Springer.

Ellis, A., & Grieger, R. (Eds.) (1977). *Handbook of rational-emotive therapy.* New York: Springer Publishing Company.

Ellis, A., & Harper, R. A. (1975). *A new guide to rational living.* Englewood Cliffs, NJ: Prentice-Hall.

Epstein, S. (1982). Conflict and stress. In L. Goldberger and S. Breznitz (Eds.), *Handbook of stress: Theoretical and clinical aspects.* New York: Free Press.

Epstein, S. (1983). Natural healing processes of the mind: Graded stress inoculation as an inherent coping mechanism. In D. Meichenbaum & M. E. Jaremko (Eds.), *Stress reduction and prevention.* New York: Plenum.

Ewart, C. K., Burnett, K. F., & Taylor, C. B. (1983). Communication behaviors that affect blood pressure: An A-B-A-B analysis of marital interaction. *Behavior Modification, 7,* 331–344.

Ewart, C. K., Taylor, C. B., Kraemer, H. C., & Agras, W. S. (1984). Reducing blood pressure reactivity during interpersonal conflict: Effects of marital communication training. *Behavior Therapy, 15,* 473–484.

Felner, R. D., Jason, L. A., Moritsugu, J. N., & Farber, S. S. (1983). *Preventive psychology: Theory, research and practice.* New York: Pergamon.

Folkman, S., & Lazarus, R. S. (1984). If it changes it must be a process: A study of emotion and coping during three stages of a college examination. *Journal of Personality and Social Psychology, 48,* 150–170.

Folkman, S., Lazarus, R. S., Dunkel-Schetter, C., DeLongis, A., & Gruen, R. (in press). The dynamics of a stressful encounter: Cognitive appraisal, coping, and encounter outcomes. *Journal of Personality and Social Psychology.*

Foster, S. L., Prinz, R. J., & O'Leary, K. D. (1983). Impact of problem-solving communication training and generalization procedures on family conflict. *Child and Family Behavior Therapy, 5,* 1–23.

Freedman, B. I., Rosenthal, L., Donahoe, C. P., Schlundt, D. G., & McFall, R. M. (1978). A social-behavioral analysis of skill deficits in delinquent and non-delinquent adolescent boys. *Journal of Consulting and Clinical Psychology, 46,* 1448–1462.

Gagné, R. M. (1966). Human problem solving: Internal and external events. In B. Kleinmuntz (Ed.), *Problem solving: Research, method and theory.* New York: Wiley.

Geer, J. H., Davison, G. C., Gatchel, R. I. (1970). Reduction of stress in humans through nonveridical perceived control of aversive stimulation. *Journal of Personality and Social Psychology, 30,* 30–43.

George, A. L. (1974). Adaptation to stress in political decision making: The individual, small group, and organizational contexts. In G. V. Coelho, D. A. Hamburg, and J. E. Adams (Eds.), *Coping and adaptation.* New York: Basic Books.

Getter, H., & Nowinski, J. K. (1981). A free response test of interpersonal effectiveness. *Journal of Personality Assessment, 45,* 301–308.

Gladwin, T. (1967). Social competence and clinical practice. *Psychiatry: Journal for the Study of Interpersonal Processes, 3,* 30–43.

Goldfried, M. R. (1979). Anxiety reduction through cognitive-behavioral intervention. In P. C. Kendall & S. D. Hollon (Eds.), *Cognitive-behavioral interventions: Theory, research, and procedures.* New York: Academic Press.

Goldfried, M. R. (1980). Psychotherapy as coping skills training. In M. J. Mahoney (Ed.), *Psychotherapy process: Current issues and future directions.* New York: Plenum Press.

Goldfried, M. R. (1982). Resistance and clinical behavior therapy. In P. L. Wachtel (Ed.), *Resistance: Psychodynamic and behavioral approaches.* New York: Plenum.

Goldfried, M. R., Decenteceo, E. T., & Weinberg, L. (1974). Systematic rational restructuring as a self-control technique. *Behavior Therapy, 5,* 247–252.

Goldfried, M. R., & D'Zurilla, T. J. (1969). A behavior-analytic model for assessing competence. In C. D. Spielberger (Ed.), *Current topics in clinical and community psychology* (Vol. 1). New York: Academic Press.

Goldstein, A. P. (1973). *Structured learning therapy.* New York: Academic Press.

Gotlib, I. H., & Asarnow, R. F. (1979). Interpersonal and impersonal problem-solving skills in mildly and clinically depressed university students. *Journal of Consulting and Clinical Psychology, 47,* 86–95.

Grimm, L. G., & Yarnold, P. R. (1984). Performance standards and the Type A behavior pattern. *Cognitive Therapy and Research, 8,* 59–66.

Guilford, J. P. (1967). *The nature of human intelligence.* New York: McGraw-Hill.

Guilford, J. P. (1968). *Intelligence, creativity, and their educational implications.* San Diego, CA: Robert R. Knapp.

Guilford, J. P. (1977). *Way beyond the IQ: Guide to improving intelligence and creativity.* Great Neck, NY: Creative Synergetic Associates.

Hamberger, L. K., & Lohr, J. M. (1984). *Stress and stress management.* New York: Springer.

Hansen, D. J., St. Lawrence, J. S., & Christoff, K. A. (1985). Effects of interpersonal problem-solving training with chronic aftercare patients on problem-solving component skills and effectiveness of solutions. *Journal of Consulting and Clinical Psychology, 53,* 167–174.

Heppner, P. P., & Anderson, W. P. (1985). The relationship between problem solving self-appraisal and psychological adjustment. *Cognitive Therapy and Research, 9,* 415–427.

Heppner, P. P., Baumgardner, A., & Jackson, J. (1985). Problem solving self-appraisal, depression, and attribution styles: Are they related? *Cognitive Therapy and Research, 9,* 105–113.

Heppner, P. P., Baumgardner, A. H., Larson, L. M., & Petty, R. E. (August, 1983). *Problem-solving training for college students with problem-solving deficits.* Paper presented at the Annual Convention of the American Psychological Association, Anaheim.

Heppner, P. P., Hibel, J. H., Neal, G. W., Weinstein, C. L., & Rabinowitz, F. E. (1982). Personal problem solving: A descriptive study of individual differences. *Journal of Counseling Psychology, 29,* 580–590.

Heppner, P. P., Kampa, M., & Brunning, L. (August, 1984). *Problem solving appraisal as a mediator of stress.* Paper presented at the Annual Convention of the American Psychological Association, Toronto.

Heppner, P. P., & Krieshok, T. S. (1983). An applied investigation of problem-solving appraisal, vocational identity, and career service requests, utilization, and subsequent evaluations. *The Vocational Guidance Quarterly, 31,* 249–259.

Heppner, P. P., Neal, G. W., & Larson, L. M. (1984). Problem-solving training as prevention with college students. *Personnel and Guidance Journal, 62,* 514–519.

Heppner, P. P., & Petersen, C. H. (1982). The development and implications of a personal problem solving inventory. *Journal of Counseling Psychology, 29,* 66–75.

Heppner, P. P., & Reeder, B. L. (1984). Training in problem solving for residence hall staff: Who is most satisfied? *Journal of College Student Personnel, 25,* 357–360.

Heppner, P. P., Reeder, B. L., & Larson, L. M. (1983). Cognitive variables associated with personal problem-solving appraisal: Implications for counseling. *Journal of Counseling Psychology, 30,* 537–545.

Hiroto, D. S., & Seligman, M. E. P. (1975). Generality of learned helplessness in man. *Journal of Personality and Social Psychology, 31,* 311–327.

Hockey, R., & Hamilton, P. (1983). Cognitive patterning of stress states. In R. Hockey (Ed.), *Stress and fatigue in human performance.* New York: Wiley.

Hokanson, J. E., DeGood, D. E., Forrest, M. S., & Brittain, T. M. (1971). Availability of avoidance behaviors for modulating vascular-stress responses. *Journal of Personality and Social Psychology, 19,* 60–68.

Holroyd, K. A., Appel, M. A., & Andrasik, F. A. (1983). A cognitive-behavioral approach to psychophysiological disorders. In D. Meichenbaum & M. E. Jaremko (Eds.), *Stress reduction and prevention.* New York: Plenum.

Hunt, J., McV. (1963). Motivation inherent in information processing and action. In O. J. Harvey (Ed.), *Motivation and social organization: The cognitive factors.* New York: Ronald.

Hussian, R. A., & Lawrence, P. S. (1981). Social reinforcement of activity and problem-solving training in the treatment of depressed institutionalized elderly patients. *Cognitive Therapy and Research, 5,* 57–69.

Intagliatia, J. C. (1978). Increasing the interpersonal problem solving skills of an alcoholic population. *Journal of Consulting and Clinical Psychology, 46,* 489–498.

Jacobson, N. S. (1977a). Training couples to solve their marital problems: A behavioral approach to relationship discord. Part I: Problem-solving skills. *International Journal of Family Counseling 5,* 22–31.

Jacobson, N. S. (1977b). Problem solving and contingency contracting in the treatment of marital discord. *Journal of Consulting and Clinical Psychology, 45,* 92–100.

Jacobson, N. S. (December, 1977c). *The role of problem solving in behavioral marital therapy.* Paper presented at the Annual Convention of the Association for Advancement of Behavior Therapy, Atlanta.

Jacobson, N. S. (1978). Specific and nonspecific factors in the effectiveness of a behavioral approach to the treatment of marital discord. *Journal of Consulting and Clinical Psychology, 46,* 442–452.

Jacobson, N. S. (1984). A component analysis of marital behavior therapy: The relative effectiveness of behavior exchange and communication/problem-solving training. *Journal of Consulting and Clinical Psychology, 52,* 295–305.

Jacobson, N. S., & Follette, W. C. (1985). Clinical significance of improvement resulting from two behavioral marital therapy components. *Behavior Therapy, 16,* 249–262.

Jacobson, N. S., & Margolin, G. (1979). *Marital therapy: Strategies based on social learning and behavior exchange principles*. New York: Brunner/Mazel.

Jahoda, M. (1953). The meaning of psychological health. *Social Casework, 34,* 349–354.

Jahoda, M. (1958). *Current concepts of positive mental health*. New York: Basic Books.

Janis, I. L. (1982). Decision making under stress. In L. Goldberger & S. Breznitz (Eds.), *Handbook of stress: Theoretical and clinical aspects*. New York: Free Press.

Janis, I. L. (1983). Stress inoculation in health care: Theory and research. In D. Meichenbaum & M. E. Jaremko (Eds.), *Stress reduction and prevention*. New York: Plenum.

Janis, I. L., & Mann, L. (1977). *Decision making: A psychological analysis of conflict, choice, and commitment*. New York: Free Press.

Jannoun, L., Munby, M., Catalan, J., & Gelder, M. (1980). A home-based treatment program for agoraphobia: Replication and controlled evaluation. *Behavior Therapy, 11,* 294–305.

Jenkins, C. D. (1975). The coronary-prone personality. In W. D. Gentry & R. B. Williams, Jr. (Eds.), *Psychological aspects of myocardial infarction and coronary care*. St. Louis: Mosby.

Jones, L. C. T. (1954). Frustration and stereotyped behavior in human subjects. *Quarterly Journal of Experimental Psychology, 6,* 12–20.

Kagan, C. (1984). Social problem solving and social skills training. *British Journal of Clinical Psychology, 23,* 161–173.

Kahneman, D., & Tversky, A. (1979). Prospect theory: An analysis of decisions under risk. *Econometrica, 47,* 263–291.

Kanfer, F. H. (1970). Self-regulation: Research, issues, and speculations. In C. Neuringer & J. L. Michael (Eds.), *Behavior modification in clinical psychology*. New York: Appleton-Century-Crofts.

Kanner, A. D., Coyne, J. C., Schaefer, C., & Lazarus, R. S. (1981). Comparison of two modes of stress measurement: Daily hassles and uplifts versus major life events. *Journal of Behavioral Medicine, 4,* 1–39.

Karol, R. L., & Richards, C. S. (November, 1978). *Making treatment effects last: An investigation of maintenance strategies for smoking reduction*. Paper presented at the Annual Convention of the Association for Advancement of Behavior Therapy, Chicago.

Kelly, M. L., Scott, W. O. M., Prue, D. M., & Rychtarik, R. G. (1985). A component analysis of problem-solving skills training. *Cognitive Therapy and Research, 9,* 429–441.

Kendall, P. C., & Fischler, G. L. (1984). Behavioral and adjustment correlates of problem solving: Validational analyses of interpersonal cognitive problem solving measures. *Child Development, 55,* 879–892.

Kendall, P. C., & Hollon, S. D. (Eds.). (1979). *Cognitive-behavioral interventions: Theory, research, and procedures*. New York: Academic Press.

Kleinmuntz, B. (Ed.). (1966). *Problem solving: Research, method and theory*. New York: Wiley.

Krasnor, L. R., & Rubin, K. H. (1981). The assessment of social problem-solving skills in young children. In T. Merluzzi, C. Glass, & M. Genest (Eds.), *Cognitive assessment*. New York: Guilford Press.

Lacey, J. I. (1967). Somatic response patterning and stress: Some revisions of activation theory. In M. H. Appley & R. Trumball (Eds.), *Psychological stress*. New York: McGraw-Hill.

Larson, L. M., & Heppner, P. P. (1985). The relationship of problem-solving appraisal to career decision and indecision. *Journal of Vocational Behavior, 26*, 55–65.

Lazarus, R. S. (1966). *Psychological stress and the coping process*. New York: McGraw-Hill.

Lazarus, R. S. (1981). The stress and coping paradigm. In C. Eisdorfer, D. Cohen, A. Kleinman, & P. Maxim (Eds.), *Theoretical bases for psychopathology*. New York: Spectrum.

Lazarus, R. S. (1982). Thoughts on the relations between emotion and cognition. *American Psychologist, 37*, 1019–1024.

Lazarus, R. S. (1983). The costs and benefits of denial. In S. Breznitz (Ed.), *Denial of stress*. New York: International Universities Press.

Lazarus, R. S., & Folkman, S. (1984). *Stress, appraisal, and coping*. New York: Springer.

Lazarus, R. S., Kanner, A., & Folkman, S. (1980). Emotions: A cognitive phenomenological analysis. In R. Plutchik & H. Kellerman (Eds.), *Theories of emotion*. New York: Academic Press.

Leventhal, H., & Nerenz, D. R. (1983). A model for stress research with some implications for the control of stress disorders. In D. Meichenbaum & M. E. Jaremko (Eds.), *Stress reduction and prevention*. New York: Plenum.

Levine, M. (in press). *Principles of effective problem solving*. Englewood Cliffs, N.J.: Prentice-Hall.

Levine, J., & Zigler, E. (1973). The essential-reactive distinction in alcoholism: A developmental approach. *Journal of Abnormal Psychology, 81*, 242–249.

Liberman, R. P., McCann, M. J., & Wallace, C. J. (1976). Generalisation of behaviour therapy with psychotics. *British Journal of Psychiatry, 129*, 490–496.

McClelland, D. C., & Clark, R. A. (1966). Discrepancy hypothesis. In R. N. Haber (Ed.), *Current research in motivation*. New York: Holt, Rinehart & Winston.

McFall, R. M. (1982). A review and reformulation of the concept of social skills. *Behavioral Assessment, 4*, 1–33.

McFall, R. M., & McDonel, E. C., & Lipton, D. (November, 1984). *Heterosocial cue reading skills in psychopathology*. Paper presented at the Annual Convention of the Association for Advancement of Behavior Therapy, Philadelphia.

McKay, M., Davis, M., & Fanning, P. (1981). *Thoughts and feelings: The art of cognitive stress intervention*. Oakland, CA: New Harbinger Publications.

McGrath, J. E. (Ed.). (1970). *Social and psychological factors in stress*. New York: Holt, Rinehart, & Winston.

McGrath, J. E. (1976). Stress and behavior in organizations. In M. D. Dunnette (Ed.), *Handbook of industrial and organizational psychology*. Chicago: Rand McNally.

McGrath, J. E. (1982). Methodological problems in research on stress. In H. W. Krohne & L. Laux (Eds.), *Achievement, stress, and anxiety*. New York: Hemisphere.

Maddux, J. E., Sherer, M., & Rodgers, R. W. (1982). Self-efficacy expectancy and outcome expectancy: Their relationship and their effects on behavioral interventions. *Cognitive Therapy and Research, 6,* 207–211.

Mahoney, M. J. (1974). *Cognition and behavior modification*. Cambridge, MA: Ballinger.

Mahoney, M. J. (1977). Personal science: A cognitive learning therapy. In A. Ellis & R. Grieger (Eds.), *Handbook of rational-emotive therapy*. New York: Springer.

Mahoney, M. J. (1980). A strategy for generating self-help. In G. L. Martin & J. G. Osborne (Eds.), *Helping in the community: Behavioral applications*. New York: Plenum.

Mahoney, M. J., & Mahoney, K. (1976). *Permanent weight control*. New York: W. W. Norton.

Maier, N. R. F. (1949). *Frustration: A study of behavior without a goal*. New York: McGraw-Hill.

Mandler, G. (1982). Stress and thought processes. In L. Goldberger & S. Breznitz (Eds.), *Handbook of stress: Theoretical and clinical aspects*. New York: Free Press.

Marquart, D. I., & Arnold, L. P. (1952). A study in the frustration of human adults. *Journal of General Psychology, 47,* 43–63.

Masserman, J. H. (1943). *Behavior and neurosis*. Chicago: University of Chicago Press.

Mather, M. D. (1970). Obsessions and compulsions. In C. G. Costello (Ed.), *Symptoms of psychopathology*. New York: Wiley.

Meadow, A., Parnes, S. J., & Reese, H. (1959). Influence of instructions and problem sequence on a creative problem-solving test. *Journal of Applied Psychology, 43,* 413–416.

Mechanic, D. (1968). The study of social stress and its relationship to disease. In D. Mechanic (Ed.), *Medical sociology*. New York: Free Press.

Mechanic, D. (1970). Some problems in developing a social psychology of adaptation to stress. In J. E. McGrath (Ed.), *Social and psychological factors in stress*. New York: Holt, Rinehart, & Winston.

Mechanic, D. (1974). Social structure and personal adaptation: Some neglected dimensions. In G. Coelho, C. M. Hamburg, & J. E. Adams (Eds.), *Coping and adaptation*. New York: Basic Books.

Meichenbaum, D., & Asarnow, J. (1979). Cognitive-behavioral modification and metacognitive development: Implications for the classroom. In P. C.

Kendall & S. D. Hollon (Eds.), *Cognitive-behavioral interventions: Theory, research, and procedures.* New York: Academic Press.

Meichenbaum, D., & Cameron, R. (1983). Stress inoculation training: Toward a general paradigm for training coping skills. In D. Meichenbaum & M. E. Jaremko (Eds.), *Stress reduction and prevention.* New York: Plenum.

Meichenbaum, D., Henshaw, D., & Himel, N. (1982). Coping with stress as a problem-solving process. In W. Krohne & L. Luax (Eds.), *Achievement stress and anxiety.* New York: Hemisphere.

Meichenbaum, D., & Jaremko, M. E. (Eds.). (1983). *Stress reduction and prevention.* New York: Plenum.

Mendonca, J. D., & Siess, T. F. (1976). Counseling for indecisiveness: Problem solving and anxiety in management training. *Journal of Counseling Psychology, 23,* 330–347.

Miller, G. A., Galanter, E., & Pribram, K. H. (1960). *Plans and the structure of behavior.* New York: Holt, Rinehart, & Winston.

Miller, R., & Pfohl, W. (1982). Management of job-related stress. In R. M. O'Brien, A. M. Dickinson, & M. P. Rosow (Eds.). *Industrial behavior modification: A management handbook.* New York: Pergamon.

Miller, N. E., & Weiss, J. M. (1969). Effects of somatic or visceral responses to punishment. In B. A. Campbell & R. M. Church (Eds.), *Punishment and aversive behavior.* New York: Appleton-Century-Crofts.

Mitchell, J. E., & Madigan, R. J. (1984). The effects of induced elation and depression on interpersonal problem solving. *Cognitive Therapy and Research, 8,* 277–285.

Moon, J. R., & Eisler, R. M. (1983). Anger control: An experimental comparison of three behavioral treatments. *Behavior Therapy, 14,* 493–505.

Mooney, R. L., & Gordon, L. V. (1950). *Manual: The Mooney Problem Checklist.* New York: Psychological Corporation.

Mowrer, O. H. (1960a). *Learning theory and behavior.* New York: Wiley.

Mowrer, O. H. (1960b). *Learning theory and the symbolic processes.* New York: Wiley.

Murphy, G. E. (1985). A conceptual framework for the choice of interventions in cognitive therapy. *Cognitive Therapy and Research, 9,* 127–134.

Neal, G. W., & Heppner, P. P. (March, 1982). Personality correlates of effective personal problem solving. Paper presented at the Annual Meeting of the American Personnel and Guidance Association, Detroit.

Newell, A., & Simon, H. A. (1972). *Human problem solving.* Englewood Cliffs, NJ: Prentice-Hall.

Nezu, A. M. (1985). Differences in psychological distress between effective and ineffective problem solvers. *Journal of Counseling Psychology, 32,* 135–138.

Nezu, A. M. (1986a). Efficacy of a social problem solving therapy approach for unipolar depression. *Journal of Consulting and Clinical Psychology, 54,* 196–202.

Nezu, A. M. (1986b). Negative life stress and anxiety: Problem solving as a moderator variable. *Psychological Reports, 58,* 279–283.

Nezu, A. M. (in press). A problem-solving formulation of depression: A literature review and proposal of a pluralistic model. *Clinical Psychology Review.*

Nezu, A., & D'Zurilla, T. J. (1979). An experimental evaluation of the decision-making process in social problem solving. *Cognitive Therapy and Research, 3,* 269–277.

Nezu, A., & D'Zurilla, T. J. (1981a). Effects of problem definition and formulation on decision making in the social problem-solving process. *Behavior Therapy, 12,* 100–106.

Nezu, A., & D'Zurilla, T. J. (1981b). Effects of problem definition and formulation on the generation of alternatives in the social problem-solving process. *Cognitive Therapy and Research, 5,* 265–271.

Nezu, A. M., & Ronan, G. F. (in press). Social problem solving and depression: Deficits in generating alternatives and decision making. *Southern Psychologist.*

Nezu, A. M., & Ronan, G. F. (1985). Life stress, current problems, problem solving, and depressive symptomatology: An integrative model. *Journal of Consulting and Clinical Psychology, 53,* 693–697.

Nezu, A. M., Kalmar, K., Ronan, G. F., & Clavijo, A. (1986). Attributional correlates of depression: An interactional model including problem solving. *Behavior Therapy, 17,* 50–56.

Nezu, A. M., Nezu, C. M., Saraydarian, L., Kalmar, K., & Ronan, G. F. (in press). Social problem solving as a moderating variable between negative life stress and depressive symptoms. *Cognitive Therapy and Research.*

Noller, R. B., Parnes, S. J., & Biondi, A. M. (1976). *Creative actionbook: Revised edition of creative behavior workbook.* New York: Charles Scribner's Sons.

Novaco, R. W. (1979). The cognitive regulation of anger and stress. In P. C. Kendall & S. D. Hollon (Eds.), *Cognitive-behavioral interventions: Theory, research, and procedures.* New York: Academic Press.

O'Leary, K. D., & Borkovec, T. D. (1978). Conceptual, methodological, and ethical problems of placebo groups in psychotherapy research. *American Psychologist, 33,* 821–830.

Osborn, A. (1952). *Wake up your mind.* New York: Charles Scribner's Sons.

Osborn, A. (1963). *Applied imagination: Principles and procedures of creative problem solving* (3rd ed.). New York: Charles Scribner's Sons.

Parloff, M. B., & Handlon, J. H. (1964). The influence of criticalness on creative problem-solving in dyads. *Psychiatry, 27,* 17–27.

Parnes, S. J. (1962). The creative problem solving course and institute at the University of Buffalo. In S. J. Parnes and H. F. Harding (Eds.), *A source book for creative thinking.* New York: Charles Scribner's Sons.

Parnes, S. J., & Meadow, A. (1959). Effects of "brainstorming" instructions on creative problem solving by trained and untrained subjects. *Journal of Educational Psychology, 50,* 171–176.

Parnes, S. J., & Noller, R. B. (1973). *Toward supersanity: Channeled freedom.* New York: D. O. K. Publishers.

Parnes, S. J., Noller, R. B., & Biondi, A. M. (1977). *Guide to creative action: Revised edition of creative behavior guidebook.* New York: Charles Scribner's Sons.

Payne, J. W. (1982). Contingent decision behavior. *Psychological Bulletin, 92,* 382–402.

Pellegrini, D. S. & Urbain, E. S. (1985). An evaluation of interpersonal cognitive problem solving training with children. *Journal of Child Psychology and Psychiatry, 26,* 17–41.

Petty, B. J., Moeller, T. P., & Campbell, R. Z. (1976). Support groups for elderly persons in the community. *Gerontologist, 16,* 522–528.

Phillips, E. L. (1978). *The social skills basis of psychopathology: Alternatives to abnormal psychology and psychiatry.* New York: Grune & Stratton.

Phillips, S. D., Pazienza, N. J., & Ferrin, H. H. (1984). Decision making styles and problem solving appraisal. *Journal of Counseling Psychology, 31,* 497–502.

Phillips, L., & Zigler, E. (1961). Social competence: The action-thought parameter and vicariousness in normal and pathological behaviors. *Journal of Abnormal and Social Psychology, 63,* 137–146.

Phillips, L., & Zigler, E. (1964). Role orientation, the action-thought dimension, and outcome in psychiatric disorder. *Journal of Abnormal and Social Psychology, 68,* 381–389.

Platt, J. J., & Scura, W. C., & Hannon, J. R. (1973). Problem solving thinking of youthful incarcerated heroin addicts. *Journal of Community Psychology, 1,* 278–281.

Platt, J. J., & Siegel, J. M. (1976). MMPI characteristics of good and poor social problem solvers among psychiatric patients. *Journal of Community Psychology, 94,* 245–251.

Platt, J. J., & Spivack, G. (1972a). Problem solving thinking of psychiatric patients. *Journal of Consulting and Clinical Psychology, 39,* 148–151.

Platt, J. J., & Spivack, G. (1972b). Social competence and effective problem solving in psychiatric patients. *Journal of Clinical Psychology, 28,* 3–5.

Platt, J. J., & Spivack, G. (1973). Studies in problem-solving thinking of psychiatric patients: Patient-control differences and factorial structure of problem-solving thinking. In *Proceedings, 81st Annual Convention of the American Psychological Association, 8,* 461–462.

Platt, J. J., & Spivack, G. (1975). *Manual for the means-ends problem-solving procedures (MEPS): A measure of interpersonal cognitive problem-solving skills.* Philadelphia: Hahnemann Community Mental Health/Mental Retardation Center.

Platt, J. J., Spivack, G., Altman, N., Altman, D., & Peizer, S. B. (1974). Adolescent problem solving thinking. *Journal of Consulting and Clinical Psychology, 42,* 787–793.

Premack, D. (1965). Reinforcement theory. In D. Levine (Ed.), *Nebraska symposium on motivation.* Lincoln: University of Nebraska Press.

Richards, C. S., Perri, M. G. (1978). Do self-control treatments last? An evaluation of behavioral problem solving and faded counselor contact as treatment maintenance strategies. *Journal of Counseling Psychology, 25,* 376–383.

Rimm, D. C., & Masters, J. C. (1979). *Behavior therapy: Techniques and empirical findings.* (2nd ed.). New York: Academic Press.

Robin, A. L. (1979). Problem-solving communication training: A behavioral approach to the treatment of parent-adolescent conflict. *The American Journal of Family Therapy, 7,* 69–82.

Robin, A. L. (1980). Parent-adolescent conflict: A skill training approach. In D. P. Rathjen & J. P. Foreyt (Eds.), *Social competence: Interventions for children and adults.* New York: Pergamon.

Robin, A. L. (1981). A controlled evaluation of problem-solving communication training with parent-adolescent conflict. *Behavior Therapy, 12,* 593–609.

Robin, A. L., Kent, R. N., O'Leary, K. D., Foster, S., & Prinz, R. J. (1977). An approach to teaching parents and adolescents problem-solving communication skills: A preliminary report. *Behavior Therapy, 8,* 639–643.

Sarason, I. G. (1980). Life stress, self-preoccupation, and social supports. In I. G. Sarason & C. D. Spielberger (Eds.), *Stress and anxiety* (Vol. 7). New York: Hemisphere.

Sarason, B. R. (1981). The dimensions of social competence: Contributions from a variety of research areas. In J. D. Wine & M. D. Smye (Eds.), *Social competence.* New York: Guilford.

Sarason, I. G., & Sarason, B. R. (1981). Teaching cognitive and social skills to high school students. *Journal of Consulting and Clinical Psychology, 49,* 908–918.

Schinke, S. P., Blythe, B. J., & Gilchrist, L. D. (1981). Cognitive-behavioral prevention of adolescent pregnancy. *Journal of Counseling Psychology, 28,* 451–454.

Schönpflug, W. (1983). Coping efficiency and situational demands. In R. Hockey (Ed.), *Stress and fatigue in human performance.* New York: Wiley.

Schulz, P., & Schönpflug, W. (1982). Regulatory activity during states of stress. In H. W. Krohne & L. Laux (Eds.), *Achievement, stress, and anxiety.* New York: Hemisphere.

Seligman, M. E. P. (1975). *Helplessness.* San Francisco: Freeman.

Seligman, M. E. P., & Maier, S. F. (1967). Failure to escape traumatic shock. *Journal of Experimental Psychology, 74,* 1–9.

Selye, H. (1983). The stress concept: Past, present, and future. In C. L. Cooper (Ed.), *Stress research: Issues for the eighties.* New York: Wiley.

Sherry, P., Keitel, M., & Tracey, T. J. (August, 1984). *The relationship between person-environment fit, coping, and strain.* Paper presented at the 92nd Annual Convention of the American Psychological Association, Toronto, Canada.

Shure, M. B. (1981). Social competence as a problem-solving skill. In J. D. Wine & M. D. Smye (Eds.), *Social competence.* New York: Guilford.

Siegel, J. M., & Spivack, G. (1976a). Problem-solving therapy: The description of a new program for chronic psychiatric patients. *Psychotherapy: Theory, Research, and Practice, 13,* 368–373.

Siegel, J. M., & Spivack, G. (1976b). A new therapy program for chronic patients. *Behavior Therapy, 7,* 129–130.

Snyder, R. C., Bruck, H. W., & Sapin, B. (1962). *Foreign policy decision-making.* New York: Free Press.

Solomon, R. I. (1964). Punishment. *American Psychologist, 19,* 239–253.

Spivack, G., Platt, J. J., & Shure, M. B. (1976). *The problem-solving approach to adjustment.* San Francisco: Jossey-Bass.

Spivack, G., & Shure, M. B. (1974). *Social adjustment of young children.* San Francisco: Jossey-Bass.

Sprafkin, R., Gershaw, N. J., & Goldstein, A. P. (1980). Structured-learning therapy: Overview and applications to adolescents and adults. In D. P. Rathjen & J. P. Foreyt (Eds.), *Social competence: Interventions for children and adults.* New York: Pergamon.

Staats, A. W. (1975). *Social behaviorism.* Homewood, IL: Dorsey Press.

Straw, M. K., & Terre, L. (1983). An evaluation of individualized behavioral obesity treatment and maintenance strategies. *Behavior Therapy, 14,* 255–266.

Tableman, B., Marciniak, D., Johnson, D., & Rodgers, R. (1982). Stress management for women on public assistance. *American Journal of Community Psychology, 10,* 357–367.

Toseland, R. (1977). A problem-solving group workshop for older persons. *Social Work, 22,* 325–326.

Trower, P., Bryant, B., & Argyle, M. (1978). *Social skills and mental health.* London: Methuen.

Turk, D. C., & Salovey, P. (1985). Cognitive structures, cognitive processes, and cognitive-behavior modification: I. Client issues. *Cognitive Therapy and Research, 9,* 1–17.

Tversky, A., & Kahneman, D. (1981). The framing of decisions and the psychology of choice. *Science, 211,* 453–458.

Ullmann, L., & Krasner, L. (1969). *A psychological approach to abnormal behavior.* Englewood Cliffs, NJ: Prentice-Hall.

Urbain, E. S., & Kendall, P. C. (1980). Review of social-cognitive problem-solving interventions with children. *Psychological Bulletin, 88,* 109–143.

Watson, D. L., & Tharp, R. G. (1985). *Self-directed behavior: Self-modification for personal adjustment* (4th ed.). Monterey, Calif.: Brooks/Cole.

Weiss, J. M. (1968). Effects of coping responses on stress. *Journal of Comparative and Physiological Psychology, 65,* 251–260.

Weiss, J. M. (1970). Somatic effects of predictable and unpredictable shock. *Psychosomatic Medicine, 32,* 397–408.

232   *References*

Weisskopf-Joelson, E., & Eliseo, A. (1961). An experimental study of the effectiveness of brainstorming. *Journal of Applied Psychology, 45,* 45–49.

White, R. W. (1959). Motivation reconsidered: The concept of competence. *Psychological Review, 66,* 297–333.

Wilkins, W. (1984). Psychotherapy: The powerful placebo. *Journal of Consulting and Clinical Psychology, 52,* 570–573.

Wine, J. D., & Smye, M. D. (Eds.). (1981). *Social competence.* New York: Guilford.

Woolfolk, R. L., & Lehrer, P. M. (Eds.). (1984). *Principles and practice of stress management.* New York: Guilford.

Wrubel, J., Benner, P., & Lazarus, R. S. (1981). Social competence from the perspective of stress and coping. In J. D. Wine & M. D. Smye (Eds.), *Social competence.* New York: Guilford.

Yerkes, R., & Dodson, J. D. (1908). The relation of strength of stimulus to rapidity of habit formation. *Journal of Comparative and Neurological Psychology, 18,* 459–482.

Zigler, E., & Phillips, L. (1961). Social competence and outcome in psychiatric disorder. *Journal of Abnormal and Social Psychology, 63,* 264–271.

Zigler, E., & Phillips, L. (1962). Social competence and the process-reactive distinction in psychopathology. *Journal of Abnormal and Social Psychology, 65,* 215–222.

Appendix A
Problem Solving Inventory (PSI)*

Purpose: This is not a test. There are no right or wrong answers. Rather, it is an inventory designed to find out how people normally react to problems and events in their daily interactions. We are not talking about math or science problems, but rather about personal problems that come up from time to time, such as feeling depressed, getting along with friends, choosing a vocation, or deciding whether to get a divorce. *Please respond to the items as honestly as you can so as to most accurately portray how you handle problems.* Don't respond to the statements as you think you *should* in order to solve problems—rather respond to the statements as honestly as you can, and in such a way so that you most accurately reflect how you actually behave when you solve problems. Ask yourself: Do I ever behave like this?

Directions: Below is a list of 35 statements. Read each statement, and then indicate in the parentheses ( ) next to the number of the statement, the extent to which you agree or disagree with that statement, using the following alternatives:

1 = Strongly Agree
2 = Moderately Agree
3 = Slightly Agree
4 = Slightly Disagree
5 = Moderately Disagree
6 = Strongly Disagree

<u>1.</u> ( ) When a solution to a problem was unsuccessful, I do not examine why it didn't work.

*Adapted from: Heppner, P. P., & Petersen, C. H. (1982). The development and implications of a personal problem solving inventory. *Journal of Counseling Psychology, 29,* 66–75. Copyright (1982) by the American Psychological Association. Reprinted/Adapted by permission of the author.

2. ( ) When I am confronted with a complex problem, I do not bother to develop a strategy to collect information so I can define exactly what the problem is.

3. ( ) When my first efforts to solve a problem fail, I become uneasy about my ability to handle the situation.

4. ( ) After I have solved a problem, I do not analyze what went right or what went wrong.

5. ( ) I am usually able to think up creative and effective alternatives to solve a problem.

6. ( ) After I have tried to solve a problem with a certain course of action, I take time and compare the actual outcome to what I thought should have happened.

7. ( ) When I have a problem, I think up as many possible ways to handle it as I can until I can't come up with any more ideas.

8. ( ) When confronted with a problem, I consistently examine my feelings to find out what is going on in a problem situation.

9. ( ) When I am confused with a problem, I do not try to define vague ideas or feelings into concrete or specific terms.

10. ( ) I have the ability to solve most problems even though initially no solution is immediately apparent.

11. ( ) Many problems I face are too complex for me to solve.

12. ( ) I make decisions and am happy with them later.

13. ( ) When confronted with a problem, I tend to do the first thing that I can think of to solve it.

14. ( ) Sometimes I do not stop and take time to deal with my problems, but just kind of muddle ahead.

15. ( ) When deciding on an idea or possible solution to a problem, I do not take time to consider the chances of each alternative being successful.

16. ( ) When confronted with a problem, I stop and talk about it before deciding on a next step.

17. ( ) I generally go with the first good idea that comes to my mind.

18. ( ) When making a decision, I weigh the consequences of each alternative and compare them against each other.

19. ( ) When I make plans to solve a problem, I am almost certain that I can make them work.

20. ( ) I try to predict the overall result of carrying out a particular course of action.

21. ( ) When I try to think up possible solutions to a problem, I do not come up with very many alternatives.

22. ( ) In trying to solve a problem, one strategy I often use is to think of past problems that have been similar.

23. ( ) Given enough time and effort, I believe I can solve most problems that confront me.

24. ( ) When faced with a novel situation I have confidence that I can handle problems that may arise.

25. ( ) Even though I work on a problem, sometimes I feel like I am groping or wandering, and am not getting down to the real issue.

26. ( ) I make snap judgments and later regret them.

27. ( ) I trust my ability to solve new and difficult problems.

28. ( ) I have a systematic method for comparing alternatives and making decisions.

29. ( ) When I try to think of ways of handling a problem, I do not try to combine different ideas together.

30. ( ) When I am confronted with a problem, I do not usually examine what sort of external things in my environment may be contributing to my problem.

31. ( ) When I am confronted by a problem, one of the first things I do is survey the situation and consider all the relevant pieces of information.

32. ( ) Sometimes I get so charged up emotionally that I am unable to consider many ways of dealing with my problem.

33. ( ) After making a decision, the outcome I expected usually matches the actual outcome.

34. ( ) When confronted with a problem, I am unsure of whether I can handle the situation.

35. ( ) When I become aware of a problem, one of the first things I do is to try to find out exactly what the problem is.

Scoring: Scoring the PSI is a matter of summing the responses (1–6) to each item. Items 9, 22, and 29 are filler items, and are not to be scored in any way. Please note that several items are worded negatively. Scoring of these items must be reversed (i.e., 1=6, 5=2, etc.) These items are underlined (e.g., 1).

Appendix B

Problem-Solving Self-Monitoring (PSSM) Form

Instructions: The purpose of this form is to record information about a significant problem which occurred in your life and how you attempted to solve it. A "problem" is defined as a situation in which you perceive a discrepancy between "what is" (present conditions) and "what should be" (conditions which are demanded or desired), but the means for reducing this discrepancy (a possible solution to the problem) are not immediately apparent or available to you. For each problem-solving situation, record the information requested below in sections A, B, C, D, and E. When describing this information, please be as *specific* and *concrete* as possible. If there is not enough room in the space provided to complete your description, you may write on the back of the page, but be sure to identify the section that you are continuing.

A. *Problem Information* (PO & PDF)

In the space below, describe all the relevant facts about the problematic situation. Your information should provide answers to the following questions:

1. Who was involved?
2. What happened (or did not happen) that was unacceptable?
3. Where and when did it happen?
4. Why did it happen? (if reasons or causes are known)
5. Why was this problem important? (What was at stake? Was there a threat? Was there a challenge?)
6. What was your problem-solving goal? (What specific outcome did you desire?)

Please answer the following questions about the problem by circling the answer which best describes your view of the situation.

   a. The *main* cause of the problem was:
   1. An obstacle or deficiency in the environment (including the behavior of other people).
   2. An obstacle or deficiency in myself.
   3. A combination of an obstacle or deficiency in the environment *and* in myself.
   b. How important was the problem for your *overall well-being* (physical, psychological, social, economic)?
   1. Slightly important
   2. Moderately important
   3. Extremely important
   c. To what extent did you view the problem as a *threat* to your well-being (potential for harm or loss)?
   1. Not at all threatening
   2. Slightly threatening
   3. Moderately threatening
   4. Extremely threatening
   d. To what extent did you view the problem as a *challenge* (opportunity for personal growth or mastery)?
   1. Not at all challenging
   2. Slightly challenging
   3. Moderately challenging
   4. Extremely challenging
   e. When you first recognized the problem, how likely did you think it was that the problem was solvable (that the factors causing the problem could be changed or controlled)?
   1. Very unlikely
   2. Somewhat unlikely
   3. Somewhat likely
   4. Very likely
   f. When you first recognized the problem, how confident did you feel in your ability to solve the problem through your own efforts?
   1. Not at all confident
   2. Slightly confident
   3. Moderately confident
   4. Extremely confident
   g. When you first recognized the problem, how much time and effort were you willing to commit to the task of solving the problem on your own?

1. No time and effort at all
2. Some time and effort
3. Much time and effort
4. Very much time and effort
 h. Compared to the time that you expected to spend on the problem, how much time did you actually spend on it?
1. Much more time than I expected
2. Somewhat more time than I expected
3. About as much time as I expected/no more and no less
4. Somewhat less time than I expected
5. Much less time than I expected

B. *Emotions*

In the space below, describe all the feelings and emotions which you may have experienced when you were first confronted with this problem (for example, fear, hope, tension–anxiety, exhilaration, anger, joy, disappointment, euphoria, depression, etc.). What steps did you take, if any, to try to minimize or control the *negative* feelings and emotions?

Rate the intensity of your negative feelings or *emotional distress* by circling a number on the rating scale below:

Low   Moderate   High
1   2   3   4   5   6   7   8   9

C. *Alternative Solutions Considered (GAS)*

In the space below, list all the possible "solutions" or ways of coping with the problematic situation that you may have considered before actually deciding what you were going to do. Please be *specific*.

D. *Solution Choice (DM)*

In the space below, describe the solution or coping method that you chose to implement in this particular situation and describe *in detail* all the reasons why you chose that particular solution.

E. *Solution Implementation and Outcome (SIV)*

In the space below, describe what happened when you implemented your solution. Your description should include the following information:

1. The specific steps involved in carrying out the solution.
2. The obstacles you may have encountered (for example, disruptive emotions, negative thoughts, lack of skills or resources, resistance from others).
3. The consequences or results of your solution, including the degree of problem resolution, effects on your emotional well-being, amount of time and effort required, and other important costs and benefits.

Rate the degree of your satisfaction with the *overall outcome* of your solution by circling a number on the following rating scale:

+5 Extremely Satisfactory

+4

+3 Moderately Satisfactory

+2

+1 Slightly Satisfactory

−1 Slightly Unsatisfactory

−2

−3 Moderately Unsatisfactory

−4

−5 Extremely Unsatisfactory

Index

Problem Solving Performance Evaluation Test (PPET), 77, 185–186
Problem Solving Self-Evaluation Test (PSET)), 74–75, 185–186
Problem-Solving Self-Monitoring (PSSM), 79–80, 81, 95, 99–100, 236–240 (form)
Problem-solving skills, assessment of, 74–80
Problem-solving training (PST), 92–142
  and adjustment, 68–69
  alternative solutions, generation of (unit 5), 122–129
  assessment, *see* Assessment
  avoidant/dependent coping style, 105–106
  and behavior modification, 8–9
  in broader therapy program, 93–94
  case illustrations, 144–171; *see also* Case illustrations
  cautions and conclusions, 214–216
  coping techniques, 111–112
  current antecedent problem, 93
  decision making (unit 6), 129–136
  definition of major components, 96
  emotions, use and control of (unit 3), 109–113
  externalization rule, 101
  future directions for, 214
  general format, 95–98
  general problems checklist, 104, 106
  goal of, 92–94, 95–98
  guided problem solving, 112
  initial structuring (unit 1), 95–103
  instruction methods, 94–95
  limited capacity of the conscious mind, 100–103
  maintenance and generalization (unit 8), 141–144
  outcome studies, 182–212; *see also* Outcome studies
  and positive reinforcement, 54
  problem definition and formulation (unit 4), 113–122
  problem orientation (unit 2), 103–108
  problem perception in, 97, 98–99
  problem recognition, 103–104
  problem-solving coping style, 104–108
  and problem-solving deficits, 93–94
  problem-solving process, overview of, 96, 97
  program schedule, 95
  PSSM method in, 99–100
  rationale for, 95–98
  recognition of value of, 3–10

simplification rule, 101–102
and social-skills training, 13–14
solution implementation and verification (unit 7), 136–139
variations in programs, 172–181
visualization rule, 101
work-related problems checklist, 104, 105
see also Prescriptive model for social problem solving
Problem-solving variables, 14–17
Problem understanding, 29, 116–118
Prospect theory, 34–35, 36–38
Pseudo-problems, 27–28
Psychiatric patients, outcome studies of, 182–186
Psychopathology
  functional definition of, 60–61
  medical definition of, 3–4
  social competence approach to, 6–7

Quantity principle, 33, 42, 125

Rapid problem-solving model, 140–141
Rational reappraisal of threat, 58
"Real" problem, 30–31, 119–120
Reappraisal of problem, 32–33, 122
Rehearsal in PST, 94–95
Reinforcers, loss/deprivation of customary, 48
Relaxation/desensitization techniques, 58, 111
Resistance stage, 57
Richards, C. S., 191–192
Robin, A. L., 180–181, 196, 197

Sarason, I. G., 55, 206
Schinke, S. P., 206
Schönpflug, W., 85, 86
Secondary cognitive appraisal, 85
Selye, H., 56–57
Selective abstraction, 27–29, 115
Self-appraisal measures, 62–63
Self-control, 38–40
Self-evaluation, 39–40, 138–139
Self-efficacy expectation, 24
Self-instruction techniques, 58, 111
Self-monitoring, 39, 137–138
Self-reinforcement, 40, 139
Self-report assessment, 74–78
Semantic abilities, 16
Sensitivity to problems, 16
Shock phase of alarm reaction, 57
Siegel, J. M., 182

Visualization rule, 101, 128
Vocational indecision, outcome studies
    of, 190–191

Ways of Coping Checklist, 84
Weight-control program, 176–177, 198–
    200

Weiss, J. M., 61
Well-being
    emotional, 35, 130–131
    overall personal-social, 35–36, 131
Work-related problem checklist, 104, 105

Yerkes-Dodson Law, 54–55